K·I·S·S

DK

The Only Guides You'll Ever Need!

THIS SERIES IS YOUR TRUSTED GUIDE through all stages and situations. Want to learn how to surf the Internet, care for your new dog? Or maybe you'd like to become a wine connoisseur or an expert gardener? The solution is simple: just pick up a K.I.S.S. Guide and turn to the first page.

Expert authors will walk you through the subject from start to finish, using simple blocks of knowledge to build your skills one step at a time. Build upon these learning blocks and by the end of the book, you'll be an expert yourself! Or, if you are familiar with the topic but want to learn more, it's easy to dive in and pick up where you left off.

The K.I.S.S. Guides deliver what they promise: simple access to all the information you'll need on one subject. Other titles you might want to check out include: Playing Guitar, Playing Golf, the Internet, Microsoft Windows, and Astrology.

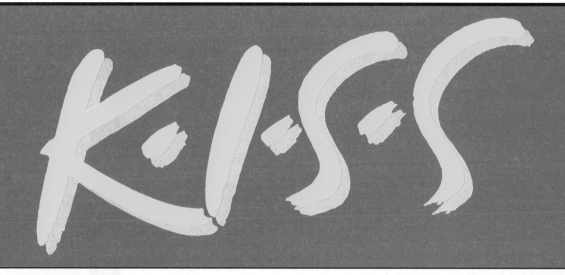

K·I·S·S

GUIDE TO LIVING WITH A

Dog

BRUCE FOGLE, D.V.M

Foreword by Wendy Richard

A Dorling Kindersley Book

Dorling Kindersley

LONDON, NEW YORK, SYDNEY, DELHI, PARIS,
MUNICH, AND JOHANNESBURG

Dorling Kindersley Limited
Editorial Director Valerie Buckingham
Senior Editor Bridget Hopkinson

Managing Art Editor Stephen Knowlden
Jacket designer Neal Cobourne

Dorling Kindersley Publishing, Inc.
Editorial Director LaVonne Carlson
Series Editor Beth Adelman
Copy Editor Cheryl Smith

Created and produced for Dorling Kindersley by
THE FOUNDRY, part of The Foundry Creative Media Company Ltd,
Crabtree Hall, Crabtree Lane, Fulham, London SW6 6TY

The Foundry project team
Frances Banfield, Lucy Bradbury, Josephine Cutts, Sue Evans, Karen Fitzpatrick,
Douglas Hall, Sasha Heseltine, Dave Jones, Jennifer Kenna, Lee Matthews, Ian Powling,
Bridget Tily, Nick Wells, Polly Willis. Special thanks to Karen Villabona.

First published in 2000 by Dorling Kindersley Limited
9 Henrietta Street, London WC2E 8PS

2 4 6 8 10 9 7 5 3 1

Copyright © Dorling Kindersley Limited, London
Text copyright © 2000 Bruce Fogle

A CIP catalogue record for this book is available from
the British Library

ISBN 0 7513 2723 9

Colour reproduction by Kingswood Steele, Modern Age, and the Foundry
Printed and bound by Printer Industria Grafica, S.A., Barcelona, Spain

For our complete catalogue visit
www.dk.com

Contents at a Glance

CONTENTS

PART ONE Finding Your Best Buddy   24

CHAPTER 1 Why We Live Together   26

CHAPTER 2 The History of Dogs   38

Foreword

IF YOU ARE ABOUT TO GET YOUR FIRST DOG, then Bruce Fogle's K.I.S.S. Guide to Living With a Dog is a definite MUST! Every page is packed with useful information, from first training – most important if you are to have a dog that will obey a command the first time, and not in its own time! – to correct feeding, and medical necessities. When people realize fully the responsibilities of being a dog owner, there will be fewer abandoned and mistreated dogs in the world.

My own dog, Shirley Brahms II (named after my character in Are You Being Served?), is a bouncy little Cairn Terrier. She has been a constant source of joy to me, even when she has eaten a whole packet of Giant Smarties and been ill all over the carpet. I wouldn't be without her for the world. She has taught me the joys of walking in all weathers, patience to stand around while every lamppost or tree is carefully examined on these walks, and, most of all, that I am not alone. There is always another heartbeat there at home with you.

Don't ever try to make your dog look foolish – it is only you who will end up looking the fool. Enjoy and cherish your dog and you will have a friend for life, who will ask you no questions and tell you no lies.

Wendy Richard

WENDY RICHARD

. Wendy Richard is a well-known and much loved actress. Most famous for starring in Are You Being Served? *and* EastEnders, *she has also appeared on the stage in plays and more recently in pantomimes. During her lengthy and hugely successful acting career she has also worked extensively on the radio. She is a longtime lover and owner of dogs, and she enjoys Greyhound racing.*

Introduction

THANKS FOR DROPPING IN. *I don't know the exact figure, but there are certainly more dogs in this country – 65 million at last count – than there are books purchased each year about dog care. So I already know you are a conscientious dog owner, or potential dog owner, because you're reading this book.*

This may sound a bit egotistical, but I deeply feel that it is important for a subject to be discussed by someone with first-hand experience. As a practicing veterinarian, for better or worse, what I can give you is more than 30 years experience with dogs and their owners. I hope, when you read this book, that you better understand the lifelong responsibilities of living with a canine companion; that a dog is not a character created by Walt Disney but a fascinating, unique species with an integrity and honesty that is profoundly admirable.

What you get

The book is organized to make it as simple as possible for you to find just the information you need. I really do hope you read the book all the way through, but later, when you want to go back and check up on something, you'll know just where to find it.

In the margins scattered throughout the book you will see some icons (see page 23 for examples). Next to each icon you'll find some text in red print – that's the text most directly related to the icon. There are four of these icons:

- *Very Important Point – be sure you don't miss these.*
- *Complete No-No – something you should avoid at all costs!*
- *Inside Scoop – experience or learning I've gained through years of practice.*
- *Getting Technical – sometimes you just need to know the details.*

In addition, you will find boxes that give specific addresses on the World Wide Web. The Internet can be a great resource for dog lovers, as long as you take note of the information source. I'll also use these boxes to provide definitions for doggy terms that you may not be familiar with, or tell some interesting bit of information that just doesn't fit in anywhere else. And finally, there will be some bigger boxes here and there that will shed light on issues indirectly related to the topic at hand.

■ **Every dog** is a unique individual.

And thank you

This has been an exciting year, working on this book. As always, my colleagues at the veterinary clinic have smoothed the path. My nurses Manda Hackett, Hester Small, and Hilary Hayward, and veterinary colleagues Bas Hagreis and Grant Petrie, are the best anywhere. When I had a sudden DK or pogopet.com deadline, Bas simply smiled and said "no problem." Writing is not possible without their background support.

So too at DK. Thank you to the regular team, and also to Beth Adelman and LaVonne Carlson in New York. Beth, incidentally, is a card-carrying petaholic – a dog writer's ideal for canine facts, figures, and trivia.

DR. BRUCE FOGLE

What's Inside?

THE INFORMATION IN the K.I.S.S. Guide to Living With a Dog *is arranged from the simple to the more advanced, making it most effective if you start from the beginning and slowly work your way to the more involved chapters.*

PART ONE

In Part One I'll give you information on the history of dogs and the reasons why the dog has become our loyal companion. I'll discuss the variety of dogs breeds and personalities to help you find your perfect friend.

PART TWO

Before bringing your new dog home read Part Two to make sure you are prepared in advance to cope with the new arrival. I will discuss dog-proofing your home and yard and explain how to think like your pet pooch.

PART THREE

Part Three discusses the importance of proper training. I will cover the key areas of house training, obedience training, and the vital retraining. I'll show you how to modify your actions to encourage your dog positively and give you an insight into why dogs behave in a certain way.

PART FOUR

A dog's health is fundamental to dog ownership and I will tell you in Part Four how to ensure your pet is in perfect condition. Diet, first aid, and grooming are all explained in some detail.

PART FIVE

In Part Five I'll explain a variety of circumstances you and your dog will come across during your future together. These vary from kenneling and breeding, to dog shows and the breeding process, all of which need careful consideration before bringing a new dog home.

The Extras

THROUGHOUT THE BOOK, *you will notice a number of boxes and symbols. They are there to emphasize certain points I want you to pay special attention to, because they are important to your understanding of your dog. You'll find:*

Very Important Point
This symbol points out a topic I believe deserves careful attention. You really need to know this information before continuing.

Complete No-No
This is a warning, something I want to advise you not to do or to be aware of.

Getting Technical
When the information is about to get a bit technical, I'll let you know so that you can read carefully.

Inside Scoop
These are special suggestions that come from my own personal experience either as a dog owner or as a veterinarian.

You'll also find some little boxes that include information I think is important, useful, or just plain fun.

Trivia...
These are simply fun facts that will give you an extra appreciation of dogs in general.

DEFINITION

Here I'll define words and terms for you in an easy-to-understand style. You'll also find a glossary at the back of the book with all dog-related lingo.

INTERNET

www.internet.com

I think the Internet is a great resource for dog lovers, so I've scouted out some web sites that will add to your enjoyment and understanding of your dog.

PART ONE

MAKE SURE YOUR DOG IS RIGHT FOR YOUR FAMILY

FINDING YOUR BEST BUDDY

OUR RELATIONSHIP WITH DOGS, the oldest *union* we have with any other mammal species, began because we were good for each other. Tens of thousands of years later, we are still good for each other, but in a whole range of new, unexpected ways. Throughout the world, dogs and people work well together in obvious but also very subtle ways. It's a great *partnership*.

If you are thinking about bringing a dog into your life, think hard. The range of sizes, shapes, and personalities of dogs is magnificent. So too are their needs. The relationship between dogs and people is *mutual*. Make sure that the dog you choose is right for you and your family, and also that you are right for your dog.

Chapter 1

Why We Live Together

I N THE UNITED KINGDOM alone there are over 7 million family dogs. There are more British dogs than there are Norwegian men and women. Is this nuts? It just does not seem logical to invite a carnivore to share our homes. But many of us do. There are reasons why so many of us choose to treat animals with big teeth, that bite, as part of the family. But make sure you understand the reasons why we should not live together. A dog will be with you for around 12 to 15 years. Do not let your dog become another statistic in the unwanted dog population.

In this chapter...

✓ Dogs are useful to us

✓ We are useful to dogs

✓ The downside

✓ The hidden side

✓ It's a great partnership

DOGS AND HUMANS HELP ONE ANOTHER TO BE MORE SOCIABLE, CALMER BEINGS

Dogs are useful to us

IT IS PRETTY SIMPLE *to see that dogs are useful to us. A dog is a sociable companion. Just think of the difference between returning to an empty home and coming back to a wagging tail. Dogs stir up the dead air of emptiness and they do a lot more. Carrying on a tradition set by their wolf ancestors, dogs, even the smallest, protect us. In surveys, about 75 percent of British dog owners say they feel safer when their dog is around. It's a nuisance to some, but gratifying to others, that a dog naturally barks a warning to the rest of his family when he hears unexpected sounds trespassing on his space.*

■ **Even the smallest** *dogs help us to feel safe by barking.*

Dogs get us out and about

Dogs are useful in other, less obvious ways. Because a dog needs exercise, dog owners find themselves getting more exercise – something doctors agree is good for our health. Dogs are also terrific at helping people meet each other. A social scientist once asked my help for a study he was doing. He asked some of my clients to walk a set route through the local park, with a dog and without. He scampered from tree to tree with his clipboard, recording what happened. Of course, if you walk in the park with a dog, it's more likely that people will smile at you, nod a hello, stop to talk to your dog and to you, or stroke your dog (but not you). Dogs are better than dating services when you want to meet people.

■ **Dogs are** *invaluable when aiding blind, deaf, and disabled people.*

Owning a dog can lead to other social or physical activities, from having your friend jog with you to joining a dog-agility club and getting more agile as your physically fit furry friend weaves through the poles and climbs the see-saw. Dogs make you laugh. That is another simple fact most dog owners agree with. And what a terrific bonus it is!

Dogs at our service

Then there are the extremely useful dogs, the service dogs that act as eyes or ears for blind or deaf people, that help disabled people in wheelchairs, even warn epileptics of impending seizures. There are also search and rescue dogs trained to work in mountain, avalanche, and earthquake rescue.

We are useful to dogs

USEFULNESS WORKS BOTH WAYS. *If you approach dogdom from the viewpoint of the "selfish gene", we are extraordinarily useful to dogs. We feed them nutritious food, house them well, and take them to the veterinary surgeon when we think they are not well. Simple! In addition, by tying their destiny to ours, dogs have spread throughout the planet, to all continents (until they were removed from Antarctica in the mid 1990s), all major islands, and most minor islands.*

There are more dogs in the world today than any other carnivore (other than us). The only other meat-eating animal that comes close to the dog's success is the domestic cat – another species that tied its future to ours.

■ **Newfoundlands** *have been bred to rescue people from water: teams of these dogs are used by the rescue services in France.*

Trivia...

In Mediterranean France there is a fleet of trained Sea Rescue Newfoundlands. They are so big and powerful that after rescuing someone who has fallen overboard from a boat, they swim back and pull the boat to shore.

Trivia...

Dogs took the first explorers to the South Pole. In 1995, to preserve Antarctica's ecology, the dogs that had remained on the continent were airlifted to new homes, mostly in Canada. Dogs will never be allowed to return to the land they helped discover.

We help dogs adapt

The genetic potential to adapt to a range of new environments was always within the dog, but by moving into our homes that ability to adapt was accelerated. It is still happening today. Only a few human generations ago, dogs were bred to have temperaments that were appropriate for specific jobs, such as working, guarding, fighting, or hunting.

Take the Great Pyrenean Mountain Dog as an example – a breed selectively bred to withstand the cold of harsh mountain nights, to be the colour of the sheep he tended, and to protect the flock from predatory wolves.

Thirty years ago, when the Great Pyrenean Mountain Dog started to increase in popularity, this was still a dangerous guarding breed. More than once in the early 1970s I could not enter the room of a family who had one, and once was pinned to the wall by one of these 55-kilo packages of luxurious fur and murderous intent. Yet within only a few generations, Pyrenean breeders successfully bred for a more easy-going personality. From time to time I still see a gleam in the eye of the occasional Pyrenean, but today, the perpetuation of the breed is assured because this "new" temperament fits in with his new purpose as a companion.

■ **The Great Pyrenean Mountain Dog** *was bred specifically to guard sheep. His coat allows him to hide from wolves among the flock and protects him from the elements.*

■ **A typical-looking** *mountain shepherd dog, the Kuvasz is a powerful animal bred to live outdoors.*

> ## Trivia...
> *The Great Pyrenean Mountain Dog in Andorra and France, like the Komondor and Kuvasz in Hungary, the Akbash in Turkey, the Tatra Mountain Sheepdog in Poland, the Maremma in Italy, or the Aidi in the Atlas Mountains of Morocco, all look similar because they have the same job: to consider the sheep as members of the family, but when a predator comes near, to trot over and say, "I ain't no sheep!"*

We calm our dogs

There is another surprising way we are useful to dogs, one that was discovered almost 40 years ago but is only now being made use of. Stroke a dog and his blood pressure drops. In fact, his skin temperature drops and his heart rate also slows down. A dog's state of arousal is diminished when he is stroked by a member of his human family. This is good for a dog's health — a fact that is only now beginning to be realized by veterinary surgeons.

Unexpectedly, we also have a positive influence on a dog's immune system. There is convincing evidence that a dog gets better faster when comforted by his human family than he does if he has to recover in the absence of social support from people. Just like us.

The downside

FOR EACH POSITIVE REASON for living with dogs, there is a negative. After all, why make an emotional and financial investment in something as odd as a competitive species that wants what you have: your food, your bed, your attention? It's easy to argue that the world would be a better place if there were no dogs. Some cities actually tried this. Rekjavik, Iceland, and (until recently) Beijing, China, banned dogs for hygiene reasons. Dogs can spread diseases, from worms to ticks to rabies. Dogs have muddy feet and, let's face it, some odious habits. Increasingly, we are becoming allergic to dogs. Let's look at the negatives for a moment.

■ **When you stroke** a dog his blood pressure drops and he becomes relaxed.

Dogs are not necessary

There was a time when the progress of human civilization was intimately tied to our dogs. Without dogs, many parts of the world, from high mountain passes to vast expanses of the Canadian, European, and Asian Arctic regions, would never have been inhabited by humans. Migrations of indigenous people to Australia and the Pacific Islands, including the Hawaiian Islands, might not have occurred without the help of dogs. Exploration of great areas of the world depended on the physical abilities of dogs. With assistance from dogs we developed livestock agriculture. Dogs helped us to tend our flocks and herds, drove them from lower to higher pastures in summer, and to market in the autumn. Dogs of war were, in their time, the most modern and fearsome weapons. Some historians argue that it was our relationship with the dog that rapidly accelerated human development.

■ **Although the Maltese** *has long hair, it does not shed, but the hair can matt.*

Dogs were of almost infinite value then, but what about now? Migration depends on Boeing 747s and copious paperwork. Exploration uses satellite imaging, a new respect for indigenous knowledge, and mechanical aids to move supplies and equipment. While dogs are still superb for guarding and moving herds and flocks, so too are horses and motorcycles. As for war, well, dogs have been superseded a zillion times by modern, fearsome weapons.

Dogs shed

In a squeaky clean culture like ours, the fact that dogs shed their hair is a considerable negative – not just because we do not like dog hair on our furniture or clothes, but because of dog hair allergies. No one knows why, but in wealthy countries such as the United Kingdom and Ireland, allergies, especially in children, are a serious problem. In developing countries such as Ethiopia and India, allergies are very rare.

■ **Consider getting** *a Bedlington Terrier, which does not shed its coat, if a family member has an allergy.*

Trivia...
These breeds do not shed, but do need clipping:
Bedlington Terrier
Bolognese
Bichon Frise
Havanese
Maltese
Poodle (all three sizes)

Dog allergies

Technically, allergic people (and that includes me) are not allergic to dog hair. We are allergic to a protein in the dander that comes off with the hair, and to a saliva protein on the hair, which is there because dogs lick themselves as a way of self grooming.

Allergic people are usually allergic to a range of things. Personally, it's only during the summer months that dogs and cats make me sneeze and I experience a tightness in my chest. Some seasonal allergen, probably a pollen, triggers my allergic reaction to my patients.

If you are allergic, choosing to bring a big, hairy dog into your home, especially a breed prone to skin conditions, does not seem sensible. If you already have a dog and allergies have become a problem, there are things you can do before considering re-homing your hairy friend.

1. Undergo allergy testing to make sure your dog is the culprit. If you have a dog and an allergy, many doctors assume the two are related. But they may not be. Get the facts.
2. Never allow your dog on fabric furniture or in the allergic person's bedroom.
3. Use a vacuum cleaner that filters out dog *dander*, pollen, and dust, rather than spreading *allergens* in the air.
4. Always groom your dog outdoors.
5. Wash your dog's bedding at least weekly.
6. Shampoo your dog frequently; weekly is ideal. Weekly shampoos reduce shedding dander and wash away other allergens.
7. Keep your dog's coat short. Clip it routinely. Other allergens, such as pollen or mould spores, catch in long or dense hair and can be a cause of allergies.

INTERNET

members.aol.com/
AHTerrier/allergies.html

This section in the web site for the American Hairless Terrier offers basic information about pet allergies, a list of breeds recommended for allergy sufferers, and a page of links to other pet allergy sites.

DEFINITION

Dander is little bits of dog skin that naturally flake off as the skin renews itself. An allergen is any substance that triggers an allergic reaction.

■ **If you are allergic**, *ensure your dog's bedding is machine washable and clean it weekly.*

■ **Weekly shampoos** *reduce shedding and can help reduce problems with allergies.*

Dogs are dirty

If you are a meticulous housekeeper, do not consider getting a dog. The contradictions are too great. Dogs have muddy feet and dirty habits. It does not matter how clean you keep your dog; dogs are naturally piggish in their thoughts and deeds. Wash your dog and what will it do? It will immediately get rid of the disgusting smell of shampoo by rolling on the ground. Let her swim and what will she do? Run over to you and shake off the water.

In Tokyo I visited an apartment building designed by a dog-loving, people-understanding architect. In the floor, just inside the front door of each apartment, is a five-centimetre-deep stainless steel sink for washing a dog's feet. But let's face it, most of us will never have thoughtful amenities like that in our homes. Living with a dog means living with muddy footprints, wet licks on your feet or face, stones and other little bits in their fur, and some unbelievably disgusting smells. All presented to you with a happy smile. I'm probably a bit of a slob myself, so none of this bothers me. If it bothers you, keep your life simple and get a ceramic dog.

■ **Dogs are naturally** *dirty, so if you are set on keeping your house spotless, do not consider getting one as a pet.*

The hidden side

I DID NOT EVEN KNOW there was a hidden side to our relationship with dogs until I started talking to psychologists, psychiatrists, and other people outside veterinary medicine. These people helped me better understand why my clients behaved the way they did with their dogs, and also why I behave the way I do with my own dog. When I married my wife Julia, did I invite her Golden Retriever, Honey, to live in our bedroom? (Julia says I married her dog and that she was just a part of a package deal.) There are fascinating hidden answers; good stuff to know when you are considering getting a dog.

We need to be needed

We tend to think of the typical dog-owning family as the old-fashioned nuclear unit: 2.3 kids and an estate outside. The only problem with that assumption is that nuclear families are now fewer than ever before. Single people living alone, single-parent families, gay couples, empty nesters – together, these make up many of the family units today. Dogs are an integral part of these families, for a variety of reasons.

The most common reason for the popularity of dogs is also the most basic: we humans have a unique need, different from perhaps all other animals, to nurture, to care for other living things.

Even those of us who have children to nurture only have them in our homes for perhaps one-third of our lives. And some of us never have children. Yet the need to give love, as well as to receive love, lasts throughout our lives. We meet that need in many ways. Playing with dolls is an early manifestation, caring for a garden comes later.

■ **Dogs fulfill our** *need to nurture and care for something.*

Dogs are almost perfect as objects of our nurturing, because in their own way they are "children" from puppyhood to old age. Aaron Katcher, a psychiatrist at the University of Pennsylvania, captured the essence of dogs when he described them as "four-legged Peter Pans caught between culture and nature." It's so true! Dogs are part of the human family, but we recognize they are still dogs. Dogs are part of nature, but we also recognize that they are more than that. We communicate lucidly with them. And they understand us. Although outwardly we look after dogs, in a hidden way, by allowing us to nurture them, they also look after us.

■ **By allowing us** *to look after them, dogs give a lot of love in return.*

Is your dog your mother?

Dr. Constance Perin, a cultural anthropologist at the Massachusetts Institute of Technology in Boston takes the "hidden" argument one step further. She says that consciously we mother our dogs, but subconsciously we get mothered by them.

Connie first looked at what physiologists discovered in the 1970s: when you stroke your dog, your blood pressure drops. Your fight-or-flight reflexes relax. Your body calms down and goes on to autopilot, exactly as your body did when you were an infant in physical contact with your mother.

■ **When we stroke dogs,**
our blood pressure drops.

Connie then looked at what suburban Americans say about their dogs. Basically, we lie. "That's not my dog barking. She'd never bark." "My dog didn't foul on your grass. My dog is perfectly trained." "My dog didn't snap at your child. He'd never do such a thing." And we fantasize. "My dog will protect me from burglars." "My dog will save me if I fall in the river."

Connie's conclusion – one that is well accepted by other "ologists" – is that subconsciously our dogs offer comfort and security that is similar to the comfort and security we got from mother during the first year of life. If she is right, this explains a number of the contradictions we have in our relationship with our dogs.

It's a great partnership

Putting theory aside, what we have is a great reciprocal relationship. Both dogs and people get rewards from living together. It's just that simple. But we have to be careful that, when choosing to live together, we make sure our personalities are compatible. Dogs do not have much choice in this matter, so success depends on us.

When we choose well, there is no doubt in my mind that we end up looking like our dogs. I jokingly call my wife Julia my own personal Golden Retriever. She is blond, dresses casually, and wags her tail when she's happy.

Ask most vets, and I am sure they will say they can look in a waiting room and match dogs to their owners. The better the match, the better the prospects for the relationship. If you understand what you want from living with a dog, you will be more successful when you start looking for one. This is such an important point that I'm going to spend the rest of this section talking about how you can make the best choice.

■ **Having a dog** *in the home makes us feel loved and protected.*

A simple summary

✓ Dogs offer a lot of positives to our lives. They are sociable companions, and help to get us out and about, meeting new people and enjoying new situations.

✓ We offer a lot of positives to dogs. Not only do we feed and house them, but our presence brings them comfort.

✓ The process of domestication has helped make dogs genetically adaptable, enabling them to change as our needs change.

✓ Dogs have their negatives as well. They get dirty and smelly and can trigger allergies.

✓ Dogs help us fulfill our need to nurture another. They also make us feel safe and protected.

✓ Getting a dog is a big commitment, because dogs can live 12 to 15 years. That's why it's so important to think long and hard about what type of dog will be the best match for you.

■ **Owning a dog** *is a huge commitment, and a responsibility that can last 12 to 15 years.*

Chapter 2

The History of Dogs

THE HISTORY OF DOGS is really the history of a strain of wolf that initially chose to live close to us. Over time, these wolves were taken into human settlements, where they proved to have a variety of uses. Eventually we controlled their breeding, domesticating them and creating the variety of dog breeds that exist today. The modern dog, our best friend, is the result of this evolving and recent relationship. The dog has become a member of the human family, but remains to the core of its abilities a wolf in disguise.

In this chapter...

✓ How dogs get started

✓ Practical dog jobs

✓ A modern dog's life

MANY DOG BREEDS RESEMBLE THEIR DISTANT COUSIN, THE WOLF

How dogs got started

WE ARE A PRETTY PRETENTIOUS *species, and although we give God recognition for the really big happenings in history, we tend to credit ourselves as the instigators of many lesser but still important events in human development. That is why the dog is always described as the first species we domesticated, and, as a result, our oldest and most constant and reliable friend.*

Right now my geriatric Golden Retriever, Lexington, is asleep at my feet. She ambled into the study, smiled (at least that is what it seemed to me), lay down, and fell into a deep, tranquil sleep. A few minutes ago her eyelids twitched and her whiskers flickered, as she chased rabbits in her dog dreams. She is, to me and to my family, a personal, reliable, and constant friend. Lexy and I don't need language to communicate. We keep things simple between us. I understand how she feels, even what she thinks. She is a member of my family.

But her ancestors were not actively domesticated by my ancestors. The dog's ancestors, wolves, chose for their own reasons to live near human communities, and by doing so domesticated themselves. It was a brilliant evolutionary move on their part.

By moving into our sphere of influence and by adapting its way of thinking, the wolf, in its modified guise as a dog, became the world's most successful carnivore.

A dog is not exactly a wolf

The most ancient dog skeletons archeologists have found are about 12,000 years old. They differ from wolf skeletons in only two significant ways. A dog's teeth are smaller and more crowded than a wolf's, and (don't let your dog take this too personally) the cavity in the skull for the brain is about one-third smaller. Those features – smaller teeth and smaller brains – remain the great anatomical differences today between dogs and wolves. In virtually all other ways, a modern dog is a wolf in disguise. Simply put, a Chihuahua in a velvet basket and a timberwolf in the woods of Minnesota share a similar set of genes. Mating a wolf and a dog produces fertile offspring.

■ **The skeleton** *of the dog reveals the small skull size which arose from domestication.*

But before you start hankering for a bigger-brained wolf as a pet rather than a dog, let me explain why I think the dog, with her smaller brain, is an infinitely better companion.

Self-domestication

When the wolf moved into the new ecological environment that developed around human settlements, it domesticated itself. This happened 12,000 to 15,000 years ago in those parts of Asia where our previously nomadic ancestors developed agriculture and created permanent human settlements. The relatively small Asian wolf was attracted to these settlements for a variety of reasons. Garbage was a good and constant source for scavenging, and the area around a settlement held fewer dangers from other, larger predators. Less danger meant the best protected breeding sites were near human settlements, which in turn gave people a greater opportunity to capture wolf cubs from their dens.

What happened to the wolf?

Wolves that settled into this new ecological niche, living on land surrounding human settlements, naturally changed in their appearance and behaviour. At first they did so without our active intervention. Domestication was an extremely simple affair. Those most likely to survive in this new niche were the least fearful and most sociable; those that were relaxed in the physical presence of our ancestors. With no large game available to eat (people captured all the large animals in this new environment), the smallest animals were the most fit to survive. Teeth got crowded. Natural camouflage in coat colour became less important because there were fewer predators to hide from. The brain shrank and changed, too, but this did not mean less intelligence than wolves.

■ **The Dingo** *arrived in Australia about 4,000 years ago; living around Aboriginal settlements, it scavenged for food, and helped keep the camp clean.*

INTERNET

www.dmoz.org/Recreation /Pets/Dogs/Origins/

Try this site for a really interesting collection of articles about the history and evolution of dogs.

■ **Wolves that lived** *close to humans changed their appearance and behaviour; eventually they were incorporated into settlements as working dogs or human companions.*

Brain changes

Scientists who study brains have shown that there is no such thing as a learning centre in the brain. There are many different learning centres. When the wolf moved close to human settlements, some learning centres (for example, the part of the brain responsible for mentally mapping territories that cover tens or even hundreds of square miles) were no longer necessary. That wolf ability, which takes up a good part of a wolf's brain, diminished as wolves evolved to live in smaller territories.

The modern dog's ability to map large territories mentally is often hopeless, but there are verifiable stories of dogs finding their way home over vast distances. These dogs probably benefit from inheriting some of their ancestors' ability to map large territories mentally.

To survive in the wild, the wolf needs a large brain to house a variety of learning centres. As well as mentally mapping territory, a wolf must understand what is good to eat and what is dangerous. A typical Labrador Retriever, who thinks she is really just a mobile stomach, seems to have completely lost this ability! The wolf must understand caution and danger, something Jack Russell Terriers often no longer comprehend. Other learning centres in the brain that help a wolf understand what makes a safe home, or a productive region to hunt, or who is best to mate with, also shrank, simply because these brain centres were no longer as important when the wolf was living close to us.

■ **Wolves have larger** *brains than dogs so that they can map territory and know where to find prey.*

Brain improvements

At the same time, self-domestication enhanced other learning centres in the brain. Brain centres responsible for learning to live and work compatibly with another species (us), for inhibiting natural hunting behaviour toward other species (our livestock), and for learning to respond to hand and voice signals from another species all increased in size and efficiency.

Brain shrinkage was a natural event in the dog, but the result is not a deficient brain. It is simply a modified and adapted one, superbly developed to serve the dog in her new environment.

■ **Domestication** *of the dog developed centres of the brain which have allowed it to learn hand and voice signals from us.*

The wolf retains its ability to mentally map its territory, to hunt rather than depend on us for its food, to defend its territory, and to intuitively understand mechanics, motions, and forces. It can be sociable with us, but not with the reliability that comes from thousands of generations of breeding that naturally enhanced the dog's affable and sociable characteristics. When it comes to the type of brain that enriches the relationship between us and dogs, small is beautiful.

Practical dog jobs

NO ONE KNOWS exactly when or where self-domesticated wolves were taken into human settlements, but human nature is not much different now than it was then. It's realistic to assume that wolf pups were as endearing then to people as canine pups are now. These pups were raised until they grew out of the puppy stage, and then were killed and eaten. Some, probably the most sociable, escaped this fate and were allowed to mate with other sociable individuals. This was the beginning of true domestication – the point in time when we actively intervened, deciding who would breed with whom.

Early dog jobs (bad)

You and I might find it an unpleasant fact, but selective breeding for the cooking pot was one of the first important reasons for our meddling in dog breeding. Historically, breeds such as the Hawaiian Poi Poi and the Chinese Chow Chow were bred for food. It is a sad fact that in some parts of the world, the ancient need to eat dog to avoid starvation evolved into a culture of eating dog as a gastronomic delicacy, or to enhance human sexual abilities. In the Philippines alone, between one and two million dogs are eaten yearly. There are similar statistics from China and Korea. To be bred for amusement, then consumption, was probably the dog's first job.

> ### Trivia…
> *Please, don't classify Japan as a dog-eating culture. In Japan, no meat from any land animal, let alone dog meat, was permissible to eat until well into the 19th century.*

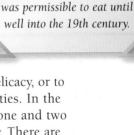

■ **The Chow Chow** *was originally bred in China for food.*

Early dog jobs (good)

It's pretty easy to guess what happened next. Some of the food animals escaped the cooking pot because they had added value to the settlement. Some pups might have barked, showing their abilities as sentries. Others might have attacked intruders, while still others might have tagged along when men went hunting, revealing their abilities to help track and attack game. It may simply have been that on occasion a runty pup, perhaps a dwarf or a midget, was born, of little practical use even for the cooking pot, but of a size that triggered our instinctive need to nurture small, helpless, adorable animals the size of our babies. These shrunken wolf-dogs may have survived to mate with other small individuals, to be kept as bed warmers or simply as companions.

*It takes only a few generations of selective breeding to enhance natural traits, such as barking, but our ancestors had a few more tricks. They probably selectively bred for **drop ears**, rather than erect ones, to differentiate their dogs from wild wolves. But they did something else that has no logical explanation.*

One of the great differences between a wolf skull and a dog skull is the size of the frontal sinuses. Sinuses are air-filled cavities in the skull. Frontal sinuses are the cavities above and between the eyes on the forehead. (Your frontal sinuses can get blocked when you have a cold, or can throb when you have a headache.) For some reason, early dog breeders selectively bred dogs to have larger frontal sinuses. This is why a dog has a more domed head than a wolf. This may make a dog look intelligent to us, but it has no survival value for the dog. It does, however, mean you can honestly call your dog an air-head.

■ **Dogs were bred** *to have a domed head, created by air-filled frontal sinuses. This look has no particular survival value.*

Breeding dogs for jobs

Through our intervention in their breeding, groups of dogs developed specific enhanced abilities. As a member of human packs, the dog's superior senses of hearing and smell made her an excellent guard and sentry. Millennia later, when people domesticated

■ **Dogs' ears that** *hang down are called drop ears.*

> ### DEFINITION
>
> **Drop ears** *are ears that hang down, like the ears on Basset Hounds and Labrador Retrievers. Ears that stand up, as on German Shepherds and Malamutes, are called prick ears. And ears that fold partway, like the ears on Greyhounds and Bulldogs, are called rose ears.*

other species, the dog was already prepared and equipped to help the shepherd guard and protect his flock. Other dogs were bred as hunting companions, to locate, chase, capture, and kill prey. As our own hunting methods improved, the dog's natural ability to track and retrieve game became more important. Still other dogs evolved as campsite scavengers, with responsibility for removing human rubbish from human settlements. The dog's digestive system finds nourishment in the waste of other animals. That is why our lovable friends disgustingly want to eat horse manure or rabbit droppings, then lick our faces.

A modern dog's life

LEXINGTON, STILL LYING at my feet dreaming sweet dog dreams, is not untypical of dogs today. Her ancestor is the wolf. Her body organs are virtually identical to theirs. She shares diseases and illnesses with wolves (but virtually none with us). Her senses, her pack instinct, even the colour of her coat, she has inherited from the wolf. She can mate successfully with a wolf and produce fertile wolf-dogs.

> ## Trivia...
> *The Inuit in northern Canada sometimes mated their Huskies back to wolves to enhance their dogs' territory-mapping abilities. A female in season was tied to a post and left for a wolf to mate with. Unfortunately, as many dogs were killed by wolves as were mated by them.*

In so many ways other than in her looks, the dog is truly a wolf in disguise. If you think of your dog this way, you'll have a better appreciation of the needs and the potential of a modern dog.

■ **The Inuits** *sometimes mated their dogs with wolves to enhance their territorial mapping skills.*

Why it's bad to be a dog

The dog's mind, inherited from the wolf, is magnificent. With such a superb inheritance, the dog is inquisitive, resourceful, energetic, and enduring. Dogs are clever. Dogs are curious. Dogs are gregariously and gloriously sociable. Just watch how well-socialized dogs behave when they meet. A sniff of the lips and bottom is the equivalent of a handshake, then it's instantly into games to calculate the social and physical strengths and weaknesses of the new companion.

■ **Dogs are naturally** *gregarious and inquisitive animals, ever ready to greet other dogs and humans.*

Dogs have a zest for life, a joy in living that we admire, perhaps even envy a little. We love dogs partly because they act out some of the freedoms we wish we had. So what do we do with our dogs? We often keep them locked in luxurious jails. A modern dog, evolved from the physically robust and dynamic wolf, is bound to find her brain shrinking to nothingness if she is never allowed to use it.

For thousands of generations we selectively bred dogs for special aptitudes and abilities. But in this century we have disregarded the dog's practical abilities and concentrated on her looks as the most important reason for choosing and living with one. It's simple to see why veterinary surgeons are seeing more and more behaviour problems in pet dogs!

Why it's good to be a dog

On the other hand, look at why it's good to be a dog today. First of all, they live with us. You might not instantly think this is a benefit, but we're a lot like dogs and so we make good companions for them. Both of us are pack animals. Given the opportunity, we both like to live in communities of blood relatives, with parents, grandparents, and our own children. We are both territorial, with a need for personal space and pack territory. Both of us are species in which members help each other, and both have pack leaders. Both of us learn best when we are young. And perhaps most unique, both of us retain throughout our lives the youthful pleasures of curiosity, of playing games, and of adventure. A dog is a delight because she never really grows up. She is always in touch with her inner puppy. If we are lucky, we have the same ability throughout life to retain our child within. All in all, we are pretty good dog substitutes, but of course, we are even more than that.

Always a dog

■ **Like us, dogs** *are pack animals and enjoy living in company.*

It's good to be a dog today because a dog is treated as a member of the human family. She is housed comfortably, fed nutritiously, and taken to the vet when she is not well. We worry about our dogs as we worry about people we are emotionally close to. So let me give a gentle reminder before we go any further: a dog is a dog.

Do not think your dog is a furry person in disguise. We may share common characteristics with dogs. We are quite good at understanding many of their needs. But they were not created by Walt Disney.

Dogs' physical needs and intellectual abilities are inherited from their pack-animal, meat-eating, predatory ancestors. With big, brown, intelligent-looking eyes and with face and ear muscles that give more expression to their looks than any species other than primates, dogs seem to understand everything. They do not. When you bring a dog into your home, you are bringing a true part of nature into your life. Your relationship with your dog and hers with you will be most rewarding if you remember that we are different species that, by an act of chance, find life enhanced in each other's company.

■ **The position of** *the dog has changed throughout history and today she is treated as a family member.*

A simple summary

✔ The dog's ancestors, wolves, chose to live near human communities. In doing this, they domesticated themselves.

✔ As wolves evolved into dogs, their teeth and brains became smaller. This does not mean dogs became dumber, though. It does mean they needed fewer survival skills than wolves, and more ability to get along with other species (us).

✔ In virtually all other ways, a modern dog is just like a wolf. Understanding this greatly enhances our ability to understand our dogs.

✔ As dogs came to be domesticated, we realized they could be selectively bred to enhance certain skills, such as guarding or herding. Dogs bred to do these jobs need activities to keep their minds and bodies engaged, even now that we no longer need them to herd or guard our flocks.

✔ We are much like our dogs in many ways; we crave company, recognize leaders among us, and still love to explore and play. But ultimately, dogs are animals and we are humans. It is unfair to expect our dogs to be like people.

Chapter 3

A Successsful Search For Your Dog

LOOKING FOR A DOG is most successful when you plan ahead. Control your impulses. That doggy in the window might be cute. He might also be ill or likely to grow into a massively expensive eating machine. Think about the environment you can provide for a dog, then let your biases about sex, colour, and size influence your plans. Be careful, even wary, of people selling dogs. Many are extremely helpful. Many are unscrupulous. If someone gives you the third degree when you ask about her dog, that is a positive sign. Dogs that have been treated like members of the family make the best companions.

In this chapter...

✓ Your first decisions

✓ Dog decisions

✓ Dogs bred for sale

✓ Dogs from people you know

REMEMBER EACH BREED OF DOG HAS DIFFERENT NEEDS

Your first decisions

YOU AND YOUR FAMILY *have decided that a dog is for you and, just as important, that you can be good dog substitutes for a dog. Now you are ready for a delicious search for the right dog. But before leaping into the world of dogdom, consider a few more basics. Don't worry, I'll keep it simple.*

■ **Pedigree breeds,** *such as Great Dane puppies, are more expensive than random crossbreds.*

Think cost

Buying a dog costs from nothing to thousands of pounds for a champion-quality show or working dog, but that initial purchase cost is small compared to the expense of keeping big eaters or dogs prone to poor health.

During the three decades I have been in veterinary practice, the life expectancy of dogs has increased faster than perhaps at any other time in their history. You should expect your canine companion to share your home and your life for, on average, almost 12 years. Many dogs live far longer lives, during which you pay for their food, medical care, and basic accessories. Add to that the costs of kennelling, training classes, and all those little doggy things you do not need but cannot live without, and you have a realistic idea of the true financial costs of bringing a dog into your life.

■ **Popularity has concentrated** *inherited defects in many dog breeds, for example, Golden Retrievers are prone to skin and eye conditions.*

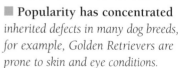

Over a canine lifetime, the typical purchase price of £150 to £400 for a purebred dog amounts to less than a pound a week. Food for a dog like my Golden Retriever adds, let's say, £5. Veterinary care adds a few more pounds, as do other hidden costs. Assume it will cost your family from £1 to £3 a day, for the next decade, to keep a dog.

Think space

If you decide that the joy of having a dog in your home is worth the cost of a daily newspaper and chocolate bar, next consider where you live now, and expect to live in the future. I know this involves a little star-gazing, but it's important. It is a cliché that small dogs fit better into small apartments, but it is not necessarily always true. Some small dogs have phenomenally high energy levels and thrive in more spacious surroundings. Simply because of bulk, large dogs need some space too, although, curiously, the really giant breeds like the St. Bernard can be content living in homes with small gardens, because they seldom indulge in terrier-type fun.

■ **A dog that conforms** *to breed standards can cost thousands of pounds.*

When you think space, think smell too. A really big dog living in a little home can make your home smell like a veterinary clinic at the end of a busy, hot day. Be realistic with your plans and be willing to compromise. Your fantasy may be to have a working Border Collie, but reality may mean that a Shetland Sheepdog better fits the lifestyle you can provide for a dog.

What does the law say?

Dog-related laws may vary from country to country. Some laws are logical and reasonably uniform, others are particular to travelling with your dog. Whether you plan to travel with your dog or not, ensure that he wears external identification in the form of an ID tag on his collar or a tattooed number in his ear or groin. A visible tag can also be proof of rabies vaccination. Alternatively you can use microchip identification on your dog.

Other bylaws restrict dog activity. A typical bylaw might say that dogs are not allowed off their leads. A better worded bylaw says that a dog must always be under your control. That permits a well-trained dog off his lead for exercise. In many places unfair bylaws universally restrict dogs from public parks or buildings. More enlightened law makers understand that playing with a dog is, after shopping, our favourite hobby. They actively create public environments for dog owners to exercise their dogs.

Trivia...

When the city of Sarasota, Florida, USA, decided to ban dogs from its public parks, it set up Paws Park, dedicated to people like me who want to throw tennis balls as far as we can, then have hairy friends retrieve them for us. (It even set up Little Paws Park, a one-acre section where doglets can exercise without being sniffed by bigger dogs.)

Other dog laws range from pragmatic to regrettable to downright unfair. In some places the number of dogs you can have, or even their sex, is restricted. Specific breeds are illegal in some countries. Blocks of flats usually have their own dog bylaws. In some there is a blanket restriction on dogs, in others dogs must be carried onto and away from designated areas. Before you start actively looking for a dog, find out from your landlord or your city, town, or county council office what your local dog laws are.

If you think the dog laws where you live are irrational or unfair, get active with others. Laws are created by people for the benefit of other people. Having a dog and giving him freedom to exercise is one of the most popular of all family activities.

Dog decisions

■ **Female dogs** *are often more demanding of affection than male dogs.*

DOG COSTS, SPACE REQUIREMENTS, *and what the law allows focuses you in the right direction. Now you can get down to more doggy basics and build on your personal preferences.*

Male or female?

We all have our preferences here. Mine is really simple: I like living with the girls. All the dogs in my childhood were females, and that tradition continues today. There is no "better" or "worse" between the sexes, but there are distinct differences in behaviour.

Female dogs are:
- ✓ Easier to obedience train.
- ✓ Easier to housetrain.
- ✓ More demanding of affection.

Male dogs are:
- ✓ More likely to be aggressive with other dogs.
- ✓ More dominant.
- ✓ More active.
- ✓ More destructive.

There are no differences between males and females in their:
- ✓ Watchdog barking.
- ✓ Playfulness.
- ✓ Excitability.

■ **Male dogs** *sometimes require more exercise than females as they are more active.*

These differences apply to dogs in general, but they are not hard and fast rules. For example, the risk of a dog, on his own territory, snapping at an unknown child is one of our great concerns.

While male dogs are statistically more likely to do so than are females, this is not the case for all breeds. In one study, male Golden Retrievers and Cocker Spaniels were more likely than the average male to snap at kids, while male Labrador Retrievers were less likely. To complicate matters even more, in Toy Poodles it is the female who is reported to be less reliable with children than the male.

I am speaking as a veterinarian when I say that a male dog's temperament remains the same all year long. Not so a female's. Her mood changes when she is in season can be striking, ranging from possessiveness over toys, to changes in food preferences, to a disinclination to do an honest day's work. Before I spayed her, with each of her twice yearly seasons Lexington became a bore, lying under the kitchen table, refusing to play tug-of-war with her buddy Liberty (another female Golden), even picking at her food, eating the biscuit but leaving the meat. It can be tough being a female.

When choosing a dog, work with your natural preferences but remember there are pros and cons to both sexes, and that neutering almost always eliminates sexual drawbacks without inhibiting the attractions of that sex.

Trivia...

The male dog's brain is masculinized by male hormones while the pup is still in the womb. A female dog's brain is not affected by female hormones until her first heat cycle.

Young or older dog

Puppy or adult? This is always a tough call – a hearts and minds decision. The advantage of a puppy is obvious. He is putty in your hands, ready to be moulded to you and your family's lifestyle. Your dog will have fewer behavioural problems if you acquire him when he is about eight weeks old and raise him in your own unique environment. If you have a cat, he learns from puppyhood that cats rule, cats demand respect, and cats are not for chasing. If you have toddlers, a puppy learns not to be afraid of the jerky movements of people-in-training. If your life is hectic and filled with a little mayhem, a puppy easily learns to accept there are times when he is not the centre of attention.

■ **To reduce** *behavioural problems, acquire your puppy at about eight weeks old.*

Adult dogs bring their own advantages. Most adult dogs are already house-trained. Many adults already have an understanding of basic doggy obedience. Costs of purchase, training, and neutering have been met.

Virtually all adult dogs, given the need or chance, are emotionally capable of building a powerful new bond with you. Dogs are more fickle than many of us would like to believe. As you read this, there are hundreds of thousands of adult dogs that, through no fault of their own, are looking for new homes. Your choice of pup or older dog is a personal one. Weigh the advantages and disadvantages.

■ **Purebred dogs are** *at high risk of developing medical conditions; Dobermanns are susceptible to heart disease.*

Purebreds

Here is another hard choice. A successful match of dog and human depends on good preparation, but let's face it, what attracts us first to dogs is their looks. That is why breeds are so popular. But looks can deceive. If you are thinking *purebred*, it's best to know why a dog looks the way he does (more about that in Chapter 4). That gives you good clues about how he behaves.

The advantage of a purebred dog is that you are getting an individual bred for a particular size and temperament – something I'll discuss in much more detail in the next chapter.

DEFINITION

According to my definitions, a purebred dog *is one produced by mating two dogs of the same breed. A* crossbred dog *is the result of mating two dogs from two different recognized breeds. A* random-bred dog *is anything else. You might already have discovered there are certain aspects of political correctness I think are silly, but let me add my own silly one. I do not like the word "mongrel". "Mutt" is OK, because it has an element of affection in it.*

■ **Certain breeds are likely** *to inherit particular medical conditions, for example, Golden Retrievers sometimes develop irritable skin conditions.*

The disadvantage is that, when breeding for certain positive characteristics, we unwittingly have bred for a higher risk of medical conditions. These risks vary from breed to breed. Health problems, such as inherited joint pain, blindness, heart disease, and allergies, are frequently breed-specific.

Crossbred dogs

Crossbreeding has proved to be a successful way to reduce the risks of inherited diseases. Labradoodles, Cockerpoos, and Pekepoos all have proved to be excellent crosses. (I guess a cross between a Collie and a Malamute is a Comute – a good breed to take to work with you. Do not ask what you get if you cross a Bull Terrier with a Shih Tzu.)

While purebred dogs make up the vast majority of the population in countries such as Sweden and Norway, in the rest of Europe our most numerous dogs remain *random-breds*. They benefit from hybrid vigour, the enhancement of good health that comes from mixing stock from different genetic backgrounds. The disadvantage of random-bred dogs is that, as puppies, it can be difficult to guess what size they will grow to. I have seen pups grow to four times their mother's size. It can be equally difficult to guess what type of personality traits an individual dog has inherited. (But remember, personality is most flexible if you get a pup and train him from early life to fit in with your lifestyle.)

> ### Trivia...
> *I hate the word "housebreaking" and I am not going to use it. To me, it has the same inference as "horse breaking", that is, breaking an animal's will. The last thing I want you to do is break your dog's spirit. Later on I'll tell you how to house-train your dog, rather than housebreak him.*

■ **These random-bred puppies** *are likely to be healthier than purebred puppies*

Where to find the dog of your life

Now it's getting even simpler. You have made some crucial decisions about the type of dog you can integrate into your life. Where will you find him or her? Do a little more homework, and the answers you need will be there. Many, if not most dogs are the results of accidents, "unauthorized alliances" as a witty radio listener once described them to me. Let's look at the others first – the dogs that are there because someone meant for them to be there.

Dogs bred for sale

DOGS ARE INTENTIONALLY BRED *as a hobby by some, and as a way to make money by others. There is no reason why someone should not make money from their hobby, but beware of the breeder who is in it only for profit.*

■ **When viewing a puppy,** *ask the breeder if you can see his mother.*

■ **The puppy should not** *leave his mother before he is eight weeks old.*

Breeders

When I started practising veterinary medicine, I cannot say, hand on heart, that I much liked dealing with dog breeders. Now, with some humility, I know that many of them are terrific and that the passionate ones who think that life revolves around their breed are magnificent.

What you are looking for is not just a breeder but a reliable breeder. A simple rule: if a breeder has a door knocker in the shape of their breed, salt and pepper shakers in the shape of their breed, sofa cushions with pictures of their breed, dog show rosettes on the walls, and dogs on the sofa, you are in the home of a true addict, someone who will want to investigate you as much as you will want to investigate him or her. This is a reliable breeder.

If you are planning to get a dog from a breeder, ask these questions:

1. May I see the mother? (You should always be able to.)
2. May I see the father? (Do not expect to. The best breeders go outside their kennels for fathers.)
3. Where do the pups live? (Pups raised indoors in a home make better pets than those raised in a kennel.)
4. Have they been seen by your veterinarian? (Good breeders have the parents examined before mating and the pups examined before they are sold.)
5. When will they be ready to go? (Six weeks is too soon. Twelve weeks is too late. Eight weeks is usually just about right.)

Pet shops

Some breeders sell their pups through pet shops. It is extremely rare for reliable breeders to do so. Unreliable breeders – the people you do not want to do business with – sell their pups this way.

Here and there are a few excellent pet shops. Most are not. Some are hotbeds of infection. Get pet supplies from a pet shop, not puppies (or kittens).

■ **To raise a champion dog,** *look for a pedigree with winning parents.*

Newspaper ads

Be very careful with the "Dogs for sale" sections of the classified ads in your paper. Some of these will be genuine ads from loving breeders, but many are private homes used as intermediaries by puppy farm breeders – people who turn bitches into puppy-making machines and who have little interest in anything other than a sale. Of course, it is always possible to get what turns out to be a great dog from a source like this, but why support their odious endeavours when you can get a dog from a more reliable source?

BEWARE OF THE SALES PITCH

When getting a pup from any of the above sources, be cautious. Do not be impressed by claims that sound great but mean nothing.

Kennel Club registered
So what? Most purebred dogs are eligible for Kennel Club registration. Registration only guarantees that the dog really is the breed he is represented to be. It says nothing about a pup's health, temperament, or how he has been raised.

Champion
Forget it! There are so many dog shows

and pedigrees are so long that there is bound to be a champion somewhere in a dog's family. Champion parent(s) is another matter. That often means quality.

Rare
If it's so rare why are they willing to sell it to you?

Must go. We deliver
You do not want an end-of-season bargain, or a puppy that is being pushed out. Reputable breeders want to meet you. They want to show you the mother and her litter. They want to discuss diet and management. They want you to keep in touch.

Dogs from people you know

FRIENDS AND FAMILY are a common source of puppies and adult dogs. We usually know exactly why a dog needs a new home, and know the dog or his parents and can get a full medical and behavioural history of the individual.

Friends

■ **Rescue dogs are** *often already house trained, so adult dogs can make excellent pets.*

Friends and neighbours have been, historically, the most popular source of pups. While this is still one of the most common ways to acquire a dog, it is declining, and for a good reason. The good reason is that more of us accept the fact we have a responsibility to prevent unwanted matings – the natural source of a neighbour's pups.

From a medical perspective, good, responsible neighbour's pups are perhaps the healthiest of all pups. They are often raised in a parasite- and disease-free environment and are played with intensively until they leave one home to move into another.

■ **Rescue associations** *house many types of dog, both purebreds and random-breds.*

Sensible neighbours are an excellent source of pups. However, if your neighbours treat their dog in a way you would never treat yours, avoid their puppies, too. Chances are you're in for problems of health, temperament, or socialization.

Veterinary clinic ads

Veterinary clinics are more than canine medical centres. The staff, especially the receptionists, run adoption agencies. Where I practice, there is a jungle telegraph that operates among clinic staff all over the city. After a dog dies, I might mention to the nurses that they should be on the look-out for a possible successor for our client – only to be told that the receptionist at a nearby practice already knows of one.

Dogs with former lives

There are, as I mentioned, hundreds of thousands of mature dogs in need of good homes. You can find these at animal shelters or through a variety of rescue associations.

It is a good thing to rescue a dog, but before you do your good deed, here are some facts, the results of five years of observations at an American animal shelter.

Shelters and pounds

Purebred dogs stray from home as much as random-breds, but mongrels are more likely to be dumped by their owners at animal shelters. Almost three quarters of strays or dogs that are given up are less than a year old. Most are guys. So if you visit an animal shelter be prepared to see lots of young male dogs.

Certain breeds show up in animal shelters more frequently than their American Kennel Club registration numbers suggest.

INTERNET

www.ncdl.co.uk

The National Canine Defence League provides valuable information on shelter dogs needing good homes and on the responsibilities of dog ownership.

www.cp.org.uk

This site provides similar information on cats needing new homes.

■ **Dogs from animal** *shelters will be used to socializing with other dogs.*

BREED	PERCENTAGE OF AKC REGISTRATIONS	PERCENTAGE OF DOGS AT SHELTERS
Labrador Retriever	7.9	14.6
German Shepherd	5.0	9.8
Golden Retriever	5.0	7.5
Beagle	3.9	7.1
Siberian Husky	1.8	5.3

Dogs from the American Kennel Club's Herding, Sporting, and Hound Groups are more likely to be found at an animal shelter. Dogs from the Working Group appear in average numbers, while dogs from the Terrier, Non-Sporting, and Toy Groups are the ones least likely to be found in shelters.

■ **Unfortunately, many random-breds,** *especially males, are unwanted and are dumped in animal rescue associations.*

Breed rescue associations

Each breed club runs one or more breed rescue associations. Dedicated breeders coordinate the re-homing of members of their breed who fall on hard times, through the death of an owner or a change in circumstances that means a family must part with a pet. Many of these rescued dogs need re-homing because of behaviour quirks: fears, phobias, and other conditions.

If you are planning to rescue a purebred, ask these questions:
1. Was he lost or given up? (Vagrants often have a lifelong wanderlust.)
2. If surrendered, why was he given up? (Many dogs are discarded because they have behaviour problems that are not apparent until you live with the dog.)
3. Has the rescue centre done any behaviour testing? (Progressive rescue centres analyze behaviour and give reports to potential adopters.)
4. Can you help with any future problems? (The best rescue centres give continuing advice on behaviour problems.)

INTERNET

www.AKC.org

The AKC maintains a list of American rescue coordinators. To find information on local UK rescue centres visit: **www.dogpages.btinternet. co.uk.**

Retired assistance and working dogs

Over the last 20 years the number of service dogs trained to assist people with disabilities has increased magnificently. I am involved with a charity that trains dogs for deaf people. We carefully select dogs according to their training potential, but still have failures. Our rejects are found good homes.

All assistance dogs eventually retire from active service. Guide dogs in particular often need new homes, and make excellent companions. So do retired racing Greyhounds when they are placed with knowledgeable, loving families.

■ **Assistance dogs make** *excellent family pets when they retire from service.*

A simple summary

✔ Before you get your dog, remember that you must make a commitment that will likely last more than a decade. Make sure you are willing to take on the cost and bear the responsibility that a dog entails.

✔ Consider the space you have available and your local ordinances when you are considering whether to get a dog, and what kind of dog.

✔ There are generalities about male and female dogs, but individuals vary. And neutering pretty much levels the playing field when it comes to choosing a sex.

✔ Adults and puppies each have their advantages. So do purebreds and crossbreed dogs. Think hard about what your family is really expecting from a dog, and make your decision accordingly.

■ **The advantages and disadvantages** *of getting a puppy, rather than an adult dog, should be weighed carefully before deciding.*

✔ If you are buying your dog from a breeder, look for a breeder who is clearly devoted to their breed. Responsible, reliable breeders will ask you lots of questions about your suitability as a dog owner. That's a good sign!

✔ It is a good deed to adopt a dog from a shelter or a rescue organization. Just make sure you learn as much as you can about the dog before you bring him home.

■ **Neutering diminishes the** *differences between bitches and dogs, making them better family pets.*

Chapter 4

Breeds:
An Unlimited Variety

DOGS COME IN A VARIETY OF SHAPES AND SIZES because these once were useful attributes for the dog. For thousands of years we selectively bred them to do specific things.

In this chapter...

✓ The dog for you

✓ The role of kennel clubs

✓ Sporting dogs

✓ Hounds   ✓ Working dogs

✓ Terriers   ✓ Toy dogs

✓ Non-sporting dogs   ✓ Herding dogs

✓ Other great dogs   ✓ Dog documents

THERE IS AN AMAZING VARIETY OF DIFFERENT DOG BREEDS TO CHOOSE FROM

The dog for you

ALL OF US have personalities, aspirations, and values we consider to be uniquely our own. The joy of dogs is that there are so many different temperaments, looks, sizes, and abilities within the species, so we can satisfy our own needs by carefully selecting a dog that fits us like a glove. Let me keep this simple: if you like dogs but the idea of wiping dog drool off the walls is unappealing, do not get a St. Bernard. If you are a control freak, if you like everything done your way, do not get a Basenji. If you like everything to be in its own place, get a small Poodle on which you can carry out canine topiary. If you love to be surrounded by those who love, honour, and obey, there is nothing better than a female Golden or Labrador Retriever.

Your choice of the sex, age, colour, coat texture, size, and working potential of your dog is vast, and can complement your own personality. But remember, looks are not everything. A breed may look good, but most look the way they look for reasons that once were important for their original working ability. And that ability may or may not make them suitable as a pet for you.

■ **Every breed** has a different temperament and characteristics, so choose the dog that matches your lifestyle.

Why are there so many shapes and sizes?

Different breeds look the way they do for a purpose. Dachshunds have short legs and big teeth because they were bred to *go to ground*. A Dachsie might appeal to you because of her size, but she retains in the core of her being the potential for mayhem.

Newfoundlands have heavy coats because once they were used in the cold north-Atlantic waters around Newfoundland to swim out to cork floats attached to fishing nets and bring them ashore. Rottweilers are muscular because they helped south-German butchers drive cattle to market. Yorkshire Terriers are small because Scottish (not Yorkshire) breeders carried their little ratting dogs in their coat pockets to rat-killing competitions. Beagles get on with other dogs because they once lived in hunting packs, where survival meant being amenable with your neighbours.

DEFINITION

To go to ground is to follow a burrowing animal into its underground den, and there to do fearless battle. Dachshunds and other terriers were bred to burrow after and kill rabbits, badgers, weasels, and foxes.

■ **Dogs are a certain size** *and shape for a reason; mountain dogs have coats that keep them warm whereas hunting dogs have short legs to be close to the ground.*

All of us are attracted to physical shapes or sizes we find aesthetically appealing, but when choosing a breed, remember that shape and size once served a purpose. Through selective breeding last century we diminished the dog's need to do what she once did, but retained her once-useful physical characteristics.

Breeding and breeds

Through thousands of years of breeding for specific abilities, we created breeds with different looks. Once that happened, we started breeding both for abilities and looks. That continued into the last century, when looks began to supersede abilities. This is when breeders began to push these physical characteristics to extremes: the densest coat, thickest neck, longest limbs, flattest face, lightest weight. Dogs suffered.

By the late 1970s breed associations began to realize the problems inherent in breed standards that promoted extremes. Many breed clubs rewrote their standards, eliminating or at least downgrading the extremes. But problems still exist, and you should be aware of these when you're choosing a purebred dog.

■ **Breeds such as the Poodle** *were originally developed for their working and sporting abilities.*

It might look cute for a dog to have the wrinkliest face, but it isn't cute for the dog's health or for your wallet. Extremes cause medical problems, and these cost money to rectify. Conscientious breeders avoid breeding dogs that suffer for their looks.

■ **Breeding to develop** *a particular characteristic, such as a wrinkly or flat face, has created medical problems in some breeds such as the Shar Pei.*

AMPUTATING TAILS AND EARS

The oldest known European dog care book, written almost 2,000 years ago, recommended cutting off a dog's tail to prevent the dog from getting rabies. This procedure is called docking. Tail docking evolved from there into a traditional procedure with some working dogs, especially terriers and spaniels, to prevent tail injuries. Today, companion dogs have their tails amputated for our vanities, not their welfare. In other countries dogs have their ears partly amputated – "cropped" is the benign word people like to use – for no other reason than to make them look fierce. This is primarily a German tradition, born out of the military origins and uses of breeds like Great Danes, Boxers, Dobermann, and Schnauzers. This mutilation – I am sorry to be so blunt, but that is what cropping is – is banned in its country of origin, and in most other FCI countries. North America remains the only significant region in the world where ear and tail amputations are still routinely performed. There is no medical or work-related justification for these procedures to be performed on pet dogs. Many dedicated, dog-loving veterinary surgeons will no longer carry out these alterations.

Trivia...
The Kennel Club registers about 260,000 purebred dogs a year. That's more than 20,000 a month!

■ **Cropped ears** *are of no benefit to the dog; they merely make her look fierce.*

The role of kennel clubs

KENNEL CLUBS ARE CHANGING. Not long ago a kennel club was a social organization that issued birth certificates and organized beauty contests for purebred dogs. Today, the best of them do much more. Kennel clubs promote responsible pet ownership, organize dog-training classes, fund veterinary research into genetic diseases, and coordinate lost and found registers for all dogs, not just their own purebreds.

■ **Sketches from the London Kennel Club** *Dog Show in April 1890.*

A choice of clubs

The world's first kennel club, still called simply The Kennel Club, is in London. The American Kennel Club (AKC) came into existence soon after. By the turn of the twentieth century most countries had their own national kennel clubs; for example, the Swedish Kennel Club (SKK), located in Stockholm.

To simplify the showing of dogs throughout Europe an umbrella organization, the Fédération Cynologique Internationale (FCI) was formed. Most, but not all, of Europe's national kennel clubs are members of FCI. (You'll find addresses of all these organisations in Appendix A). But The Kennel Club remains very much leader of the pack, top dog, larger and more influential than all other European clubs combined. The Kennel Club's influence elsewhere in the world is as great, on a par with the American Kennel Club.

How kennel clubs classify breeds

Each kennel club classifies breeds in its own idiosyncratic way. Because more purebred dogs in the United Kingdom are registered with The Kennel Club than with all other European registries I will use their classification system, which organizes dogs into sporting (gundog), hound, working, herding (pastoral), terrier, toy, and non-sporting (utility) groups. This division is based somewhat on common characteristics the breeds in each group share, but is also somewhat arbitrary. It does not include breeds not recognized by The Kennel Club. Those breeds will be my eighth group – along with the breeds that are still awaiting full Kennel Club recognition.

Sporting dogs

THE KENNEL CLUB classifies this group as Gundogs; the group is sub-divided into four categories: retrievers, spaniels, hunt/point/retrieve, and setters. Gundogs were originally bred to work with the hunter, to be part of the team, flushing birds from hiding then retrieving game that had been shot or wounded.

Of all the groups, these breeds were in the best position to evolve into family companions — active, amusing, and with a gentleness of spirit. Many continue as dual-purpose dogs, detecting drugs or helping disabled people by day and lounging on the sofa by night.

In this group you'll find:

50 pounds/23 kilos and under

American Water Spaniel
Brittany
Cocker Spaniel
English Cocker Spaniel
English Springer Spaniel
Field Spaniel
Kooikerhondje
Spanish Water Dog
Sussex Spaniel
Welsh Springer Spaniel

BRITTANY

SUSSEX SPANIEL

ENGLISH COCKER SPANIEL

Over 50 pounds/23 kilos

Bracco Italiano
Chesapeake Bay Retriever
Clumber Spaniel
Curly Coated Retriever
English Setter
Flat Coated Retriever
German Longhaired Pointer
German Shorthaired Pointer
German Wirehaired Pointer
Golden Retriever
Gordon Setter
Hungarian Vizsla
Irish Setter
Irish Water Spaniel
Italian Spinone
Labrador Retriever

Large Munsterlander
Pointer
Weimaraner

HUNGARIAN VIZSLA

CHESAPEAKE BAY RETRIEVER

GOLDEN RETRIEVER

LABRADOR RETRIEVER

GERMAN SHORTHAIRED POINTER

WEIMARANER

Hounds

THE HOUNDS CLASSIFICATION *includes breeds originally used for hunting either by scent or by sight and includes such varied breeds as the fleet-footed Afghan and the more plodding Basset. Many have names that explain what they once did for a living.*

Some hounds have limitless energy, while others are quite laid back. Yet others, in my opinion, are not hounds at all. Dachshunds for example are really terriers, developed to hunt vermin in burrows. I think they got classified here just because their name ends in "hund."

Under 20 pounds/9 kilos

Miniature Dachshund

20 to 50 pounds/9 to 23 kilos

Basenji
Basset Bleu de Gascogne
Basset Fauve de Bretagne
Basset Hound
Beagle
Finnish Spitz
Ibizan Hound
Norwegian Elkhound
Petit Basset Griffon
　　Vendéen
Salukt
Segugio Italiano
Standard Dachshund
Whippet

MINIATURE DACHSHUND

BEAGLE

50 to 80 pounds/23 to 36 kilos

Afghan Hound
Bavarian Mountain Hound
Foxhound
Greyhound
Hamilton Stövare
Pharaoh Hound
Rhodesian Ridgeback
Saluki

Over 80 pounds/36 kilos

Bloodhound
Borzoi
Irish Wolfhound
Otterhound
Deerhound

BLOODHOUND

AFGHAN HOUND

OTTERHOUND

RHODESIAN RIDGEBACK

Working dogs

Working dogs have been bred for centuries to guard but also to assist in a variety of other ways. Most working dogs are big and while many evolved as guards or cart-pullers the group also includes the gentle, drooling giant Newfoundland.

As we become more concerned with our own protection, the popularity of working dogs increases. Generally speaking, many of these breeds are not suitable for canine novices. There are some firm personalities in this group that need experienced handling.

Under 50 pounds/23 kilos

Portuguese Water Dog

50 to 80 pounds/ 23 to 36 kilos

Boxer
Dobermann
Giant Schnauzer
Hovawart
Siberian Husky

GREAT DANE

BOXER

Over 80 pounds/36 kilos

Alaskan Malamute
Beauceron
Bernese Mountain Dog
Bullmastiff
Eskimo Dog
Great Dane
Leonberger
Mastiff
Newfoundland
Rottweiler
St. Bernard
Tibetan Mastiff

ST. BERNARD

ROTTWEILER

Terriers

DO YOU WANT a dog with a sense of humour? This
is your group! But be wary. "Terrier" is like "terror".
Many (but not all) of these dogs were bred to kill. They
have big teeth and use them – frequently. Many terriers are
small, so they make intemperate little nippers. My worst
nightmare is a Rottweiler with the temperament of a classic
rat-hunting terrier.

BORDER TERRIER

Under 15 pounds/7 kilos

Border Terrier
Cairn Terrier
Norfolk Terrier
Norwich Terrier

WELSH TERRIER

15 to 25 pounds/7 to 11 kilos

Australian Terrier
Bedlington Terrier
Cesky Terrier
Dandie Dinmont Terrier
Lakeland Terrier
Manchester Terrier
Scottish Terrier
Sealyham Terrier
Smooth Fox Terrier
Standard Manchester Terrier
Welsh Terrier
West Highland White
    Terrier
Wire Fox Terrier

BEDLINGTON TERRIER

LAKELAND TERRIER

25 to 50 pounds/11 to 23 kilos

Irish Terrier
Kerry Blue Terrier
Miniature Bull Terrier
Glen of Imaal Terrier
Skye Terrier
Soft Coated Wheaten Terrier
Staffordshire Bull Terrier

Over 50 pounds/23 kilos

Airedale Terrier
Bull Terrier

KERRY BLUE TERRIER

AIREDALE TERRIER

STAFFORDSHIRE BULL TERRIER

SKYE TERRIER

Toy dogs

The ultimate companions, toy dogs appear never to have worked for an honest penny. Not true. Pampered for centuries, some of these breeds originally had very specific purposes, such as controlling fleas on their lady owners or acting as soft, always-available hot water bottles.

Toy dogs often make good first choices for novice dog owners, but remember: some use subservience to dominate their owners. A dog may be called a toy, but she can still boss around a human household.

All toy breeds are under 20 pounds/9 kilos

Australian Silky Terrier
Affenpinscher
Bichon Frise
Bolognese
Cavalier King Charles Spaniel
Chihuahua

CHIHUAHUA

CAVALIER KING CHARLES SPANIEL

AFFENPINSCHER

Chinese Crested
Coton De Tulear
English Toy Terrier
Griffon Bruxellois
Havanese
Italian Greyhound
Japanese Chin
King Charles Spaniel
Lowchen (Little Lion Dog)
Maltese
Miniature Pinscher
Papillon
Pekingese
Pomeranian
Pug
Yorkshire Terrier

PUG

CHINESE CRESTED

POMERANIAN

YORKSHIRE TERRIER

SHIH TZU

Non-sporting dogs

The Kennel Club's catch-all classification for dogs that do not fit other categories is also known by the kinder name the utility group. Many of the dogs have non-sporting origins and were bred for specific functions.

Some, such as the Bichon Frise and the Standard Poodle, are among the very best of all canine companions, ideal for first-time dog owners. Others, such as Chow Chow, are only for dog experts. Other dogs in the group include:

Under 20 pounds/9 kilos

German Spitz
Boston Terrier (although some can
    weigh up to 11 kilos)
Japanese Spitz
Lhasa Apso
Schipperke
Tibetan Spaniel

20 to 50 pounds/9 to 23 kilos

Canaan Dog
Bulldog
Mexican Hairless
French Bulldog
Japanese Shiba Inu
Keeshond
Miniature Poodle
Tibetan Terrier

Over 50 pounds/23 kilos

Chow Chow
Dalmatian
Japanese Akita
Shar Pei
Standard Poodle

LHASA APSO

MINIATURE POODLE

DALMATIAN

CHOW CHOW

Herding dogs

ALSO KNOWN AS the Pastoral group, these are responsive dogs, relatively easy to train, like the sporting breeds, but with harder personalities – closer to the working dogs. After all, their job, herding sheep or cattle, required them to work with the shepherd but also to intimidate and control animals much bigger than themselves.

BEARDED COLLIE

This group includes the breed consistently voted "most intelligent dog", the Border Collie. The way a Border Collie works is amazing. Such intelligence! But working intelligence does not make her a good pet dog. A Border Collie in a modern household, with no sheep to herd, can be a very unhappy dog and one that is difficult to control. Dogs in this group include:

Under 50 pounds/23 kilos

Australian Cattle Dog
Bearded Collie
Border Collie
Cardigan Welsh Corgi
Hungarian Puli
Lancashire Heeler
Pembroke Welsh Corgi
Shetland Sheepdog

**GERMAN
SHEPHERD DOG**

Over 50 pounds/23 kilos

Australian Shepherd
Belgian Malinois
Belgian Laekenois
Belgian Tervuren
Bergamasco
Briard
Collie
German Shepherd Dog
Hungarian Kuvasz
Old English Sheepdog

HUNGARIAN PULI

BELGIAN TERVUREN

Other great dogs

WHILE THE KENNEL CLUB *recognizes 192 breeds in its seven groups, that is fewer than half of the breeds recognized by other kennel clubs both in the United States and in other countries. The American Rare Breed Association and the Fédération Cynologique Internationale (FCI) are excellent sources for information on non-Kennel Club recognized breeds. My favourites include:*

Jack Russell Terrier

These 4- to 7-kilo balls of muscle can be snappy and aggressive, but are resilient, healthy doggy dogs, still untainted by selective breeding for beauty rather than brains. City dwellers beware: although small, Jack Russells have a lot of energy and require a great deal of exercise. The 6- to 8-kilo size is currently in The Kennel Club's Miscellaneous Class.

INTERNET

www.arba.org

The home page of the American Rare Breed Association.

www.fci.be/english/

The home page of the FCI, the largest international purebred dog association. If you're up to it, you can also view this page in French, German, or Spanish.

Munsterlanders

Germany's equivalent of spaniels, they come in large and small varieties. The small Munsterlander in particular, at 14 to 16 kilos, is a good-natured, responsive, high-energy companion, equally willing to retrieve or play with the family. She is an excellent first dog.

Polish Lowland Sheepdog

Also in The Kennel Club's Miscellaneous Class, this is an ancient breed brought back from near extinction after World War II by dedicated Polish breeders. Fairly small, only 13 to 16 kilos, they are good companions. Much like Bearded Collies, the coat needs constant attention.

AMERICA'S MOST POPULAR BREEDS

According to the most recent Kennel Club registration figures, these are the most popular breeds in the United Kingdom.

1. Labrador Retriever
2. German Shepherd (Alsatian)
3. West Highland White Terrier
4. Cocker Spaniel
5. Golden Retriever
6. English Springer Spaniel
7. Cavalier King Charles Spaniel
8. Staffordshire Bull Terrier
9. Boxer
10. Yorkshire Terrier

BOXER

GOLDEN RETRIEVER

UNDERESTIMATED BREEDS

These are my favourite underestimated breeds. All make excellent family dogs.

1. Legatto Romagnolo
2. Hamiltonstövare
3. Hungarian Vizsla
4. Bichon Frise
5. Papillon
6. Petit Basset Griffon Vendeen
7. Norwegian Elkhound
8. Italian Spinone
9. Polish Lowland Sheepdog
10. Australian Shepherd

AUSTRALIAN SHEPHERD

PAPILLON

POLISH LOWLAND SHEEPDOG PUPPY

NORWEGIAN ELKHOUND

Dog documents

A PUREBRED DOG usually comes with two documents: a pedigree and a form for kennel club registration. Good breeders will always provide you with both papers, which you will need if you wish to show your dog.

The pedigree

The pedigree lists the registered names, going back at least three generations, of your dog's ancestors. All dogs have pedigrees. It's just that those registered with a kennel club have theirs written down in a standard format. "Ch." before a dog's name means the dog is a champion.

The more times you see Ch. on both the mother and father's sides of the family, especially in the more recent generations, the more likely it is that your dog is good-looking according to kennel-club standards.

Your dog's name will be all the way on the left of the pedigree, and as you move right, you'll be going back in generations. Mother and father are presented in pairs, with the father's name on the top. Pedigrees are fun to read, especially when you meet other owners of your breed and realize that your dog has a second cousin three times removed who lives just down the street. But that is all it means.

The registration application

This is a form you must fill in to register your purebred dog with The Kennel Club. Or it may be a form used to transfer ownership of an already named and registered dog from the breeder (or present owner) to you. Without the registration application, you cannot register your dog. If this is important to you, do not buy the dog unless the breeder can give you the registration application.

Don't accept a vague promise that "the papers will be along later". An honest, conscientious breeder has the registration papers ready for you when you buy the dog.

Once a dog is named on one of these forms, that name is carved in granite in The Kennel Club records. It can never be changed. When I got my first Yorkie, she had already been registered as Moonmist Starfire Jewel. Try calling your dog by that name in the park.

That was her *registered name*. What you call your dog is up to you. To us, Moonmist Starfire Jewel was just Sparky. My kids had a chance to name one of our Golden Retrievers, and chose Liberty Olympia Sweetpea Chewingdog Fogle. Her *call name* is Libby. If you have the chance, enjoy yourselves when you choose the registered name of your dog.

Other documents

In addition to the kennel club papers, conscientious breeders will give you health records for your pup, information on the health of the parents, an invoice or sales contract, and detailed care instructions.

Health records

Some genetic diseases are hereditary, such as certain types of blindness, deafness, hip dysplasia, and arthritis. Looking at the health records of the parents, while not foolproof, will give you some idea of the potential your puppy has to develop certain diseases. Look for results from the British Veterinary Association (BVA), and The Kennel Club (KC) health schemes for dysplasia, elbow dysplasia, and inherited eye diseases. All 20,000 yearly results are recorded on The Kennel Club database and published on progeny registration certificates. DNA tests for inherited medical conditions in the Irish Setter, Springer Spaniel, Briard, Dobermann, and Bedlington Terrier are carried out for breeders at the Animal Health Trust.

You should be given worming and vaccination certificates that tell you when a pup has been treated, what she was treated with, and when the next treatment or inoculation is due.

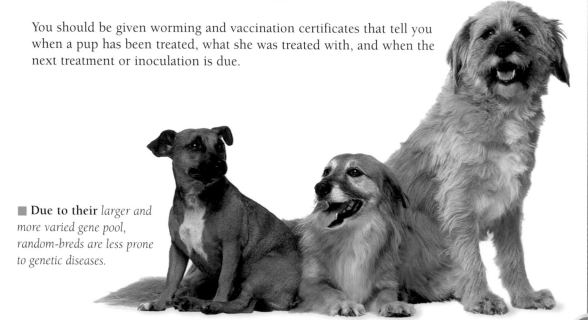

■ **Due to their** *larger and more varied gene pool, random-breds are less prone to genetic diseases.*

Care instructions

Good breeders will give you detailed instructions on what to feed your dog, how much and when, and how to manage your pup in her transition to her new home. The best breeders don't wait for you to phone them with questions; they call you to check up on how their baby is getting on. Don't feel they are interfering. The more interest a breeder takes in her pups, the more information you will have on how to raise your new family member.

Sales contract

Most sales contracts are straightforward. They should contain a health guarantee. Some breeders include a temperament guarantee. There may be a neutering clause in the contract, requiring you to agree to neuter your pup when your veterinary surgeon believes the dog is old enough for this to be done.

Breeders are very protective of their kennel names. If you buy a puppy that the breeder believes has great show potential, he might want to leave the possibility of future breeding open, but retain rights to use his kennel name for show purposes. This will make for a more complicated sales contract, sometimes involving legal co-ownership of a pup.

If you are interested in a dog simply as a companion, avoid these legal knots. Keep it simple! On the other hand, if you are interested in the dog world as a hobby, in working your dog in breed-specific areas, such as herding or hunting, in obedience or agility trials, or in the show ring, cultivate your relationship with your dog's breeder. A good breeder is the best mentor for understanding more about your dog and the wider world of dogs.

■ **Some purebred dogs,** *such as the Shar Pei, inherit genetic diseases from their parents; if possible check their parents' records.*

■ **Dalmatians are susceptible** *to inherited deafness, so make sure the parents have been tested.*

A simple summary

✓ Dogs come in a greater variety than any other animal. Although looks are appealing, temperament is more important in choosing a dog that will fit in with your family.

✓ Kennel clubs register purebred dogs, and also fund research into canine health issues, have ID registries for helping owners find lost dogs, and sanction a variety of canine competitions.

✓ The Kennel Club organizes dogs into seven groups, not always logically. Although the Herding and Sporting groups mainly describe the breeds included, the Hounds aren't all strictly hounds, and Non-Sporting is just the place for whatever didn't fit into the other six categories.

✓ Unless a registration certificate comes with the dog, you won't be able to register your dog with most kennel clubs.

✓ Purebred status and kennel club registration are not guarantees of health or sound temperament. Look at the health records of a pup's parents, ask questions, and shop carefully.

✓ Good breeders will provide a pedigree, registration certificate, health records, and care instructions, and will call to check that you are living up to being worthy of their pup.

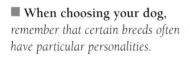

■ **When choosing your dog,** *remember that certain breeds often have particular personalities.*

Chapter 5

Personality Testing – Your Dog & Yourself

LOOKS ARE NOT EVERYTHING, but they sure are important. You have decided what type of dog you want and have found breeders or rescue groups that have dogs available. How do you choose one from another? Pups in a litter can look very similar but, in fact, each one has his own unique personality – a product of the genes he inherited, together with the way he has been treated by his mother, his siblings, and his surrounding humans, and the experiences he has. With a little time and patience, you can test the personality of a dog. But remember, your personality is equally important when considering a dog's future.

In this chapter...

✔ Does the test work?

✔ Simple puppy tests

✔ Simple adult dog tests

✔ Test yourself, with honesty

✔ Involve the family

CHOOSE A DOG THAT MATCHES YOUR PERSONALITY

Does the test work?

BEHAVIOUR TESTING WORKS on us, and on mature dogs, but not so well on puppies. The idea of behaviour testing a pup at a young age to determine the personality he will develop became popular in the 1970s. Lots of fascinating tests were developed, and books are still written advocating newer, more sophisticated methods of puppy testing.

The concept of puppy behaviour testing was logical. After all, as I mentioned in the previous chapter, breeds were originally created by selecting for certain types of behaviour. Inherited dispositions to dig, to hunt, to attack, to retrieve, are the raw material you will be working with. This is why it is easier to predict the behaviour of a purebred dog than that of a random-bred individual.

But, of course, like us, a pup is influenced by the environment he finds himself in. Behaviour testing a pup tells you what his personality is like now. When puppy tests were examined independently, it was realized they did not predict adult behaviour, except in one very important area.

■ **Dominant puppies** *grow up to become dominant adult dogs.*

Pups that have dominant personalities grow up to be adults with dominant personalities. For that reason alone, it is wise to test pups for this inherent behaviour. Pushy puppies may be cute. Pushy adult dogs are frustrating to live with and downright dangerous if not properly controlled.

■ **Do not buy** *two puppies at the same time, as training them would be almost impossible.*

Trivia...

Do not get two puppies at the same time. Training them simultaneously is virtually impossible. While training one to listen to you, unwittingly you train the other, if he is within earshot, not to listen to you. If you want two dogs around the same age, get one, train him, then get another.

Simple puppy tests

ONE OF MY NURSES *admonishes bossy dogs, "Don't be so bold!" It's the perfect word to describe the type of pup you should avoid if you are a first-time puppy buyer. The boldest pup is the one who marches out of the litter to examine you. This is endearing, but it can also mean trouble. So too can the shyest pup, the one who hangs back with a sign around his neck saying, "Help! I need you to care for me." This pup may just be having a bad day, but he may also be overly submissive – the opposite of dominant. He will be better off in the hands of an experienced dog person who knows what is necessary to enhance his self-esteem.*

■ **First-time dog owners** *should avoid bold puppies in favour of ones with quiet temperaments.*

THE TEST

Test pups for inherent dominance by trying these three simple exercises. Give the puppy a score from 1 to 5 for each test.

1   Pick up the puppy and observe his behaviour.

CRINGES	TENTATIVE	RELAXED	RESISTS	BITES
1	2	3	4	5

2   Take the pup to a quiet area away from his litter, put him down, and watch the way he explores.

TERRIFIED	TENTATIVE	RELAXED	INQUISITIVE	SUPER CHARGED
1	2	3	4	5

3   Roll the pup on his back, hold him there for a minute, and see what he does.

TERRIFIED	TENTATIVE	RELAXES	WRIGGLES	ANNOYED
1	2	3	4	5

In all aspects, the "median" pup, the individual who scores 3 every time, is on his way to becoming the easiest pup to bring into your family. Puppies that score 1 are submissive and potentially fearful. Pups that score 5, especially on the third test, are inherently dominant. These make fine dogs, but only in the hands of experienced dog handlers.

Socialization and fear

Pups go through specific fear periods, when new sights and sounds can really unnerve them. They usually start to become fearful at about seven to eight weeks of age. Testing earlier, at six weeks, is ideal, although of course not always practical.

Good breeders are aware of the value of early socialization for their pups, and expose them under controlled circumstances to a variety of sights and sounds. Ask the breeder if she has carried out an active socialization program for her pups, and if so what it involved.

The best start for a pup is to live in a busy, lively, even noisy household where he is carefully handled each day by children and adults, is played with by visitors, and meets other dogs and cats.

Beware of pups raised outdoors, in show kennels, pet shops, farms, or puppy mills, where there has been no effort to socialize them. Pups that have never lived in a home are disadvantaged from the start, and are more likely to have temperament problems.

■ **Puppies become** *fearful around seven weeks old; test a puppy's behaviour at six weeks old.*

Hearts versus minds

Our hearts go out to the underdog. He needs us. He depends on us to protect him. I know it is easier to say than to do, but try to be logical. Submissive pups often grow up to be fearful, tentative adults. If you want to avoid this problem, pick a pup with an equable temperament.

INTERNET

users.bigpond.com/ winron/training.html

For an overview of canine socialization needs, visit Collar & Lead Obedience Training at this site.

■ **Make sure** *your puppy socializes with adults, children, and other dogs from an early age.*

Some breeds that are great with children

These breeds are among the most easy-going and least likely to snap when provoked – ideal for families with young children.

Basset Hound

Bernese Mountain Dog

Bloodhound

Cavalier King Charles Spaniel

Collie

Golden Retriever

Labrador Retriever

Newfoundland

Norwegian Elkhound

Hungarian Vizsla

Ten breeds likely to snap at children

These breeds, primarily terriers, are the ones that in several studies top the list of dogs most likely to snap at children.

Chihuahua

Chow Chow

Cocker Spaniel (solid red or tan)

Fox Terrier

Irish Terrier

Jack Russell
    Terrier

Pomeranian

Scottish Terrier

Welsh Terrier

West Highland
    White Terrier

Yorkshire Terrier

■ **The sociable** *Cavalier King Charles Spaniel is an ideal dog for large families.*

Simple adult dog tests

THE MOST APTLY NAMED *dog I see at my veterinary clinic is called WYSIWYG – "what you see is what you get." That, in a nutshell, is what I find so attractive about dogs: their total, frank honesty. Dogs don't lie. They don't beat around the bush. Love, hate, apprehension, contentment, excitement, boredom, fear, mellowness – a dog's temperament is visible and true. It just doesn't get any simpler.*

Testing an adult dog gives reliable answers to your questions about temperament, simply because all dogs are WYSIWYG. Test a dog's reactions to people, circumstances, and other animals, and you'll see exactly what you're getting.

REACTIONS TO PEOPLE

■ **Introduce your** *dog to people wearing hats to test her reaction.*

Here are some ways to test an adult dog. Score his reaction from 1 to 5.

CALM	TENTATIVE	UNNERVED	AGITATED	VERY AGITATED
= 1	= 2	= 3	= 4	= 5

Strangers ____
Babies ____
Preschoolers ____
School-age children ____
Teenagers ____
Adults ____
Disabled or infirm ____
Loud people ____
Shy people ____

Joggers ____
Delivery people ____
People in uniform ____
People wearing hats ____
People wearing
  motorcycle helmets ____
People of another race
  or nationality ____

■ **Test your** *dog's reaction to meeting school-aged children.*

It is self-evident that the best family dogs, the most equable, score low in as many categories as possible. Low scorers make the best "people dogs."

The advantage to this type of temperament testing is that you know from the time you bring your new dog into your home what problems you may face and what training may be necessary to overcome those problems. Good rescue groups and shelters test dogs in a variety of ways. Ask how many of these tests they carried out.

■ **Accustomize your** *dog to car rides so that she does not react badly on journeys.*

REACTIONS TO NEW SITUATIONS AND CIRCUMSTANCES

CALM = 1	TENTATIVE = 2	UNNERVED = 3	AGITATED = 4	VERY AGITATED = 5

Car rides ____	Moving vehicles ____	Pat from a stranger ____
Umbrella opened ____	Slippery floor ____	Grooming ____
Pushchairs ____	Walk on busy street ____	
Loud noises ____	Visit to veterinarian ____	
Unfamiliar cat ____	Visit to friend's house ____	
Livestock ____	Eye contact	
Horses ____	from a stranger ____	
Moving bicycle ____		
Moving motorbike ____		

■ **A moving bicycle** *should not scare or unnerve your dog.*

Once more, dogs with low scores are well socialized and not fearful – a perfect combination for a new canine family member. Modify this test to your specific circumstances. For example, if you plan bus trips each day with your dog, test him out on buses. See what happens. Unlike with puppies, where a whole range of behaviours change as a dog matures, an adult dog's response to these tests is a true reflection of his temperament.

■ **Ask shelter personnel** *whether the dog has ever snarled or barked at a child.*

AND BE SURE TO ASK...

If you are rescuing a dog from a shelter, try to get answers to as many of these questions as possible.

Does the dog respond to commands?	yes __	no __
Is he friendly with visitors?	yes __	no __
Is he friendly with other dogs?	yes __	no __
Can you take food away without trouble?	yes __	no __
Can you take a toy away without trouble?	yes __	no __
With kennel staff, has the dog:		
growled or barked?	yes __	no __
snapped?	yes __	no __
bitten?	yes __	no __
With children, has the dog:		
growled or barked?	yes __	no __
snapped?	yes __	no __
bitten?	yes __	no __
When left alone, does the dog:		
bark or howl?	yes __	no __
dig or scratch?	yes __	no __
constantly pace?	yes __	no __
chew objects?	yes __	no __
urinate or defecate inappropriately?	yes __	no __

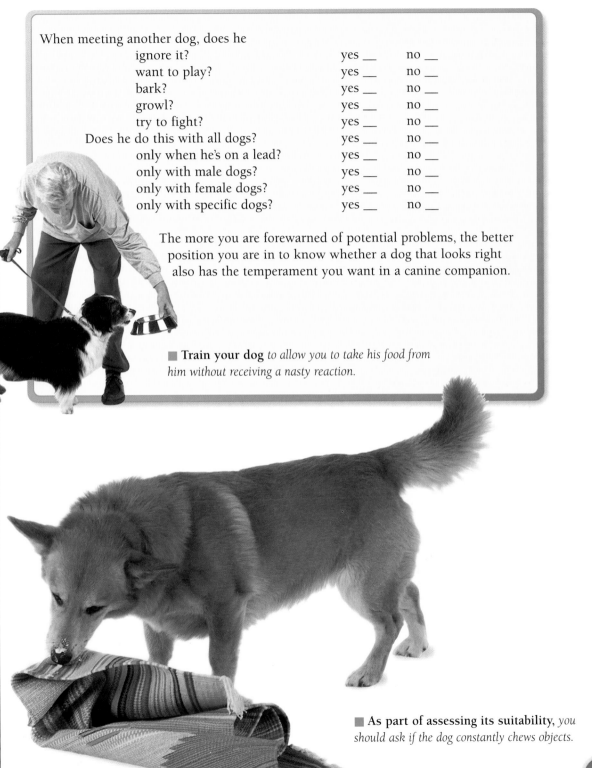

When meeting another dog, does he

ignore it?	yes __	no __
want to play?	yes __	no __
bark?	yes __	no __
growl?	yes __	no __
try to fight?	yes __	no __
Does he do this with all dogs?	yes __	no __
only when he's on a lead?	yes __	no __
only with male dogs?	yes __	no __
only with female dogs?	yes __	no __
only with specific dogs?	yes __	no __

The more you are forewarned of potential problems, the better position you are in to know whether a dog that looks right also has the temperament you want in a canine companion.

■ **Train your dog** *to allow you to take his food from him without receiving a nasty reaction.*

■ **As part of assessing its suitability,** *you should ask if the dog constantly chews objects.*

Test yourself, with honesty

DO NOT JUST TEST the dogs. Test yourself. What do you really want from a dog? We have talked about this already, but it is worth revisiting. Do you want a companion, a protector, a status symbol, an ego booster? Be as truthful with yourself as a dog is with you. Here are some simple questions you can ask yourself about what you want from your dog.

HOW IMPORTANT ARE THESE ATTRIBUTES?

Mark your dog's score below, ranging from 1 (not very important) to 5 (very important)

Friendly with strangers	____	Does not chase livestock	____
Friendly with pre-schoolers	____	Responds to commands	____
Friendly with school-age children	____	Content at being home alone	____
Friendly with teenagers	____	Enjoys family activities	____
Friendly with other		Likes to be stroked and petted	____
unknown dogs	____	Strong-willed	____
Does not chase cats	____	Confident and independent	____
		Active	____

Low scores mean you are sensible about your canine requirements, but I sneaked in three contradictions in these questions – common ones, because we often have contradictory aspirations for our dogs. It's the last three questions. We want our dogs to be good canine citizens, but at the same time we are proud of family members who are active, energetic, confident, independent, strong-willed individuals. The problem is that a strong-willed, confident, independent, active dog is a handful. This is not the type of dog that responds well to commands. He may pay attention to a deep masculine voice, but pay no heed to a soft feminine one. Here is where we must compromise.

■ **If you already** *have a pet, find out whether your new dog gets on with other animals.*

A trait that is attractive in a person can be problematic in a dog. Please, be sensible. And while I am on the subject, let me reiterate a few more points. I do not want to put you off getting a dog, but I do want to make sure you understand exactly what you are doing.

■ **Remember that** *an adult dog requires physical and mental stimulation.*

Dogs have lifelong needs

Puppies grow up. Some will grow to be bigger than you are. A mature dog has physical needs for exercise and activity, and an equal need for psychological stimulation. You are responsible not only for his physical health, but also for his emotional well-being.

And here is where there is a problem. More and more, veterinary surgeons are seeing emotional problems in dogs, for example *separation anxiety*. We cause these problems by bringing dogs into our homes and expecting them to adapt to a sedentary, solitary lifestyle. Your playful, cute puppy will become an adult very quickly, and will need you throughout his life. A dog is for life, not just for the moment.

> **DEFINITION**
>
> Separation anxiety is *an extreme reaction some dogs have when their owners leave the house. They may react by being very destructive or self destructive (licking or chewing themselves), or by excessive barking or whining. Dogs with separation anxiety need the help of a well thought-out programme of training, behaviour modification, and lifestyle enrichment.*

■ **Very lively** *dogs often respond better to a deep voice.*

■ **Dogs can** *suffer from separation anxiety; remember that they are pack animals and need company.*

Dogs cost money

Do some financial planning, especially if you are thinking of getting a big dog or one who needs constant extra attention, such as frequent professional grooming. It is not difficult to project the costs of keeping a dog. Food and dog equipment are easy costs to calculate.

Yearly preventative health care – vaccinations and parasite prevention – are also predictable. But medical emergencies are another matter. Consider pet health insurance or, as an alternative set up a bank account and make a regular deposit each month, as your own insurance policy against a pet health emergency. Whatever you do, be prepared financially for 10 to 15 years of dog expenses.

■ **Although dogs** *are inexpensive to keep, be prepared for the cost of any medical emergencies.*

Trivia...

Dogs and other canines, such as foxes, coyotes, and wolves, can carry a 90, Toxocara canis, *that is potentially dangerous to us.* Toxocara *is most common in newborn pups, and is easily eliminated using veterinarian-supplied worming medication. If we humans swallow* Toxocara *larvae, these microscopic stages of the parasite can migrate anywhere in the body, including into the back of the eye. Rarely, this can cause blurred vision in the affected eye. To eliminate this risk, make sure all pups are wormed routinely, following your veterinarian's instructions.*

Dogs can cause problems

While I am telling you about all the drawbacks of having a dog, Lexy, my aging friend, has quietly climbed on the sofa and fallen into a deep doggy sleep, exaggerated because she is almost stone deaf. I look at her and find it almost incomprehensible to think that such a gentle, giving soul is a wolf in disguise. But she is. Pushed far enough, she would bite. So will other dogs. In fact, dog bites are the most common health hazard to owning a dog.

Do not think that dogs usually bite the bad guys. Not so. Owners are bitten more often. In affected parts of Europe if your dog is not up to date with his rabies inoculation, this creates an even more complicated problem. Allergies are another increasing problem. Think about your whole family. It is heartbreaking to get a dog, then be advised to part with him because someone in the family is allergic.

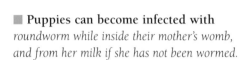

■ **Puppies can become infected with** *roundworm while inside their mother's womb, and from her milk if she has not been wormed.*

Our lives change, so plan ahead

A dog might fit in with your family plans now, but what about in five, ten, or even 15 years time? When the kids are gone and you are empty-nesters, do you want a dog or do you want your freedom? (As for me, I want both. I love the freedom, but just cannot imagine coming home to an empty house without something there – even if she's old, a bit smelly, and snores a lot.)

■ **If pushed** *far enough dogs will bite. This is a potential health hazard.*

Involve the family

A dog is a new member of the family. He may become the responsibility of one person in particular, but he belongs to the family, not to one person alone. Getting a dog is a family decision. Do not get one as a surprise for anyone, especially if you are not going to be the one who looks after the dog.

When you do get a canine companion, leave nothing to chance. Write down house rules that outline the do's and don'ts of living with your new friend. Discuss with the whole family the need to be firm in the face of expressive, pleading eyes. All of you are pack leaders, although one will be supreme commander. Finally, involve the entire family in choosing a name for your dog. It helps bring all of you together and sets the stage for bringing your new dog into your lives.

SUGGESTED HOUSE RULES

1. Sparky will be restricted to _____ (specify area).

2. Sparky will sleep in _____ (specify area).

3. Sparky will be the primary responsibility of _____ (specify who).

4. Exterior doors to the house will always be kept closed.

5. Everyone makes the time to attend Sparky's puppy obedience classes.

6. Do not give Sparky treats until he obeys a command.

7. Always use Sparky's name first when you want his attention.

8. Sparky is a member of the family. Consider him when making plans or arrangements.

■ **Agree where** *your dog will sleep before he comes home with you.*

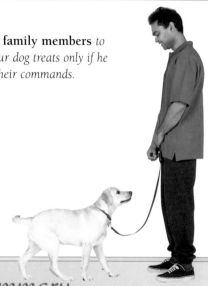

■ **Ask family members** *to give your dog treats only if he obeys their commands.*

Trivia...

Dogs respond best to short, snappy names. I gave my dogs pretentious names – Lexington and Liberty – but when speaking to them we simply say "Lex" and "Lib". Single-syllable names that do not sound like other words you regularly use are best: Rex, Bones, Ben, Meg. If you are going to call your Cocker Spaniel "Cheeseburger", be prepared to call her Cheese for short.

A simple summary

✓ Puppy testing can be a useful exercise, but it does not predict adult personality other than some measure of dominance or submission.

✓ Early socialization is important, and puppies raised in loving homes have a better chance of being calm, reliable companions.

✓ Testing an adult dog's responses to specific circumstances is a good way to gauge the dog's true personality.

✓ Your own expectations are also important in forming a good relationship with your dog.

✓ Plan on having your dog with you for his life, which can be ten to 15 years.

✓ Dogs cost both time and money. Be prepared to spend both.

■ **Avoid confusing** *your dog by agreeing on where he is allowed to sit in your home.*

PART TWO

BE PREPARED SO YOUR NEW DOG ADJUSTS QUICKLY

BRINGING YOUR BEST FRIEND HOME

LIVING WITH A DOG is immensely *rewarding*. It reminds us that we are part of nature, and brings love and *companionship* to our lives. Bringing a dog into your life also includes responsibilities, for your dog's well-being and to your family, friends, and neighbours. Plan ahead with a thoughtful introduction of your dog into family and neighbourhood life.

Read about dog care, too. Think about your dog's indoor and outdoor *environment*. Eliminate potential hazards and, at the same time, carefully plan where your dog will sleep and how training will begin. Make sure the equipment you get is practical, not just attractive. Try to think like a dog when shopping for your new friend. And keep it simple!

Chapter 6

The First Night

L ET'S KEEP THIS VERY SIMPLE. Think of yourself as a school teacher. The best teachers understand the importance of focusing and directing their students' enthusiasm and youthful energy. Good teachers know how vital it is to remain focused on goals. Your goal is to integrate your new dog into your family smoothly. If you are going to be successful, you will have to control some of your own emotions, control your family's behaviour, and channel your new dog's energy in positive ways.

In this chapter...

✓ Be leader of your own pack

✓ Who sleeps where?

✓ Beds, bedding, and barriers

✓ A crate is not a jail

✓ Outdoor kennels

✓ Routines and rituals

Be leader of your own pack

Yes, a new dog is a member of the family, but there is always one person – you – who is primarily in charge. You are responsible for your new dog, but you are also responsible for moulding and channelling the behaviour of your children, your spouse, even your other pets. Follow one cardinal rule: keep them all under control. Do that, and the rest is simple.

Control your children

Your young kids will think of a new dog, especially if she is a pup, as an exciting toy. Naturally, they will want to play with her, carry her around, invite friends over to see the new puppy. You may have told yourself that the dog is for your children. That may be so, but the responsibility for getting your dog off to a good start is yours.

TELL YOUR CHILDREN

Set these rules on the very first day:

✓ The puppy is not to be picked up.

✓ The puppy is not to be disturbed while sleeping.

✓ No screaming or jumping around the puppy.

✓ No feeding.

✓ No yanking, tugging, or pulling.

A pup, or a more mature dog, needs time to explore and investigate her new home. She should be able to do so quietly, without fuss. Consider buying your children an exciting new game or toy when you bring your new dog home, to distract them a little and give your dog some time and space.

■ **Make sure** *children play gently with a new dog, and that there is no screaming or pulling her tail.*

Control your spouse

I hate to admit it, but husbands are sometimes far worse than children in doing the wrong thing. Kids usually pay attention to you. Husbands often say, "Oh, it doesn't hurt if I put her up here on the bed just this once," or "I let her out of her *dog crate* because she was crying." When it comes to parenting there is no doubt, us fellas are the weaker sex. We give in faster. We are inconsistent. We are emotional pushovers. I really do not know what you can do about this, other than to understand that with all your good efforts in dog training, you might have a saboteur in your home subverting all your hard work!

■ **Your family** *must agree on house rules for the dog and not give in.*

Control the meeting with your resident dog

If you already have a dog, assume that initially, your resident dog will not be too happy about sharing her home with a new canine arrival. If your dog accompanies you in the car when you collect your pup, keep them separate on the return journey. The first introduction of the resident to the newcomer should take place on neutral territory, not in your home, and after your own dog has had some good exercise. The advantage of new territory is that your dog will be interested in investigating its new sights and smells. Your new pup is simply one of those interesting distractions. Let them sniff and investigate each other. Do not interfere unless either looks very agitated. If they do, distract them and move to a more interesting location.

Once you are home, let them meet again in the garden if you have one. Remove any bones, toys, or other canine possessions from the garden. You do not want your dog to get jealous or possessive if the pup sniffs or picks up a treasured object. Let the puppy loose first, and while she is exploring, let your resident dog go too.

Do not let your pup get too excited. Generally speaking, older dogs do not much like pups running like malevolent fleas around their legs. That behaviour may provoke a snarl or a snap. If you think your dog might attack the puppy, avoid the garden. Instead, go straight inside and put the pup in a playpen or dog crate.

■ **When your new pup** *meets the resident dog, let them investigate one another.*

Control the meeting with your resident cat

Most resident cats know exactly what to do when meeting a pup. A hiss, a spit, and perhaps the swipe of a paw tells the newcomer who the boss is. Most dog-cat introductions go very well. Typically, the puppy retreats and learns to respect cats.

If you have a terrier pup, or any other individual full of bravado, be ready to distract the pup so that she is not tempted to chase your cat. First lessons are vital. If there is any sign of possible chasing, do not leave the dog and cat together when you cannot supervise them. Put your pup in her playpen or crate.

■ **Cats are** *good at defending themselves; but always supervise their first meeting with your new dog.*

■ **If your dog** *chases the resident cat, leave her in a crate while she is unsupervised.*

Chasing is more likely to occur when your pup has settled in to her new home and is more confident. If she develops that gleam in the eye, keep a long, thin line attached to your pup's collar so you can step on it (the line, not the pup) at the first sign of a chase. If your boisterous pup develops the game of jumping at your cat (a great puppy game because it often makes the cat run away, creating an opportunity for a chase game), interrupt your dog's activity with a tempting toy. You want to teach your pup that you and other people, not cats, are the source of games.

Who sleeps where?

A PUPPY IS A NATURALLY *sociable individual. She enjoys companionship, thrives on playing with others, and feels relaxed and content when surrounded by her family. For the first eight weeks of her life, she snuggled in close with her mother and siblings when she slept. It is only natural for a pup to be upset when she is separated from the security of this satisfying physical contact. You have to decide what type of sleeping arrangements*

■ **A comfortable,** *spacious, and hygienic bed is important for puppies and adult dogs.*

you want for your pup and then, as best you can, abide by that decision. Many dog owners feel it is best to start as you plan to continue, with the new pup sleeping in the kitchen, utility room, or other chosen and comfortable place in the house. If this is what you want to do, be consistent. Ignore your pup's howling or crying. If you respond, you are teaching her that making noise works; that it gets a response.

A sensible start

Personally, I prefer pups to start off with temporary sleeping arrangements in a high-sided cardboard box, or playpen, or crate in your bedroom. While the pup no longer has physical contact with the rest of the pack, she is comforted by the sight, sound, and smell of her new family.

Sleeping in your bedroom accelerates your pup's bonding to you, regarding you as the leader of the pack. Pups, and even adult dogs, are extraordinarily flexible. It takes only a short time for a dog to look upon you as someone to listen to, respond to, and respect.

The night-time routine

If possible, before you take your pup home, bring a blanket to the breeder, to be left with the mother and puppies in their bedding. Within a day, this will pick up lots of familiar scent. Bring this blanket home and use it in your pup's bed. The smell will be comforting and reassuring.

Follow this routine on the first and subsequent nights:

1. Make sure your puppy is as sleepy as possible. Play with her, feed her a warm meal, take her outside to relieve herself, then put her in her temporary sleeping box.
2. Do not fuss. Be quiet. Be calm. Lie down and read a book. Do not even look at your pup. Eye contact will only provoke a mournful demand to be picked up.
3. Disregard whimpers, howls, and cries.
4. During the night when she wakes up, cries loudly, and tries to get out of her box, it probably means she needs to relieve herself. (Pups do not like to soil their own beds.) Have what you need on hand so you can quickly get up and take her outside or to her designated indoor toileting area. When she relieves herself, praise her, give her a treat, then quietly, without fuss, put her back in her sleeping box.
5. Stick ear plugs in your ears for the next ten minutes. She will want to play. If you are resolute, she'll quickly learn that vocalizing does not get her what she wants.

Permanent arrangements

Within a week your pup will be ready to sleep on her own, in the room you want her to sleep in. Of course she will be unsettled, but much less so than if she was obliged to sleep alone in a room from the day she entered your home. Please do not banish your puppy to any place that is cold, damp, or otherwise uncomfortable. And make sure she has a nice, soft bed to sleep on. Otherwise, if she howls all night it serves you right.

After choosing where she will sleep, if possible cover the floor with a large plastic sheet — the type you get from a hardware store if you are painting the room — and then lay two to three layers of newspaper over it. (Some puppies will have a lovely time shredding the plastic for you, even with the newspapers on top.)

Lay the sheet on the floor and cover it with two to three layers of newspaper. During the day, when your dog urinates in the yard or on the street, dab some Kleenex, a ball of cotton, or a Q-tip in it, pop the soiled article in a plastic bag and bring it indoors. Swab this article on the newspaper in the location where you want your pup to toilet, away from her bedding. This smell will attract your pup when she needs to toilet during the night.

Some pups, especially large breeds like German Shepherds, Labrador Retrievers, and Golden Retrievers, just do not want to toilet in the house. If your pup yaps or cries the way she did when she was in her cardboard box in your bedroom and wanted to relieve herself, get up, let her outside but do not make a fuss. Be silent. Just accompany her, let her toilet, then go straight back to bed. You do not want to teach her that crying leads to play or other rewards.

■ **A soft bed** *with a machine-washable cover is recommended for most dogs.*

Beds, bedding, and barriers

REGARDLESS OF WHERE *you want your pup to sleep, she needs a bed and bedding. Plan ahead. Consider her adult size before investing in a permanent bed. Plan where she will eventually sleep, not just where she sleeps during her first weeks with you. And think of teething. Pups go through a real nuisance chewing stage. A wicker basket might look gorgeous, but for most pups it is just too great a temptation.*

Dog beds

Dogs love the security of their own bed. Throughout life, whenever there is cloud on the canine horizon, a dog will retreat to the comfort and security of her nest. Large dogs like retrievers enjoy lying flat on their sides with their legs extended. When choosing a bed, make sure it is large enough for your dog to lie in this position.

Most dogs also enjoy the security of a solid perimeter they can lie against. I guess to a dog it means that if she's lying against a wall nothing can creep up on her from that direction. Many beds have sides, like a cup.

■ **Provide your dog** *with a chew toy to prevent her from chewing her bedding, especially during her teething period.*

When it comes to looks you have lots of options, from wicker, to wood, to replicas of the White House. If you want your dog to sleep in a fashion statement, or at least in a bed that is more like nice furniture, do not buy it until your pup is close to a year old. Concentrate instead on the type of bedding you provide.

■ **Large dogs** *prefer lying on their sides with their legs stretched out.*

Bedding

Bedding should be hygenic, washable, comfortable, and protecting. Rectangular, round, or oval "bean bags" filled wih lightweight styrofoam beads are ideal. They usually come with zippered covers that can easily be thrown in the washing machine. And if they get soaked with urine or other liquids, the whole bean bag can be washed in the washing machine and dried on the clothesline.

Many dogs like to prepare their own beds before lying down. Some dogs act like they have degrees in mechanical engineering, digging, and scratching in a dedicated fashion to create an architecture they have in their own minds, but one that is usually lost on us. A blanket helps these dogs enormously. It can be formed into mountains, nosed into corners, excavated, rotated, manipulated. Dogs like blankets.

Barriers

The stair gate, or door gate, or baby gate is one of those great underestimated inventions. Placed in the right locations, baby gates restrict your dog to the parts of the house you want her to stay in, while at the same time letting her see through to other rooms. Use baby gates for general restrictions or added security when you have visitors, or if your own baby is on the floor.

INTERNET

www.nashelter.
org/crate.html

There's more information here on crate training your dog.

Trivia...

Lexy sleeps on a dog bed in a wicker basket. Each time we wash her bed cover and blanket and make her bed, she spends the following evenings moving the blanket until it drapes over the back of her basket. We assume she likes leaning against it. When we watch her working away, she looks at us and you can see what she is thinking: "Dummies! Don't you know where the blanket belongs?"

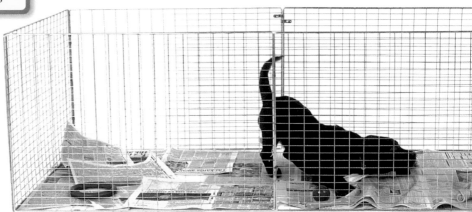

■ **The puppy's pen** *should be a fun place for her; make sure she has toys and chews.*

A crate is not a jail

A playpen, or better still a walk-in dog crate, is a must-have piece of equipment. Get one before you bring your pup home. Then use it properly. A crate should be a pleasant place for your dog to spend her time; her own personal den.

Never use it for discipline. Let me say that again. Do not let your dog associate the crate with punishment. A crate is home. Talk to your dog when she is in her crate. Choose a crate that will be big enough for your grown dog to stretch out in.

One of the great advantages of crates is that they ease your travel problems. If you have a hatchback, estate car, or utility van, the crate provides safe and secure personal transport for your dog.

■ **Leave the crate door** *open with chew toys or a treat inside and your puppy will soon investigate.*

Introducing the crate

Have the crate ready when your dog comes home. Line it with newspaper, cover part of the newspaper with soft bedding, then put food and a toy in the crate. Leave the crate door open. Your pup will willingly investigate, find the toy and treat, and consider the crate a good place. The best position for your dog's crate is a busy place like the kitchen. Do not put it in an isolated part of the house. That defeats its purpose.

Crate training

Once your pup has become accustomed to walking into the crate and playing in it, you can train her to use it by saying "crate" as she walks in or is enticed in with a treat. Eventually, close the crate door for a few minutes while she plays or relaxes in the crate.

If your pup barks while in her crate or playpen, do not even look at her. Do not scold, admonish, or talk to her. Pay no attention until she is quiet once more. (If you do pay attention, you are teaching her that noise gets results.) After she is quiet for a few minutes, take her out and play with her. The only exception to the "pay no attention" rule is if you think she has to relieve herself. If you think this is so, wait for a break in the yapping or barking, then whisk her into the garden.

■ **When your pup** *is relaxed in the crate, close the door so that she becomes accustomed to it.*

Outdoor kennels

THERE ARE VERY FEW *circumstances where you should consider keeping your dog primarily outdoors. Living outdoors dramatically interferes with proper socialization with the family. It inhibits learning. Outside dogs develop their own ways of distracting themselves, such as digging and endless barking.*

Honestly, I do not like the idea of a family dog living outdoors. Dogs are pack animals, and they get lonely without you. If you feel your dog really must spend time outdoors, plan for a combination of indoor-outdoor living.

During the first important and deeply impressionable months of your puppy's life with you, restrict her to your kitchen and crate train her. At the same time, introduce your pup to her dog house in the garden. Dogs have no difficulty learning that both the dog house and the crate are safe, secure homes.

Dream house

The dog house should be free of drafts and damp, with hygienic, washable bedding. It should be large enough for your giant breed to stretch out flat on her side.

She should use her dog house only for short periods of time. Just because she spends part of her day outside does not mean you spend any less time with her. If there are unavoidable reasons that mean your dog must be kenneled outdoors, always ensure that during inclement weather she can sleep in the kitchen. Make sure that you and your family spend as much time as possible outdoors in the garden with her.

■ **Make sure** *your dog is only kept in an outside kennel for short periods of time and that she has food, water, and toys with her.*

Routines and rituals

Just like kids, dogs thrive when there are routines and when they know the limits. Dogs are creatures of habit. They like order in their lives. They think, "I did it this way before, so I'll do it this way again."

Consistency

It's important to establish routines and rules right from the start. It's not fair to let your puppy do all sorts of things that you would not allow your adult dog to do. When you start scolding her for things that used to make you laugh, she'll wonder why she's suddenly out of favour.

Besides, give them an inch and they'll take a mile. Put a pup on the sofa and she thinks this is where she should stay. Allow her on the bed and she will assume it is hers. Give her some food while you are eating and she will expect it again.

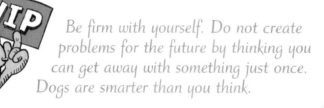

Be firm with yourself. Do not create problems for the future by thinking you can get away with something just once. Dogs are smarter than you think.

■ **Be consistent:** *even if your dog begs or whines, stick to your rules. If you decide not to let her on to the sofa, do not give in.*

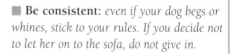

■ **Make your dog** *wait for her food until you have eaten and she will soon learn who is pack leader.*

Sparky's day

Write down your dog's daily routine so that even in your absence, nothing is missed. It may seem time-consuming, but that is only because everything you do is on the list. Here is an example for a very young puppy. This is just my suggestion, and it's OK if your dog's routine is a bit different.

7:30 am	Out for a short walk and a short, constructive play session
8:00 am	Family breakfast
8:30 am	Sparky's first meal
9:00 am	Walk – play – rest
10:30 am	Longer walk – meeting others – rest
12:00 noon	Walk – training – rest
12:30 pm	Family lunch
1:00 pm	Sparky's second meal
1:15 pm	Walk – rest
2:30 pm	Walk – play – grooming – rest
4:00 pm	Walk – training – rest
5:00 pm	Sparky's third meal
5:15 pm	Walk – rest
6:45 pm	Walk – rest
7:00 pm	Family dinner
8:00 pm	Walk – socializing – rest
9:00 pm	Sparky's fourth meal
9:15 pm	Walk – play – rest
10:30 pm	Walk – vigorous play – bed

■ **Your dog's** *daily routine will change throughout her life as her needs change.*

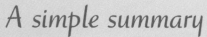

A simple summary

✓ It's very important to start as you plan to continue when setting rules and routines for your dog.

✓ You must control not only your dog, but your family, and your other pets as well.

✓ Give serious consideration to where you want your dog to sleep, and the bed you will provide.

✓ The dog should live indoors with your family.

■ **Remember that a** *controlled situation is preferable for your dog and cat to meet.*

✓ A crate is a wonderful tool and can be a cosy den for your dog, but should not be used for punishment or excessive confinement.

✓ Dogs appreciate routine, so be consistent.

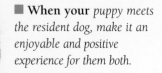

■ **When your** *puppy meets the resident dog, make it an enjoyable and positive experience for them both.*

Chapter 7

Accessorizing Your Dog

SOCIAL SCIENTISTS TELL US that shopping has become our favourite pastime. Well, here is your chance to shop like you have never done before. Use initiative and flair but remember, you are buying dog products for your dog. His practical and even aesthetic needs are different from your own. Function is vitally important. Is the clip on the lead safe, but still light enough in weight to not be a burden for your dog? Is the food bowl attractive but heavy enough not to travel across the floor when it is used? When shopping for your dog, think about his practical needs. Keep it simple.

In this chapter...

✓ Dog essentials

✓ Grooming and cleaning

✓ Fun and safe toys

✓ Travel accessories

✓ Seasonal neccesities

ACCESSORIZE YOUR DOG WITH DIGNITY AND ACCORDING TO THE REQUIREMENTS OF THE BREED

Dog essentials

Deep down inside, we humans still behave the way we have evolved to behave. We are instinctive hunter-gatherers, and just love to shop. Shopping for your new dog is extra exciting, because you can search for and find items you never knew existed.

There are essentials that all dogs need – bedding, which I have already described; bowls for food and water; collars, ID tags, and leads for security and control. When buying these items do not let style and cost be the only factors in your decision. What an article looks like is important, but even more important is the practicality of the design. Choose items that are designed according to your dog's needs as well as your fashion sense and your wallet.

■ **High-sided** *ceramic and metal bowls are preferable to plastic bowls.*

Food and water bowls

As pack animals, dogs evolved to be competitive eaters. The fastest consumer gets the most nourishment. Other than the tiny breeds (doglets like Yorkies and Chihuahuas), dogs naturally eat quickly. Choose food bowls that are wide and heavy on the bottom, ones that are unlikely to travel across the kitchen floor as your dog vacuums up his meal. Heavy ceramic or metal bowls on non-slip rubber bases are excellent. So, too, are double food and water bowls also mounted on rubber bases.

Be as hygienic with your dog's utensils as you are with your own. Wash the food and water bowls every day. If you feed your dog canned food, keep a separate can opener for your dog's food and wash it routinely. Keep any partly used can of food covered with a plastic lid, in the refrigerator, for a maximum of three days.

Dogs are sloppy, especially when drinking. Place an absorbent, washable mat under the food and water bowls to catch the majority of the drips.

■ **Make sure your** *dog has a constant supply of fresh water, and wash his bowl daily.*

Introducing collars and leashes

Your dog should learn to wear a collar and ID tag from the day you get him. A pup usually scratches his neck a lot when he first wears a collar. Do not give in to his exasperation with feeling something strange on his neck. He will get used to the sensation very quickly, almost always within days.

Choose a collar that's the right size for your dog's neck, and do not fasten it too tightly. You should be able to slip two fingers under a well-fitted collar. With all but the thickest-necked breeds, this means the collar is comfortably loose but will not come off if your dog tugs backward.

At first, put his collar on just before feeding time. His mind will be distracted by the sight and smell of food. Take it off immediately after he eats. Use the same method with his lead.

Once he is used to wearing his collar, clip the lead on just before feeding and call him to his food, applying very gentle tension to the lead. By associating these accessories with something as thrilling as food, your dog will not resent wearing either item.

EXTENDING LEAD

2-METRE COTTON WEBBING LEAD

LEATHER LEADS

Collar types

Collars (and leads) vary enormously in quality, price, and design, and are usually made of woven nylon, leather, or metal. For pups who will outgrow their first collars, woven nylon with a simple buckle is comfortable and inexpensive, an ideal first choice. (Some dogs are allergic to nylon – if the scratching and fussing persists, the collar may be making the dog itchy.) Wide, flat leather collars are excellent for long-necked breeds such as Whippets and Greyhounds, while rolled leather collars are perfect for breeds with heavier coats of hair.

DESIGNER COLLAR

REFLECTIVE BUCKLE COLLAR

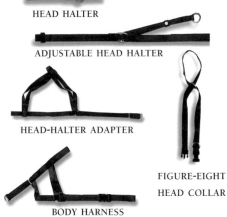

Avoid leather if you have a canine swimmer. Leather gets mouldy when wet. Metal choke chains, still popular with disciplinarian obedience trainers, really have no place on dogs. Half-check collars, on the other hand, designed to control a dog without causing discomfort or danger, are excellent for big, boisterous dogs. I will talk about these more in Chapter 13.

HEAD HALTER

ADJUSTABLE HEAD HALTER

HEAD-HALTER ADAPTER

FIGURE-EIGHT HEAD COLLAR

BODY HARNESS

Leashes for work or play

To begin with, you will need two different types of lead: a standard short one for walking and a much longer one for training. I find that a long nylon cord with a lightweight bolt snap that attaches to the collar is perfect for indoor training. If your budget allows, get one of these, and also a 6-metre cotton-webbing lead for outdoor training.

An extending lead (the original and still most popular brand is called a Flexi), used properly, serves two purposes. It acts as a short lead for walking and a longer one for outdoor training. If you get an extending lead, also get the lightweight nylon cord for indoor training. I will describe how to use all these valuable accessories (and also some alternative training aids, such as head halters) when I talk about basic training in Chapter 12.

Body harnesses

Some dogs are not the right shape for collars. For example, breeds such as Bulldogs and Pugs often have necks as wide as their heads. If your dog's shape is not right for a collar, provide him with a body harness. The most comfortable are made of woven nylon. More flamboyant models are made of leather.

Some small breeds, especially Yorkshire Terriers, have softer than normal windpipes. While a Yorkie can wear a collar to carry his ID, it is best to use a body harness for walking. Tension from any forward movement is then transferred to the body, not to the sensitive neck. Never use a half-check or choke chain on a dog with a delicate windpipe.

■ **Some dog breeds** *cannot wear a collar because their necks are the same width as their head, so try using a body harness instead.*

Canine ID

It's common sense that your dog always carries ID. Two forms are better than one. The most visible ID is an engraved name tag. At my veterinary clinic we prepare tags with the dog's name and owner's telephone number on one side and the number of the local emergency veterinary clinic on the other.

Plastic or metal ID capsules are ideal for carrying more detailed information. When travelling away from home, you can include any relevant information such as a local telephone number to contact. The metal cylinders have a tendency to unscrew. Overcome this by applying a drop of nail polish at the join after tightening the cylinder.

Tattoos on the ear or inner thigh, once very popular as permanent methods of ID, have a tendency to get blurry with time, and may be covered by the dog's hair. Still, they are quite popular with some breeders and shelters.

Microchips

The most successful recent method of canine ID is the microchip, an electronic transponder the size of a grain of rice that is injected by your vet just under the skin between the shoulder blades (I mentioned these in Chapter 3, remember?). The transponder emits a signal, read as a number when a handheld reader is run over a dog's shoulders. Many dog rescue groups and shelters now scan lost dogs for microchips.

The microchip has also become the internationally accepted method of canine identification for dogs travelling abroad. Make sure your vet uses ISO standard microchips if you plan a trip out of the country. (There are several brands of microchips, and not all are compatible, so be sure to ask.)

Both tattoos and microchips are useless unless your dog's number is registered with an agency that will track you down if your dog ever gets lost. Some registration agencies charge a single fee for life, while others have an annual renewal fee.

■ **The most visible ID** is an engraved name tag attached to your dog's collar.

123

Grooming and cleaning

OUR INTERVENTION IN *dog breeding has resulted in the great variety of coat lengths and textures. Some of these coats require more frequent attention than others. Canine body maintenance is so important that Chapter 19 is devoted to the subject, but here I want to talk about how choosing the right tools for your dog's coat gets grooming off to a good start.*

Coat types, combs, and brushes

A smooth coat like the Boxer's is the easiest to care for. Get a rubber brush or a hound glove and use it twice a week, stroking against the lie of the fur, to remove debris, dirt, and any loose hair. Afterwards, use a chamois cloth, stroking with the lie of the coat, to bring out the natural shine.

Trivia...

Grooming your dog is extraordinarily important, not just to keep him clean, but also as a natural way for you to reinforce your leadership. Picking up your dog, holding him still, gently brushing him – all of these are dominance gestures.

CHAMOIS CLOTH

RUBBER BRUSH

SOFT PIN BRUSH

TRIMMING SCISSORS

SYNTHETIC BRISTLE BRUSH

■ Grooming equipment

CANINE TOOTHPASTE

NARROW-TOOTHED COMB   TARTAR REMOVER   NAIL CUTTERS

COTTON BALLS

A short, thick coat like a Labrador Retriever's needs different tools: a slicker brush used twice a week to remove tangles, followed by a regular bristle brush to remove any remaining dirt and debris. A longer coat, like the Golden Retriever's, needs to be brushed with both the slicker and bristle brush more frequently, preferably for short periods every day to get your dog used to this type of attention. You will also need a metal comb with widely spaced teeth for combing through the feathery hair, especially on the legs and tail. The long hair around the feet, chest, and hind legs needs occasional trimming with scissors.

Some breeds (the Yorkshire Terrier is a fine example) have long, silky coats but no protective undercoat like the Golden Retriever or Rough Collie have. Take extra care when grooming these single-coated dogs. Without insulating downy hair, it is very easy to scratch or irritate the skin. Dogs like Yorkies should be brushed with a slicker brush, then combed daily to prevent knots from forming, especially behind the ears.

■ **Slicker brushes** *are preferable for silky-coated dogs, such as Yorkshire Terriers, as they have no protective undercoat.*

■ **Use a rubber brush** *to clean the smooth coats of dogs such as Boxers, and brush against the lie of the fur.*

INTERNET

www.identichip.co.uk

This site gives information on both the microchip and the Pet Travel Scheme.

Finally, if you have a Poodle, or Bichon Frise, or a similar breed with constantly growing hair, he needs clipping, usually every six to eight weeks. If you want to do this yourself it is best to get one-to-one instruction from an experienced groomer. If you are unsure about what to do with your dog, watch a professional dog groomer do it once before you try yourself.

■ **Dogs with constantly** *growing hair need clipping every six to eight weeks.*

Nail cutters

Dogs often hate it, but nail trimming is necessary to prevent overgrown nails in lightweight dogs. Heavier dogs that get good exercise are usually able to wear their nails down naturally, but it's best to check and make sure.

■ **The best time** *to trim your dog's nails is after a bath as they are soft.*

Trivia...

Unexpected and excessive nail growth is sometimes associated with an underactive thyroid gland. If your dog's nails are growing excessively, discuss this with your veterinary surgeon.

The best time to trim your dog's nails is after a bath. Their nails are made of the same substance as ours – keratin – which is brittle when dry and softer when wet. Use a guillotine-type clipper. This gives a cleaner cut with less pressure. Replace nail clippers routinely to avoid problems with blunted or loose equipment.

While the tip of the nail consists only of keratin, most of the nail contains living tissue, called the quick, which contains blood vessels and sensitive nerves. If you cut the quick it hurts.

Some dogs have translucent nails, making it easy to see the quick, but most have darker nails that make clipping a bit more difficult. If your dog has dark nails, cut just where the nails begin to curve downwards.

Quick

Nail

Cutting line

■ **Clip the nail** *gently, avoiding the quick.*

Fun and safe toys

TOYS ARE FUN, *and are also among the most important items you provide for your dog. Each toy has a purpose: to be chewed, to squeak, to be chased, or to play tug-of-war with. Use toys as rewards for your dog, just the way you would use food treats.*

INTERNET

www.petspyjamas.
co.uk

Pets Pyjamas sells an extensive range of tools and equipment.

Your dog should always have chewable toys available. These are his own toys, ones you do not get involved with. The squeak and chase toys, on the other hand, are yours, not your dog's. Keep them to yourself. That makes them more interesting when you bring them out. Always take the toy you have been playing with away at the end of a game. The not-so-subtle message you give your dog when you do this is that you are in charge.

FRISBEE

■ **Different types of toys**

ROPE

BALL

Finally, do not overwhelm your dog with toys. If he has a million to choose from, he will find it difficult to differentiate between what is a toy and what is not. The result is he will think he can play with and chew on anything.

TUG

127

Chew toys

All dogs, not just puppies, need to chew. Meat-flavoured nylon bones, rubber rings, a rubber ball on a nylon rope, rawhide chews, and Kongs are all excellent chew toys. Avoid rawhide from countries where unknown preservatives might be used.

Sterilized bones and hooves can present problems. There is no question that these "natural" chew toys are a dog's favourite, but as a vet I see teeth fractured by chewing hard bones. I have always given my own dogs sterilized bones under supervision, but one of my Goldens did fracture a molar tooth and needed surgery as a result.

An ideal chew toy is hollow inside, like a Kong, allowing you to put something exciting, like peanut butter or cheese spread, into it. This is an ideal toy to give your dog when you go out. Getting the food out gives him something mentally stimulating to do. Some toys (the Buster Cube is a good example) are designed to be nosed around the floor, dropping morsels of food out as they are rolled around. These, too, are ideal for leaving with a dog who is home alone for a period of time.

■ **Types of chew toys**

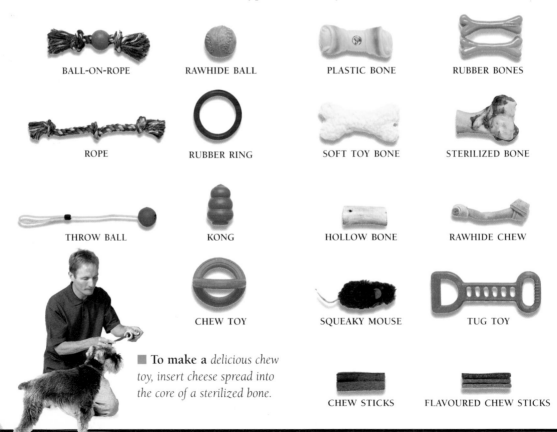

BALL-ON-ROPE   RAWHIDE BALL   PLASTIC BONE   RUBBER BONES

ROPE   RUBBER RING   SOFT TOY BONE   STERILIZED BONE

THROW BALL   KONG   HOLLOW BONE   RAWHIDE CHEW

CHEW TOY   SQUEAKY MOUSE   TUG TOY

■ **To make a** *delicious chew toy, insert cheese spread into the core of a sterilized bone.*

CHEW STICKS   FLAVOURED CHEW STICKS

Squeak toys

Squeak toys belong to you, not your dog. They also last longer when your dog plays with them for only a short time, especially when a puppy is teething. Soft sheepskin-like material surrounding a squeaker makes an ideal toy. So do very thin-skinned rubber balls with squeakers inside. Dogs are less inclined to chew on squeak toys that collapse under the slightest pressure. Give this toy to your dog as a treat, for a short period of time, using a food reward as a distraction when taking it away.

■ **Leave the chew** *toy for your dog when he is in the house alone.*

Fetch and tug-of-war toys

A tennis ball, ball-on-a-rope, braided nylon rope, Frisbee, or any other safe toy you can throw makes an ideal fetch toy. Do not expect your dog to fetch a toy and bring it back without training. If you are using fetch toys to give your dog exercise and have not yet started training him to retrieve, arm yourself with a variety of fetch toys to throw for your dog.

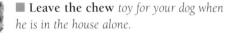

Strong-willed dogs want to win tug-of-war games, so be sensible when playing tug-of-war. You should win most of the time, but if you win all of the time your dog will probably lose interest in the game. If, on the other hand, you always let the dog win, he will think he is stronger or more clever than you – the beginning of loss of respect and consequential problems.

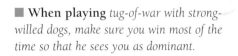

■ **When playing** *tug-of-war with strong-willed dogs, make sure you win most of the time so that he sees you as dominant.*

Travel accessories

CHANCES ARE YOUR DOG will travel somewhere with you, either just for his daily exercise or when you go on holiday. Plan ahead. A car trip can be just as dangerous for your dog as it is for you or your child. In fact, it's even more dangerous, because you have your young child in a car seat and you wear a seat belt. But if you have to stop suddenly, a dog in the back of the car becomes a flying missile. It's dangerous for your dog, and just as dangerous for the people in the car.

■ **Have the dog gate** *installed professionally to ensure that it is secure.*

A variety of canine seat belt body harnesses are available. They attach to the standard seat belt anchors in your car. If you have an estate, use your dog crate or buy a crate designed especially to fit in a car. If your dog is left free in the back of your estate car, have a dog gate installed professionally, one that your dog will not knock out if his body slams against it.

Active dogs love going on long walks with you. If you plan all-day or overnight hikes, take portable food and water bowls. Some are inflatable, while others simply fold open. An athletic dog can carry his own equipment in a backpack.

■ **Canine seat belts** *may save your dog's life.*

Finally, you might think this is dumb, especially for dogs like Labradors, but if you go boating with your buddy make sure he is wearing a life jacket. Yes, I know, dogs are great dog paddlers, but even a dog can get in trouble in turbulent water. A brightly coloured life jacket makes it easier to see your dog if he's fallen overboard or is caught in a heavy current.

■ **Although dogs** *are good swimmers, use a canine life jacket when on boating trips as there may be turbulent water.*

Seasonal necessities

DEPENDING ON WHERE you live and what type of natural coat your dog has, he may benefit from a little clothing. Yes, I know it sounds silly, but if you are a Whippet living in The Lake District, the rain can be miserable. If you are a Yorkshire Terrier in London, the autumn damp can get into your bones. If you are a Boxer in the Highlands, winter ice can freeze your feet.

Choose rainy weather wear and winter coats according to your dog's needs, not just according to their style. A well-designed coat has a waterproof exterior and a soft interior that is gentle to your dog's skin. If winter is harsh where you live, consider Muttluks for your dog – well-designed insulated dog boots developed in Canada. Muttluks are also useful for dogs with paw injuries.

■ **As they grow,** *older dogs may need winter coats even if they did not when they were puppies.*

In hot, sunny climates, a curiously useful accessory for light-skinned dogs and Collies is sunscreen. Just like us, dog skin burns when exposed to too much sunlight. Collies in particular are prone to sun damage to their noses.

Wherever you live, there is no need for indoor clothing for any dog. Other than a ribbon in his hair and a collar on his neck, your dog only needs his natural coat indoors. Peach satin baby doll outfits are for dog owners, not dogs. Dressing like a sumo wrestler is for people, not pugs. Do not demean your dog by dressing him in needless accessories. Reserve the symbolism for yourself.

■ **Choose a coat** *that serves a purpose, be it rainproof or a winter jacket, rather than style.*

A simple summary

✓ A variety of accessories is essential to your dog, including a collar and lead, food and water bowls, and identification.

✓ The right grooming tools – and their correct use – is another requirement.

✓ Make sure the toys you choose for your dog are safe.

✓ Other necessary items could include a doggie seat belt, life jacket, and possibly sunscreen or some cold-weather wear.

■ **Remember your dog** *needs a variety of stimulation; every toy can be used in different ways for physical or mental exercise.*

Chapter 8

Think Dog Thoughts

YOUR PUP DEPENDS UPON YOU, completely, for her safety and security. Think like a dog when preparing your home and garden for your new arrival. That means pretty much thinking like a child. So keep it simple. If you understand the impetuousness and curiosity of the toddler, you have a pretty good idea of how a puppy views life. You must avoid common dangers, especially during the most inquisitive stage of her life – her first year. Channel natural energy in productive ways, avoid potential dangers, and remember that whatever she is doing, she is always learning.

In this chapter...

✓ How dogs learn

✓ Good timing

✓ Dog-proofing your home

✓ A taste for the great outdoors

✓ Household items can be deadly

MAKE SURE YOUR HOME AND GARDEN ARE SAFE FOR YOUR NEW DOG

How dogs learn

ANY DOG, PUPPY *or adult, female or male, from the town or country, learns about life the same simple way: through trial and error. A dog inherits certain characteristics from her parents, but her own uniquely individual personality is formed by the successes and failures of life, especially her experiences before she is three months old.*

There is really no difference in understanding (or training) a puppy or an adult dog, but there is one overwhelmingly useful fact that influences how a young dog or a mature dog thinks and behaves. A puppy is still wet clay, ready to be moulded to the lifestyle you want for her.

Older dogs have already experienced a whole variety of successes and failures. The older dog's personality has been set by these experiences. Training an older dog is harder than training a pup because it often means unlearning something, then learning again. I will talk in detail about training your dog in Chapters 10 to 13, but I want to mention the importance of early learning now, because if you control your dog's first learning experiences, training will be so much easier. If you think like a dog, it's really simple to understand what motivates your new friend's behaviour.

Natural curiosity

Dogs are a joy because they are so gregariously curious about life. As I write this, I have a ten-week-old Labrador pup, Inca, living with me. (Inca is my son Ben's pup, and leaves our home in a few months, when Ben moves to Scotland.) Did Inca mind leaving her mother and litter? If she did, she did not give us any hints. Her natural curiosity is so potent that the rewards of investigating a new environment dramatically outweigh the loss of her previous playmates.

Young pups will investigate anything, but forget about giving a puppy total freedom. Natural curiosity may lead to unexpected and unpleasant early experiences. Your responsibility is to channel your dog's curiosity.

For example, we let Inca approach Lexy and allow Lexy to show irritation when her ears are chewed, but we are there hovering to prevent Inca's curiosity from provoking Lexy too much. We want Inca to learn there are limits, but do not want the relationship to go wrong.

Taste is important

Smell may be a dog's most important sense, but during puppyhood taste reigns. Be prepared. Puppies taste life. If a magazine or letter is on the floor, it will be chewed. If you come into your home and leave your coat over a kitchen chair (as my daughter Tamara does), the hem will be chewed (as Inca did).

Puppies must chew, so it is up to you to provide appropriate chew toys. Remember that trial and error, success and failure, is the natural way dogs learn. Eventually you will spend time actively training your dog, for example, to be obedient or not to bark. But remember that during every waking hour, quite independent of training sessions, your dog is learning. You can shape and channel your dog's learning by planning ahead. It's that simple.

A positive relationship

I like to think that our relationship with our own parents evolves from total dependency to mutual friendship. From the very beginning, your relationship with your dog should involve both of these characteristics – leadership and friendship. Dogs innately understand status. Make sure that in all your relationships with your dog she understands by your actions and deeds that you are superior.

■ **Show your dog** *who is boss during her training and with your actions; train her to come to you, eat after you, and pass through a door behind you.*

At the same time, if you want formal training to be fast, productive, and fun for both of you, your dog should be relaxed, not apprehensive, in your company. Relaxed dogs learn faster. They appreciate your praise. They want to please you.

Some people feel that old-fashioned punishment training, such as pushing your dog's nose in her urine when she messes in the wrong place or choke-chains to control boisterousness, works. Yes, it sometimes can work, but at the expense of creating needless fear in your dog.

Over the last 20 years, trainers and behaviourists such as John Rogerson, Roger Mugford, John Fisher, and Gwen Bailey have shown us that using motivation and rewards works better, works faster, and is more productive than harsher methods that were originally developed for military dogs.

Good timing

Even when you think you are not training your dog, good timing is important. Give rewards such as toys, food, or praise as soon as you see your dog is thinking about doing the right thing. That might sound abstract, but it's really quite simple. When I come home from the clinic and crouch down to say hello to Inca, as soon as she gets up to move towards me I'm already rewarding her with words of praise.

Rewards, and discipline, should be immediate, not even seconds later. If you find a puddle on the kitchen floor, forget even mentioning it to your dog. It's too late. Harsh words just mean you are angry, but your dog will have no idea what you are angry about.

Dogs are amazingly intelligent, but do not expect your dog to think in the abstract in the way we do. I wish they did, but dogs do not understand conditional ideas. I might say, "If you do that again Inca, I'll be really, really cross", but all Inca understands is what Gary Larson put in his ever-so-accurate cartoon about what dogs hear, "Blah blah blah blah blah Inca blah blah blah blah blah".

INTERNET

www.cyberpet.com/
cyberdog/articles/

For tips on pet-proofing your home, especially during the holidays, check out the articles on Cyberpet.

■ **Do not give** *your dog an old shoe to chew;
she will learn that all shoes are toys.*

Dog-proofing your home

Training will be easier and life for your pup a lot safer if you plan ahead and dog-proof your home. Think "safe for children" and you are almost there. What you are doing is controlling your dog's environment. If you do that, it is more likely you can anticipate her behaviour and be prepared for the consequences.

Here are some suggestions for what to do indoors:

1. Remove live electrical cords to prevent electric shocks.
2. Avoid dangling electrical cords. They are fun to tug on, which can lead to damage to the appliance and the pup.
3. Move all household cleaners out of reach. Most are dangerous, each in its own way.
4. Think about how you store your rubbish. A bin with a pedal to lift the top is less enticing to a dog than a hanging plastic bag.
5. Do not give your dog an old shoe or slipper to chew on. A pup cannot differentiate your cast-offs from your new Gucci shoes.
6. Check out where your chewable surfaces are. Wooden kitchen table legs are ideal. Do not let your pup chew on them.
7. Temporarily remove throw rugs and small carpets. They are too chewably attractive and difficult to clean when soiled by your as-yet-untrained puppy. Keep it simple and remove the temptation.

■ **Seemingly secure** *homes can be full of hazards to inquisitive dogs.*

Heavy iron can be pulled down

House plant is toxic

Household chemicals are harmful

Live electric flex is dangerous

■ **Here, all sources** *of danger have been placed out of the dog's reach.*

Dangerous substance, toxic plant, and live flex are out of harm's way

A taste for the great outdoors

IF YOU HAVE A GARDEN (or a balcony or a patio) think dog thoughts while you investigate it. Check the perimeter fence or rail to make sure it is dog-proof in two ways: secure enough to prevent puppy escapes now, and strong enough to withstand the actions of your dog when she is mature. (I have met several dogs named Houdini. Guess why!) A one-metre fence is fine for many small dogs, but you will need a 2.5-metre fence for agile large breeds. Make sure your fence is well secured, especially if you have a natural digger such as a terrier. Examine your gates to ensure they lock shut and do not have gaps underneath that a puppy or small dog can crawl through. The safest gates spring shut automatically after opening. And don't put anything near the fence that the dog can climb on. Many an escape has been engineered this way.

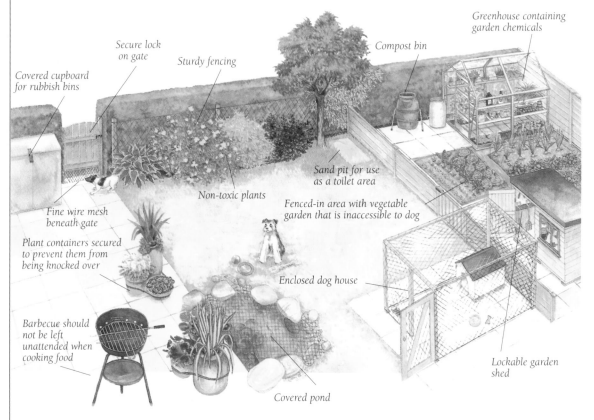

Greenhouse containing garden chemicals

Compost bin

Secure lock on gate

Sturdy fencing

Covered cupboard for rubbish bins

Sand pit for use as a toilet area

Non-toxic plants

Fenced-in area with vegetable garden that is inaccessible to dog

Fine wire mesh beneath gate

Plant containers secured to prevent them from being knocked over

Enclosed dog house

Barbecue should not be left unattended when cooking food

Lockable garden shed

Covered pond

■ **Dog-proof your garden** and pay particular attention to preventing your dog from escaping.

FOLLOW THESE RULES IF YOUR DOG GOES OUTDOORS

1. Prevent access to the barbecue area when cooking food.
2. If you have a garden pond, temporarily cover it with wire screening to prevent access.
3. Avoid placing potted plants and other plant containers where they can be knocked over.
4. Fence off the vegetable garden and compost heap.
5. Dogs love to dig. If you do not mind earthy paws and noses, consider installing a fresh earth digging zone or a sand box.
6. Dogs do crazy things. If you treasure your garden, from the first day you let your dog in it, restrict her to the area where she cannot cause damage. This may mean a fence or an *invisible fence*.

Check the pool

Once more, think child when you look at security. If you have a swimming pool (if you do, I already feel a slight pang of envy), make sure that the safety fence around the pool area is puppy-proof as well as child-proof. If you use a pool cover, make sure it is absolutely dog-proof.

Safe storage

Store all your garden chemicals and equipment in a secure area your dog cannot wander into, break into, or chew into. Rubbish bins are fun to knock over. Think about keeping them in a latched shed.

Planning the garden

If your dog is to have the enjoyment of outdoor access, examine your garden for potentially poisonous trees, shrubs, and flowers. Make sure your dog does not have access to dangerous areas of your garden. Plan where you want to place an outdoor water bowl and make sure there is a shaded area your dog can easily find in hot weather.

■ **Allocate your dog** *her own digging area in which she can play.*

> **DEFINITION**
>
> Invisible fencing *is wiring buried under the ground around the perimeter of your garden. Your dog wears a special collar that receives a signal from the buried wiring. The signal causes your dog's collar to buzz. The buzz is a warning that if the dog continues, she will receive an electric shock. The dog must be trained to understand what the whole thing means, of course.*

141

Dangerous vegetation

Flowers, plants, shrubs, trees, and ornamentals can be toxic. Most of these just cause an upset stomach but some are deadly. Make sure they are out of reach of your dog.

AMARYLLIS LEAVES AND FLOWERS

Amaryllis leaves and flowers
Autumn crocus bulbs
Azalea stems and leaves
Bird of paradise stems
Bleeding heart flowers and stems
Boxwood bark, stems, and leaves
Castor bean seeds (very dangerous)
Cherry laurel wood and branches
   (very dangerous)
Chinaberry tree wood and branches
Clematis stems and leaves
Daffodil bulbs
Delphinium plants
Dumb cane leaves (very dangerous)
English ivy fruit
Flower bulbs of any kind
Foxglove stems and flowers
Holly berries

FOXGLOVE STEMS AND FLOWERS

HOLLY BERRIES

Trivia...

Never put your dog's or cat's faeces on the compost pile. Nasties in carnivore faeces can multiply there, creating a health hazard for your dog and for you. On the other hand, waste from herbivores such as guinea pigs and rabbits can safely be put on the compost pile.

PROTECT YOUR GRASS

Prevent burnt patches on the grass by installing a sand pit toileting area for your dog. Nothing prevents acidic dog urine from burning grass. The best treatment is prevention. Train your dog to urinate in a specific area (I will discuss how in Chapter 12). If your new adult dog already urinates on the lawn, the best you can do is keep a water container handy to dilute her urine once she has emptied her bladder.

LILY OF THE VALLEY
LEAVES AND FLOWERS

Jasmine leaves
Jerusalem cherry leaves and flowers
Jimsonweed or thorn apple
    (very dangerous)
Larkspur stems
Laburnum bark, flowers, seeds,
    and leaves
Lily of the valley leaves and flowers
Locoweed
Lupine stems and flowers
Mistletoe berries (very poisonous)
Mushrooms – any you cannot
    identify as safe
Oleander bark, stems, and leaves
    (very dangerous)
Poinsettia leaves
Pokeweed
Privet bush stems and leaves
Rhododendron leaves
Rhubarb leaves
Skunk cabbage leaves and flowers
Tomato vines
Virginia creeper bark and stems
Wisteria bark and leaves
Yew bark, needles, and seeds
    (very dangerous)

RHODODENDRON LEAVES

SKUNK CABBAGE LEAVES AND FLOWERS

MISTLETOE BERRIES

YEW BARK NEEDLES AND SEEDS

143

Household items can be deadly

A PUPPY IS NATURALLY INQUISITIVE. We have a responsibility to ensure that the risks she is exposed to are minimal. The greatest physical risk comes from road traffic, but there are home risks that can be equally deadly. Here are lists of common household cleaners, chemicals, and drugs your dog might inadvertently come in contact with, and what to do if she does.

Remember, think like a dog. All she knows is that an item is new and needs to be investigated, usually by chewing.

Common household poisons

POISON	SOURCE	SIGNS	ACTION
Alkaline cleaners	Walked in by accident.	Inflamed skin.	Do not induce vomiting.
Solvents or paint stripper	Wrongly used to clean paint from dog's coat.	Vomiting, diarrhoea, possible convulsions, ulcers on the tongue.	Wash skin and coat with soap and water. Get immediate veterinary attention.
Antifreeze	Leaking from car radiator (dogs like the taste of it).	Wobbling, collapse, convulsions, coma.	Induce vomiting with a lump of baking soda. Get immediate veterinary attention. *Can be fatal.*
Aspirin	Scavenging, or given by owner.	Appetite loss, depression, vomiting (possibly blood-stained), convulsions.	Induce vomiting. Get veterinary attention. Very toxic if eaten in large quantities.
Anti-depressants or sedatives	Scavenging, or given by owner.	Depression, staggering, incoordination, coma.	Induce vomiting if just eaten. Get immediate veterinary advice.

Most of these drugs are not life-threatening, but are more dangerous to very small dogs.

POISON	SOURCE	SIGNS	ACTION
Cannabis (marijuana)	Scavenging.	Incoordination, fear, agitation, biting, dilated pupils.	Avoid sensory stimulation. Give a sedative recommended by your veterinarian.
Carbon monoxide	Car exhaust, faulty gas heating, indoor barbecues.	Cherry-red gums, staggering, unconsciousness.	Fresh air, artificial respiration.
Chlorine	Water sterilizers, scavenging near the pool (normal chlorinated swimming pool water is safe).	Red eyes and mouth.	Wash eyes thoroughly with water or saline solution. Flush mouth with water or milk.
Liquid detergents	Cleaning solutions.	Foam or froth from mouth.	Wash mouth with clean water.
Flea repellents (chlorinated hydrocarbons or rinses with malathion or older products such as lindane, gammexane, chlordane, toxophene)	Sprays, powders, dips.	Agitation, twitching, restlessness, salivation convulsions, coma. *Can be fatal.*	If not convulsing, wash off as much as possible. If twitching or convulsing, avoid light. Take to a veterinarian immediately.

■ **Remove solvents immediately** *from your dog's coat with soap and water.*

■ **Keep aspirin** *and other medication out of your dog's reach as she may chew the plastic containers.*

POISON	SOURCE	SIGNS	ACTION
Flea repellents (organo-phosphates)	Sprays, shampoos, collars, "spot-ons", old-fashioned wormers.	Muscle tremors, drooling, difficulty breathing, increased urination and/or defecation.	Wash off substance well. Take to a veterinary surgeon immediately.
Kerosene oil	Heating fuel, cleaning fluids.	Abdominal discomfort.	Do not induce vomiting; feed a milk and vegetable oil solution, then get a veterinarian's advice on an immediate purgative.
Lead	Old paint, old pipes, lead fishing weights, batteries, curtain weights, solder, putty, old linoleum, some lubricants.	Vomiting, diarrhoea, abdominal pain, followed by worried look, nervousness, whining, sensitivity to light, staggering, paralysis.	Induce vomiting if lead has been eaten recently. Get immediate veterinary attention. This is a problem with youthful, curious dogs.

■ **Ensure that all repellents** *have been thoroughly washed off your dog's coat.*

■ **Take your dog** *straight to the vet if the poison has already taken effect.*

POISON	SOURCE	SIGNS	ACTION
Phenol	Wood preservatives, some fungicides, disinfectants, photodeveloper.	Staggers, twitching, depression, coma.	Do not induce vomiting. Give milk and vegetable oil, followed by a purgative. Wash off any skin contamination Get veterinary attention. *Never use disinfectants on your dog unless the label says it is safe to do so.*
Slug and snail bait (metaldehyde)	Dogs sometimes eat bait because they like the taste.	Tremors, salivation convulsions, coma. *Can be fatal.*	Induce vomiting if just eaten. Get veterinary attention if there are signs of poisoning. Slug bait is used by malicious poisoners.

■ **If appropriate,** *give your dog an emetic of salt water.*

■ **Wash the coat** *so that your dog cannot ingest any chemicals.*

POISON	SOURCE	SIGNS	ACTION
Strychnine	Pesticide, illegal coyote bait.	Apprehension, tension, stiffness. Leads to seizures, convulsions, and death.	Induce vomiting. Get immediate veterinary attention. Strychnine is used by malicious poisoners. In any case of suspected poison, take the suspect material to your vet.
Tobacco	Scavenging cigarettes, pipe, or cigars.	If swallowed, may cause vomiting.	Soothe irritation by giving charcoal tablets.
Warfarin	Rodent bait or poisoned rodent.	Bruising, bleeding gums. *Can be fatal especially to small dogs.*	Induce vomiting if just eaten. Your vet will give injections of vitamin K to control bleeding.

DO NOT INDUCE VOMITING IN THESE CIRCUMSTANCES

Vomiting will cause even more danger if your puppy has swallowed an acid, alkali, or petroleum-based product. Do not induce vomiting if your pup has swallowed any of the following:

Caustic soda
Chlorine bleach
Dishwasher detergent
Drain cleaner
Kerosene
Concentrated detergent powder or tablets
Lye

Oven cleaner
Paint stripper or remover
Paint thinner
Petrol
Furniture, floor, or shoe polish
Toilet cleaner
Wood preservative

A simple summary

✓ Dogs learn through trial and error. That means you need to be patient and consistent.

✓ Learning should be a positive experience for your dog and for you.

✓ Dog-proofing your home is simple but essential – both indoors and out. Look around your home and garden with a dog's-eye view, and try to imagine all the mischief your pup could get up to. Then prevent it before it happens.

✓ Many plants and household items are toxic – you need to keep them safely away from your dog.

■ **Place tin cans** *or other noise-intervention equipment to deter your dog from jumping over the fence.*

■ **Remember that** *your dog can probably jump higher and dig deeper than you thought, and secure your garden accordingly.*

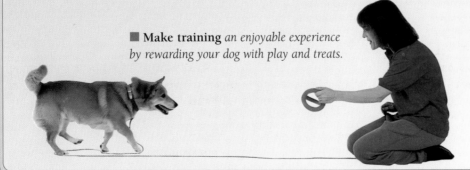

■ **Make training** *an enjoyable experience by rewarding your dog with play and treats.*

Chapter 9

Think of Those Next Door

BRINGING A DOG INTO YOUR HOME is not an isolated event. It affects your family and your neighbours, now and for the next decade or more. Be considerate. Plan ahead.

Fortunately, the majority of western homes already house dogs and cats, and even more would like to do so if their social circumstances permitted. Chances are your neighbours will welcome your new addition, but do not leave the results to chance. Tell your neighbours that you are getting a dog, and obey both local laws and common sense.

In this chapter...

✓ Be community minded

✓ Scooping poop

✓ Barking and biting

✓ Home alone

✓ The canine vagrant

✓ Family planning

BRINGING A NEW DOG INTO YOUR HOME WILL AFFECT ALL YOUR FAMILY AND NEIGHBOURS

Be community minded

DR. CONSTANCE PERIN, a cultural anthropologist, in her study of neighbouring in America, came to a fascinating, and to you and me an important, conclusion. She found that cats and dogs act as "the glue or the solvent" of relationships between neighbours. You may feel that bringing a dog into your home is a personal matter involving only your immediate family, but it is not. Of course, the feelings of your family are paramount, but you should also consider how your neighbours will be affected, especially if only a single wall separates you from them.

■ **Your dog will** *need time to adapt to a new environment. He will probably bark, so warn your neighbours in advance.*

Plan ahead

Explain to your immediate neighbours that your family will be increasing shortly. And assume that your new dog will whine or bark a little. I suggest to my clients that, before there are problems, they give their neighbours a symbolic little gift with an apology that during the first few days and nights the new family member may be a bit noisy.

With any new dog, and especially a young pup, invite your neighbours to visit once your dog is settled in. A squiggly new pup melts all but the hardest hearts. Take the initiative in forestalling problems. It is all part of respect. We humans do not like being taken for granted. Keep your neighbours informed and your pup will become the glue rather than the solvent of your immediate community.

■ **Introduce your new puppy** *to the neighbours to ease any reservations they may have about his arrival.*

Scooping poop

YES, IT IS A MESSY SUBJECT, *but it's not as bad as it sounds. Poop, and dog noise, are the two things that annoy neighbours most about dogs. From day one, train your family to clean up after your dog when he poops, whether it is in your own garden, on the road, or (heaven forbid!) on your neighbour's property.*

Trivia...

From my perspective as a veterinary surgeon, there has been a curious medical benefit to cleaning up after our dogs. When you come in close personal contact with your dog's stool, you know immediately when there is any change to its consistency – a change that is often an early warning of bowel disorders.

Pooper scoopers come in a variety of materials and styles, most of which are designed to appeal to your aesthetic rather than practical needs. Hand-held scoopers contain disposable bags. Like alligator jaws, the scooper engulfs your dog's deposit. You remove the bag and dispose of it in an appropriate rubbish bin. If bending down is difficult for you, other models come on poles, with a rake-like base for grass or a smooth base for pavement. These are fine, but practically speaking they are cumbersome and, guaranteed, there will be times when you need to clean up after your pooch and you will not have your gadget with you.

I advise people to get over their aesthetic qualms and simply use a plastic bag. Keep it simple! Rolls of poop scoop bags are commercially available from pet supply stores, supermarkets, or veterinary surgeons. Personally, I use thin plastic supermarket shopping bags. The handles are ideal for tying the bag shut. The psychological hill you have to climb when using a plastic bag to scoop the poop is the fact that the poop is fresh from the oven. It's still warm, and you will feel that through the bag.

■ **Always take** *a pooper scooper with you when you are out with your dog.*

153

Barking and biting

BARKING AND BITING *are natural canine inclinations, part of standard canine communication codes, but ones that are socially unacceptable to us. It is up to us to control both activities. Dogs, if they are not well socialized, also bark at strangers or other dogs. I will tell you in Chapter 14 how to prevent this, and in Chapter 15 how to overcome this problem if it is already happening.*

■ **Socialize your dog** *with other animals and humans from an early age so that he does not bark at strangers.*

Barking is socially destructive, but it is a problem that in most circumstances can be controlled with proper training. Dogs bark when they are left home alone and are bored. I will tell you in Chapter 14 how to prevent that problem.

Home alone

THERE WILL BE TIMES *when your new dog will be home alone. Boredom almost always leads to creativity on your dog's part. He will invent hobbies such as digging, or he will commune with others by barking or howling. You have a responsibility to your neighbours and to your dog to do your best to ensure canine contentment in your absence. Consider the following alternatives.*

■ **Provide your dog** *with a variety of toys and do not leave him unattended for long periods, as this will lead to boredom and destructive behaviour.*

Dog door

If you have a secure garden, consider installing a personal dog door so he can go in and out as he chooses. The most secure doors are activated by a magnetic tag your dog wears on his collar.

Dog walker

If you are routinely out, find a professional dog walker who will visit, play with, and exercise your dog. Many dog walkers are also excellent dog handlers. Check references thoroughly. Speak with other dog owners using the service before you sign on.

Doggy day care

This is a great concept. By parking your dog each day at his day-care centre, a couple can have a dog and still continue working. Investigate and interview the centre thoroughly. Is play supervised? Are there rest periods? Is there a barking policy? What type of training takes place? Are there health issues?

Dog sitter

Most veterinary practices know of individuals who will move into your home to care for your dog when you are absent. Animal Aunts is a well-established professional association of vetted and insured individuals. Many of these men and women can help with canine social problems as well, such as barking, weight problems, and lack of obedience.

INTERNET

www.animalaunts.co.uk

This is the website of Britain's largest pet (house and plant) sitting agency.

www.petsit.org

The home page of Pet Sitters International, an American educational organization for professional pet sitters.

■ **If you work** *during the day, find a reliable and professional dog walker to take your dog out through the day.*

The canine vagrant

This is a simple problem to solve. Do not let your dog wander. It is unsafe for your dog and discourteous to your neighbours.

I am old enough to remember when many urban dogs were allowed to wander. I would accompany my mother to the delicatessen and hear the owner comment that Angus, our Scottie, had visited earlier for his daily slice of corned beef. The barber would tell us that Angus dropped by for a drink of water. There is no doubt that Angus had a delightful life, but then again, one car passed by every 27 years.

Post-war in Toronto it was relatively safe, and also culturally acceptable, to let your dog act like a vagrant. The Yorkshire Terriers who succeeded Angus roamed free as well, disappearing into the woods, returning smelling of skunk or with porcupine quills hanging from their forlorn faces.

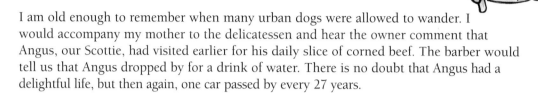

But what was okay then is irresponsible now. For most of us who live in urban, suburban, or rural communities, it is no longer socially acceptable to let dogs wander. Your responsibility to your neighbours is to know where your dog is at all times and have him under your control.

Your legal obligations

In your relationship with your neighbours remember that under the law you are responsible for your dog's actions. If your dog damages property, you are responsible. Check that your home-insurance policy covers you for dog damage. Dog damage includes direct damage, such as trashing your neighbour's flower beds or biting your neighbour's cat (or your neighbour), or indirect damage, for example to a car that swerves to avoid your dog and ends up crashing into a tree. Of course, there are also laws to protect your dog from you if you cause unnecessary suffering through neglect or cruelty.

■ **When outdoors,** *keep your dog on the leash at all times.*

Family planning

THIS IS A TOPIC *I will mention again, but I want to touch on it now because it has so many ramifications. It is good to decide at the beginning of your relationship with your dog whether you want to use him or her for breeding. Neutering – spaying females or castrating males – is an emotional subject that is influenced by our culture, tradition, sex, and even religion. Here are some facts.*

■ **Decide early on** *if your dog is to breed; consider the implications of your decision such as her health, finding homes for puppies, and if she is to be shown.*

What neutering does

Neutering prevents reproduction by removing the organs that produce eggs or sperm. Castrating a male involves making a small surgical incision in front of the scrotum and removing the testicles – the source of sperm and also the major source of the male hormone testosterone. A vasectomy, cutting the spermatic cords to prevent conception, is an uncommon operation in male dogs.

Spaying a female is a more invasive procedure. Through an incision in the abdomen, the ovaries (where eggs are manufactured) and the uterus or womb (where pups would develop) are removed. The ovaries are the major source of female hormones. Tying the Fallopian tubes to prevent conception is a rare operation in female dogs.

Vasectomies and Fallopian tube ligations are uncommon in dogs because, today, the main reason for neutering is to make life more pleasant for the dog. Sexually active dogs living under the restrictions and confines of life with us get frustrated because they are not given outlets for their natural needs.

■ **Sexually frustrated dogs** *have more energy and require more exercise than neutered dogs.*

The social consequences

Male dogs are less likely to act as vagrants. They wander less and are more responsive to the voice of their owners. They spend less time urine-marking their territory. They empty their bladders because they are full, rather than to leave scent messages for other male dogs. Neutered male dogs retain natural territorial guarding behaviour, but indulge in less inter-male dog aggression.

Neutering eliminates the risk of a male dog fathering pups and of a female becoming pregnant. Neutering also eliminates most sex hormone production in dogs, and this has many positive social consequences.

Spayed female dogs no longer experience heat cycles twice a year. The mood changes related to the production of female hormones no longer occur. Virtually all service dog-training organizations know that neutered dogs, male or female, are easier to train and more responsive to their owners, handlers, and others.

■ **After castration,**
guard dogs will retain their normal behaviour.

Potential problems

By far the most common problem associated with neutering is weight gain. One out of three dogs gains weight after neutering. This happens because energy is no longer being used in sex-related activities. Weight gain can and should be controlled by immediate calorie control. Neutered dogs should be fed fewer calories. It's that simple.

The right time to neuter

Many books say that females should be neutered after having one heat season and males before sex-hormone related problems develop. Neither of these statements has survived scrutiny. There is now enough cumulative evidence to show that neutering a female before her first season has virtually no drawbacks and many advantages. The incidence of urinary incontinence is lower. The incidence of hormone-related behaviour problems, such as possessive aggression, is lower. And the incidence of mammary tumours, the most common cancer in dogs, is zero when neutering is done before the first season.

VIP

In males, there is good evidence that neutering to control vagrancy, male dog fighting, and excessive urine-marking works just as well after a problem has developed as it does before any problems surface. In other words, if your male is showing hormone-related problem behaviours, it is never too late to neuter him. Finally, males and females neutered before puberty are less likely to have weight gain problems than those neutered after puberty.

■ **If your dog** urine-marks excessively, consider having him neutered as this will curb his behaviour.

■ **Neutering male dogs** decreases some natural instincts such as dog fighting, and helps control vagrancy.

A simple summary

✔ Dogs become part of your neighbourhood as well as part of your family. Make sure you have a good relationship with those around you.

✔ Part of being a good neighbour is scooping poop promptly.

✔ Dogs should not be allowed to wander.

✔ Barking dogs can disrupt entire neighbourhoods – don't let your dog be one of them.

✔ Neutering your dog will prevent many problems, both medical and social. Not neutering your dog will leave him frustrated and may encourage him to develop some annoying habits.

PART THREE

PLAYING CAN BE A LEARNING EXPERIENCE

HOUSE RULES

YOU ARE FORMING an exciting and deepening partnership with your dog, but it is different from your relationship with other people. With your dog you must always be the *leader*, the individual your dog obeys. Dogs naturally live in packs, and understand how to fit into a chain of command. They thrive when they know what their limits are. Happy, obedient dogs virtually never become delinquents.

Begin with house training. Be *positive*, and never use threats or discipline during training. With that good start, it is easy to apply the same rewarding approach to basic good manners – training your dog to behave obediently, for you, your family, and friends. Life as a dog is *exciting*, so expect problems. Most of these are normal dog attitudes we can mould to our liking with just a little further training.

Chapter 10

Be a Leader, Not a Boss

NOW THE FUN BEGINS. Your dog has arrived in your home as a stranger. Soon she will become a member of your family. To develop a wonderful relationship with your dog, read this chapter carefully, then read it again. If you understand how your dog thinks and interprets action, you are on your way toward enjoying a fruitful relationship with her.

Keep things simple. If you set up impossible house rules or are inconsistent with your approach to your dog, you are creating problems that are difficult to undo. I know I've said this before, but it's worth repeating yet again: it is better to spend time learning to interact with your dog than to create problems that need to be unlearned later.

In this chapter...

✓ Never too young

✓ Think dog

✓ Be consistent, be positive

✓ Proper discipline

TRAINING SHOULD BE ENJOYABLE FOR YOUR DOG

Never too young

ANY DOG IS TRAINABLE, *but the younger your dog is, the easier it will be. Young dogs are like unwritten books, and you can control their early learning. By letting them explore new situations and protecting them from developing unwarranted fears, their confidence develops as well. If you want your dog to be sure of herself around all types of people, introduce her early in life, indoors and out, to as wide a variety of people as possible – toddlers, kids, people with canes or walkers, people in uniforms or wearing hats or motorcycle helmets, mothers with babies in prams, people of different colours. The more she takes in, the less likely she is to develop idiosyncratic fears or phobias.*

■ **Introduce pups** *to children at as young an age as possible.*

Early socialization is of overwhelming value, but there is a problem. Young pups only have temporary immunity, inherited from their mothers, against certain infectious diseases. This is boosted with puppy inoculations.

Although some vaccine manufacturers now produce vaccines meant to be given at eight and ten weeks of age, there is still a two-week interval, finishing at 12 weeks, when a puppy is at risk of contracting diseases from unvaccinated dogs because they haven't yet fully developed the immunity that the vaccine is meant to stimulate. Your vet will know what the risk is in your area.

■ **Make sure** *puppies are inoculated before meeting other dogs.*

I advise my clients to take their puppies out immediately, under controlled circumstances, and let them visit safe places. This means with friends' healthy dogs in their homes and gardens, in your car, on your lap in outdoor cafes, or on the pavement in areas where you know other dogs are routinely vaccinated.

Good socializing early in life is probably the most important way to ensure good manners in adulthood.

LEARNING STAGES

Your dog's ability to learn will change as she grows through well-defined stages of development. All dogs go through these stages, but the speed of progress varies from one individual to another. Never expect more from your dog than she is capable of.

Three to 12 weeks

The experiences of this critical period in a dog's life will shape her life-long attitude. From around eight weeks, when you take over from the mother and breeder, your pup will show a genuine desire to please. At the same time, she is working out her proper position in your pack. The right signals now will teach her that all family members rank above her in the pack. Give the wrong signals and she will try to find a higher position in the household hierarchy.

■ **Teach your puppy** *to stay and sit while you leave the room.*

Three to six months

In human terms, these are the pre-teen years. At the beginning of this stage, your pup depends on you and is still eager to please. By the six-month mark she is much more independent. It is best to start your training early.

Simple obedience training is easiest when your pup has the greatest desire to please, early in the juvenile period. Training becomes increasingly more complicated as your pup develops a mind of her own.

Six to 12 or 18 months, and beyond

The teenage years. Just as with us, sexual maturity arrives before emotional maturity. Many dogs will, at some time during adolescence, challenge your authority. Territorial behaviour develops. This is difficult but if you laid down a foundation of good behaviour earlier in your dog's life, adolescent exuberance will only be a temporary blip in relationships. Physical and sexual maturity are eventually followed by emotional maturity. This arrives at different times in different dogs, and varies considerably according to breed. In Golden Retrievers, emotional maturity arrives early, while Boxers have the longest adolescence in dogdom!

■ **Boxers remain** *adolescent for up to three years.*

Think dog

YOUR DOG SEES *the world very differently from the way you and I see it. Teaching methods you might use with your kids send different messages to dogs. When they were young, I stroked my kids' heads as a sign of affection. To a dog, a pat on the head is a sign of dominance. Especially with shy pups, who already have low self-esteem, avoid head pats. Express affection by stroking the chest or back, instead.*

■ **Avoid patting** *dogs on the head as they see it as an overtly dominant sign.*

Body language

From puppyhood, a dog uses the position of her tail, body, and ears, combined with eye contact and facial expressions, to communicate. She also uses her voice – barks, howls, growls, and whines – but sound is much less important.

Dogs are more acutely aware of body language than voice. This is why puppies learn to respond to hand signals so well. Improve the way you communicate with your dog by using sensible body language, accompanied by verbal signals. For example, standing over your dog and looking straight down at her will be interpreted as a threat. Getting down on your haunches, more at her level, and spreading your arms wide is an inviting gesture that carries no threat. Most dogs will naturally respond by walking toward you. As your pup does, say "Come." Soon she will come to you whenever you say the word. It's simple!

Do not misinterpret your dog's body language. Staring at you may indicate interest, but in certain circumstances it is a sign of dominance. Showing the teeth is usually a sign of canine dominance, but some dogs show their teeth in a greeting grin – really a submissive sign of appeasement. Get to know your dog by watching her carefully. You'll soon be able to "read" her as well as she can read you.

Tone of voice

When using your voice, think about the sounds a dog might naturally respond to. Wolves howl at night to locate each other. Dogs also howl to communicate. A singsong "Spar—ky" (your personal howl) will attract Sparky's attention. If a pup does something wrong, bites her mother too hard for example, mother responds with a growl. A low-pitched, quick "Sparky!" delivered in a deep tone, like her mother's growl, communicates a wholly different meaning to your dog. If, during play, Sparky bites a litter-mate too hard, her brother or sister will yip in pain, call it quits, and stop playing. Do the same. Say "Ouch!" in a sharp way and walk away. Your pup will understand your inflection and your body language.

■ **When in the wild**, *wolves communicate at night by howling.*

Sound

Dogs have better hearing than we do – four times more acute, the experts tell us. Dogs certainly hear at the high end of sound frequency, the ultrasonic end that is inaudible to us. This creates disadvantages and advantages for dogs. A disadvantage is that some dogs are too sound-sensitive and develop a fear of sounds, such as distant thunder. The advantage, to us in dog training, is that most dogs respond quickly to simple sounds such as a whistle or a clicker. Think about using a distinctive sound to cue your dog. Whistle or *clicker training* is simple. Think shepherds and sheepdogs. With a whistle you can control your dog at a great distance without developing laryngitis.

"No" is a powerful word; strong medicine. Use it wisely, only when you see your dog doing something wrong. Do not shriek it, mumble it, whine it, or use it so frequently that your dog disregards it. Growl it, deeply and sharply.

■ **Growl the word** *"No" sharply and gruffly when your dog has transgressed.*

Forget about democracy

Here is the great difference between training children and training dogs. As our children grow, we can reason with them. They come to understand what is fair and unfair. Kids develop an innate understanding of democratic decision-making. They understand that conditions may apply. Three strikes and you're out is a situation kids learn to understand, but dogs never do. Your dog does not have the ability to learn through abstractions. I wish she did, but she will never develop democratic ideals.

Dogs are naturally possessive, naturally territorial, and sophisticated observers of hierarchies. Dogs are natural opportunists, and will take advantage when they can. In your relationship with your dog, forget about consensus and democracy.

Do not be a boss, but be a natural leader. Above all, be consistent. Never underestimate your dog's ability to see your inconsistencies and to work on them.

The shy pup

Take special care with shy pups. They need extra care and attention. Some breeds (German Shepherds and working Collies immediately come to mind) are more likely to be inherently shy than others (for example, Labrador Retrievers or Jack Russell Terriers). Shy breeds or individuals benefit just as much from socializing as do gregarious ones, but the introductions to the sights, smells, and sounds of life need to be monitored more closely.

■ **Tempt shy dogs** *out from behind the furniture with a trail of treats.*

Do not overprotect a shy dog. Protecting her from visiting children will only increase her apprehension when visitors arrive.

Ask the kids to be less noisy. Tell them to avoid eye contact with your puppy and give them food or toy treats to leave in a trail and eventually to give to your pup. Do the same outdoors. Control your natural inclination to comfort your pup when she is frightened by a noise or movement. If you pick her up and mutter soothing words, you are teaching her that she gets a reward when she shows signs of fear.

If you have a shy pup, it is always useful to mention this to your veterinary surgeon. He or she may recommend you get a little professional help to ensure that shyness does not develop into lifelong fearful behaviour.

Be consistent, be positive

ALL OF US (well, most of us) thrive on consistency. As we get older, the need for consistency becomes even greater – the reason why people my age are less inclined to accept change than are people the age of my kids. The same applies to dogs. They need to know the rules, what is allowed and what is not. Inconsistency is very confusing. Later in life, like us, consistency becomes even more important for them. The time for food, the time for exercise, the importance of possessions, the need to bark, all work on this principle. "I did it before so I'll do it again" becomes a mantra for most dogs, because it reinforces their natural need for order and consistency. Dogs like to keep it simple.

Using rewards

INTERNET

www.clickandtreat.com

This site shows you how to use clickers and treats for effective dog training. You can make some clickers yourself.

Be precise with the words you use when speaking to your dog, as well. She understands black and white, not shades of gray. Think "Yes" or "No," never "Maybe" when speaking, or for that matter interacting in any way with your dog.

In all your house rules (and by house rules I mean how you control your dog at home and away), be consistent and be positive. This is most important when giving rewards or meting out verbal discipline. Rewards are obviously positive, but when using discipline never leave your dog on a negative note. Even after a reprimand, let yourself cool down, then do something positive. Respect and friendship are the keys to a happy relationship. (Is it not fascinating how so much of this applies to human relationships as well?)

■ **Be consistent** *in your behaviour or your dog will easily become confused.*

Tasty food

When selecting rewards, a tasty treat is just about the most potent reward you can give most dogs – especially if it is gloriously smelly, like crispy, hard bits of microwaved liver. Dogs do not need conceptual food rewards (like chocolate), as we do. Just about anything is fine, as long as it tastes good. With many dogs, just a piece of regular dinner kibble is a sufficient reward. It's almost a symbolic gesture.

Keep food rewards with you wherever you go with your dog. I find that Pet-tabs, a yeast-based vitamin and mineral tablet, are really excellent. They smell sufficiently disgusting for dogs to love them, while not too disgusting to keep in your pocket, purse or bag.

RUBBER BONE AND TUG TOY

Enjoyable toys

Do remember that not all dogs are foodies. Some will need other kinds of rewards. Toys are almost as powerful rewards as food, especially chewable or squeaky toys. Use toys as rewards for dogs that are not piggish by nature. As a breed, German Shepherds respond well to toys as rewards. So do Border Collies. An ideal toy is one small enough for you to hide in your pocket, but big enough that your dog can't possibly choke on it.

Sometimes you have to build up interest if you want to use a toy. If this is the case, do silly things with it. Take it out of your pocket, sniff it, and put it back. Talk to it. Wave it at your dog, then put it on a shelf. Your aim is to trigger your dog's interest.

Trivia...

There is an inherent problem with furry mice, squeaky pigs, balls on ropes, and any toy you use specifically as a reward. Eventually, you want them back. They are yours. This is because your dog must learn that rewards come from you. They are what she earns for her good behaviour. So make sure that at the end of the training session, the reward toys end up back in your pocket. (Of course, the everyday chew and play toys can be left around all the time.)

SQUEAKY BALLS

■ **Tempt your dog**
into playing by teasing her with a toy to trigger her interest.

A gentle touch

A soothing lick her from mother was comforting to your puppy. So too is a gentle stroke on her body from you.

Use contact comfort as an important reward when your dog responds well.

Associate touch with food rewards and words of praise. It is always good to train a dog to be touched while she is eating. Later, I will show you how training your dog to let you take her food away while she eats reduces the risks of her becoming possessive and guarding it from people or other animals.

■ **A mother soothes** *her puppies with a comforting lick while they are feeding.*

Soothing words

At the same time you give a potent reward such as food, a toy, or touch, give a verbal reward. Your dog soon learns that the words "Good girl!" or "Good boy!" are satisfying on their own. In your relationship with your dog, start with a potent reward and graduate to using less powerful rewards, such as words alone.

PROBLEM SOLVING

If your dog becomes too excited by food or a toy as a reward, ignore her and go away. Repeat what you were trying to do when she is calmer using a less potent reward such as words alone. If she is not interested in responding to any of your rewards, schedule activities just before feeding time, when she is most alert.

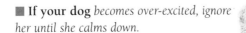

■ **If your dog** *becomes over-excited, ignore her until she calms down.*

Proper discipline

THERE WILL *be occasions when discipline is needed. Use it wisely, as you use rewards. Your reason for discipline is not to get even (although there will be times when your dog pushes you so far that you want to).*

Use a variety of different forms of discipline so that your dog always has the potential to be surprised by what you do.

And remember that the only purpose of discipline is to help your dog learn what is acceptable and what is not. Notice that I have not said your dog should learn right from wrong, because that is not what you are teaching her. To her mind it is right to howl when separated from her family. It is right to chew on hard objects. It is right to guard her own food. What she learns from you is not right and wrong, but acceptable and unacceptable.

Harsh words

As I have mentioned, do not overuse the word "No" when giving verbal discipline. "Bad dog," said crisply, is a good phrase. Personally, I like "Arghhh!". It is a bit like what a pup's mother used to say to her misbehaving pup. One of my nurses, Jenny Ward, brought her Italian Spinone puppy to work each day. All of us giggled ourselves silly as we heard "Arghhh!" coming from all parts of the clinic. The end result, however, was great. All Jen has to do now is lift her right lip as if she's going to "Arghhh!" and her dog stops what he is doing and returns to his bed.

The evil eye

This is a subtle form of discipline, but one that dogs naturally understand. They know the difference between being looked at and being given the eye. Dominant dogs stare down others. You can do the same, especially because you have a height advantage. Standing over your dog, saying "Bad dog," then maintaining your stare is an excellent form of discipline. Eventually, just the look will be enough.

■ **Dominant dogs** *stare down others in their pack, who soon learn to submit.*

My Golden Retriever Liberty was the world's best scavenger, and we lived with a McDonald's, a Burger King, a KFC, and two Starbucks within a two-minute walk. To an urban retriever, this is dog heaven. Lib scavenged what she could, but if she saw a chewed hamburger on the road and caught my eye, she didn't wait for a "No." My look told her to leave it alone and just walk on.

Isolation

Dogs are intensely social. They do not like being separated from family activity. That means you can use symbolic isolation as a potent form of discipline.

By symbolic I mean for its shock value, not as a form of retribution. If, for example, your pup bites you too hard during play, emit your well-practised, high-pitched shriek, get up, leave the room, and shut the door. Wait half a minute then go back in, disregard your dog for another minute, then do what you want. If too many other people are in the room, take your dog to an empty room, the bathroom for example, shut the door, count to 30 then let her out, disregarding her for another minute or so. A minute is all it takes!

■ **Use brief periods** *of segregation as discipline when your dog has misbehaved.*

Theatrics

There will be times when harsh words, the evil eye, or isolation are not enough. Something more dramatic is needed to get your dog to pay attention or to stop what she is doing. This is where water pistols, noise makers, even a *scruff shake* are effective. The key to success with all these methods is that they should be unexpected. "What happened?" is what you want your dog to think. Theatrics stop unwanted behaviour and get your dog's mind back on listening to you.

DEFINITION

A scruff shake is similar to what mother does when she is annoyed by puppy mayhem. You hold some loose skin around the neck and give your dog a gentle shake. Use this form of discipline sparingly and wisely. You do not want your dog to become shy of your touch, nor do you want to provoke an aggressive response.

■ **Spray your dog** *gently in the face as a last resort for bad behaviour.*

Good timing

Whatever the rewards or discipline, good results depend on good timing. Give the reward, food, toys, touch, or praise as soon as your dog tries to do the right thing.

Rewards (or discipline) given too late, even three seconds after the event, cause confusion, especially in young pups. Good timing is a skill that some people naturally have and that others have to learn. Fortunately, older dogs understand that some people can sometimes be a bit clumsy with timing. Unfortunately, puppies don't understand this as well. Stay alert. Concentrate. Poor timing is confusing and gets your relationship off to a bad start.

A successful relationship

Whatever happens, no matter how much your dog amuses you or irritates you, try to remember that you are both her leader and her friend. Good relations, and obedience, from your dog depend on her seeing you as the individual who makes decisions and issues commands. If she thinks she is your equal, you lose her respect. And if you lose her respect, she will not respond to you as a leader.

■ **Encourage** *all members of your family to handle your dog.*

SUBTLE SIGNS OF LEADERSHIP

1. All members of the family routinely handle your puppy.

2. Your puppy sees that you eat first. Give your pup her meals after you have eaten yours.

3. People go through doors first. Puppy waits.

4. Groom your pup daily. Pick her up. Examine her mouth, ears, and eyes. Handle her feet and tail. Brush her body. Turn her around. (Your vet will give you a million thanks for doing this!)

■ **Never forget** *to show your dog that you are the leader.*

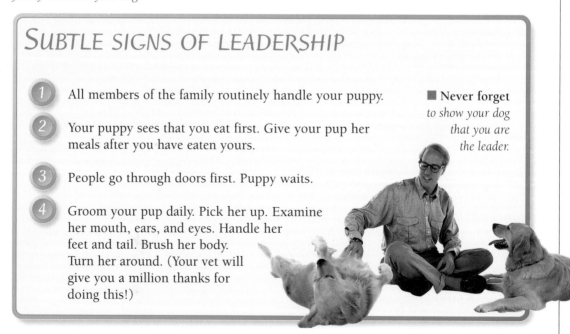

You want your dog to be relaxed so do not make her tense. If you are her friend, she will want to please you because she so much enjoys your praise when she does something right.

And that, simply put, is the attractiveness of dogs: their open, giving desire to please. Do not turn it into fear through punishment or disdain through inconsistency. A wonderful relationship will develop, but it depends upon you using calm logic, understanding, a positive attitude, and consistency.

One final hint: if you can, take a week or two of your holiday time now. Time devoted to good training now pays dividends for years to come.

■ **Make sure you** *build a relationship with your dog while she is young.*

A simple summary

✓ Puppies are ready to learn at a very early age, which means you can start training yours as soon as you bring her home.

✓ Dogs excel at interpreting body language. You can use this to your advantage by using your body to convey praise or your displeasure.

✓ You can use your tone of voice to mirror canine communications for better effect.

✓ Consistency in how rules are set and enforced is extremely valuable to dogs, and will prove a huge benefit in training.

✓ Discipline does not need to be harsh – a growly word, the evil eye, or a moment of isolation are all powerful.

✓ Dogs require a leader – you must be one for your dog.

Chapter 11

House Training

THIS IS WHAT MAKES OR BREAKS your relationship with your dog. If house training goes well, obedience training will also develop quite nicely. But if your dog constantly messes in the house, it won't matter if he also sits on command. House training is simple, but it depends on your vigilance. If your dog has difficulty learning house training, I can virtually guarantee that it is not your dog's fault. Dogs are instinctively clean animals, unwilling to soil their nest. It is up to you to teach your dog that your entire home is "the nest."

In this chapter...

✓ A practical start

✓ Accidents will happen

✓ Apartment training

✓ House training an adult dog

✓ There will be lapses

✓ Submissive urinating

DOGS ARE CLEAN ANIMALS AND PREFER TO TOILET AWAY FROM THEIR NEST

A practical start

IT IS EASIEST to house train a dog if you have immediate access to a park or garden. Flat dwellers and disabled people have a few more logistical problems, but wherever you choose, aim for the following:

1. Select a toileting area away from activity and distractions.
2. In the garden or a public place, choose an area that is easy to clean. Scooping is simpler from a hard surface than from grass.
3. Have poop scoops (such as a plastic bag) always available. Clean up immediately after your dog eliminates.

Work with your dog

Your pup arrives pre-programmed for house training. He does not want to soil his nest, and naturally wants to relieve himself at the following times:

1. After eating (sometimes within a minute).
2. After play or exercise.
3. After any excitement, such as a greeting.
4. After waking up.

As a young puppy he will need an opportunity to empty his bladder every hour. He will also need a toilet time last thing at night.

■ **Plastic bags** *make excellent poop scoops.*

What your pup tells you

Watch your puppy's body language for these clues:

1. Sniffing the floor.
2. Circling.
3. Running with his nose to the floor.
4. Getting ready to squat.

When you see any of these activities, interrupt him and take him outside. If you can, avoid picking him up. You want him to learn he should walk to the back door when he wants to relieve himself.

■ **Sniffing the floor** *often indicates that your puppy needs to urinate.*

Crate training

Dogs (and cats) are inherently clean animals – a powerful reason why we chose them (and not monkeys) as our favourite house pets.

A dog instinctively feels comfortable in the security of his own den, and does not want to mess in it. (Perhaps one of the first lessons a puppy learns is the need to be houseproud when his mother consumes all the waste her pups leave in the nest.)

A crate is a natural den. It looks like a cage to us, but it is not to a dog – unless we use it incorrectly. Dogs like crates, the same way dogs like going under kitchen tables, or behind sofas, or under beds. Your dog's crate should be comfortable and contain activities for his amusement, but not be so large that he can mess in one part and sleep or play in another. Plan ahead when getting a crate so that it's useful for your dog when he is adult size. If that means the crate is too big for your puppy, use a cardboard carton to block off a section of the crate until he is bigger.

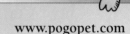

INTERNET

www.pogopet.com

Search the word "crate" on this site and find extensive step-by-step advice on how to crate train.

Crate training speeds up house training enormously, because a dog is either:

- ✓ in his crate,
- ✓ out of his crate toileting where you want him to toilet,
- ✓ safely discovering the rest of the world because he has emptied both tanks.

A crate gives you time to concentrate on matters other than your pup 24 hours a day.

■ **This crate** *should be larger and contain toys for your puppy to play with.*

Word cues

Choose a word cue you would be happy to say in public, and then use it every time your dog eliminates. In time your dog will associate these words with the need to go. "Hurry up" is a practical word cue. So is "Do it," although personally, I like the sporting edge to "Just do it." It does not matter what the word cue is, as long as you use the same one every time. Whistle a tune if you want, as long as you associate a specific sound or word with toileting. By doing so, you will be able to control your dog's toileting activities (for obvious reasons, this is something elephant trainers have always understood).

■ **Let your dog** *sniff around outside the house before urinating.*

Back yard training

This is the ideal. At the times I have mentioned, take your pup outdoors. Sorry, but you must go out with him. Just letting him out the back door is not enough. You want him to be relaxed. If he is out and you are in, he may concentrate on wanting to get back to you rather than on relieving himself. He sees you standing inside the door and gets stressed because he wants to be with you. He gets excited trying to get in. You conclude that he is not going to relieve himself because he is not sniffing around and doing the other things dogs do before they eliminate, so you let him in. Within a few minutes he has messed inside (because of the excitement and stress). The result is a mess for you to clean up and a pup who has attended the wrong school.

Wear warm clothes, take an umbrella if necessary, but be prepared to be outside for four or five minutes while he sniffs and wanders. Patiently wait. Do not play games. Be still and silent. As he starts to relieve himself, say the cue words that you have chosen to be associated with the dog relieving himself. Later, hearing these words will stimulate him to relieve himself. After he has finished, give him enough praise to make his tail wag.

If the weather permits, stay out a little longer. Play a game. Most dogs love the opportunity to be outdoors.

If, after five minutes, he has not relieved himself, return indoors but keep an eagle eye on his activity, so you are prepared for a quick return outside.

■ **Teach your dog** *to recognize chosen words when relieving himself; this will encourage him to go quickly and at specific times.*

Accidents will happen

WHEN YOU SEE *your dog relieving himself in the house, get his attention by shouting – not to frighten or punish him, but rather to get his mind on you. If you frighten him or if he thinks you are angry, you will teach him to be more selective about where he toilets, but not in the way you might hope. He will learn to sneak away to relieve himself, making it harder for you to train him.*

As soon as you have his attention, call his name then run, skip, or cartwheel to your back door. You want to encourage him to willingly follow you outside where, after the excitement of watching you has subsided, he will complete what he started earlier. When you return to the house, keep him in another room while you clean up his mess.

Training more than one dog at a time is extremely difficult, and only worth attempting if you can concentrate totally on your puppies. A crate becomes almost imperative for easy house training of two or more pups at the same time. As with all training, it is important that only one dog at a time hears appropriate word signals.

■ **A puppy play pen** *will ease house training if you have two or more puppies.*

No punishment

Forget about punishing your dog for what he has done earlier. He will not get it. What he will understand is that you are angry with him, and he will respond by acting submissively. He does this to appease you, to extinguish the flame of your anger.

We make the mistake of thinking that his signs of appeasement are signs of guilt. They are not. Your dog does not remember what he did six seconds ago.

I cannot emphasize this enough. Punishing after the fact is counterproductive. You are only teaching him that you are irrational and unpredictable. Punishment when you return to a mess in the house is interpreted as punishment when you return. This can lead to anxiety whenever your dog is left home alone, and to other problems.

Apartment training

THIS IS A BIT MORE *complicated, and more time-consuming on your part, but it follows the same principles as back yard training. First, choose the area near your flat where it is safe and acceptable for your dog to toilet. The closer the better, but of course this is not always possible. That makes the hourly visit to the great outdoors even more important. You have got to be extra vigilant.*

If an hourly trip outside is not practical, then indoor paper training to newspaper, a litter box, or commercially produced disposable pet pads becomes the pragmatic second choice.

TERRY RYAN'S SLEIGH BELLS

Terry Ryan is a dog trainer's trainer. She has a neat trick she teaches dog trainers to teach dog owners, who then teach it to their dogs. When a dog wants to go outside the dog rings a string of sleigh bells. This is how it's done.

Most dogs learn to go to the door when they want to relieve themselves, but many just sit there in the hope they will be seen. Terry hangs a string of bells from the door handle. Then she holds a smelly treat like a piece of microwaved liver in her hand close to the bells. Eventually the dog uses his nose or his paw to try to get the treat out of her hand. When this happens, Terry rings the bells, says "Good Dog" as she gives the dog the treat, and both go outside. Gradually she rewards only moves that take the nose or paw closer to the bells, until finally, only contact with the bells gets the verbal and food rewards. Often, when they go out she plays with the dog – a really great reward.

With a couple of two-minute training sessions each day, it is possible within three weeks to train a dog to ring the bells when he wants to go outside.

■ **Paper training** *puppies is good for people without gardens, but better avoided if you have easy access outdoors.*

■ **Praise** *your puppy after he has relieved himself.*

Paper training

Paper training is a practical way to train puppies that are growing up in a flat, but remember, if you use this method you prolong the training period. You are training your pup to mess on paper inside the house, then later when he has control of his bladder and bowels, you must retrain him not to mess on paper, but rather to mess outdoors.

If you're not using a crate (why not?), the easiest way to paper train is to restrict your pup to one room or one area of a room where the floor has been covered in plastic sheeting, on top of which you lay lots of newspaper. In these circumstances, your pup can only relieve himself on the newspaper. You will see over a few days that he prefers several specific spots.

When removing soiled newspaper, save small bits to place in the areas where you want your dog to urinate. It takes less than a week for a pup to be trained to eliminate in these areas. Day by day you reduce the paper-covered areas, until only a few are needed.

At the same time, take your dog out as frequently as possible so that he learns to use his outdoor toilet as well. Just as with any other form of house training, only let your pup investigate other parts of your home after he has pooped and peed on his litter box (fine with small dogs), piddle pad, or newspaper. The frequency of his need to empty his bladder and bowels decreases as your pup matures.

SMELL AND STAIN REMOVERS

The sensitivity of a dog's nose is simply beyond our comprehension. Routine cleaning and disinfecting may mask odours for us, but will not get rid of the residual odours left by messing. These natural smells draw your dog back to the same site, so it is vitally important to eliminate odour molecules. Avoid any cleanser with ammonia. Ammonia is a natural by-product of wastes. It will attract rather than repel a dog from a site.

If carpet is soiled, the underlay, and even the floor beneath should be treated with any odour-eliminating product. White vinegar and water is good for removing stains from carpets.

■ **Clean up well** *after your dog has messed or the smell will attract him back to soil in the same place.*

House training an adult dog

IN MY EXPERIENCE, *odour and stain products that contain enzymes work pretty well. You can find a wide variety of these on the market. As an alternative, mix a laundry detergent that contains enzymes (several brands do) with hot water and liberally soak the area. Alcohol will also break down odours.*

All the principles of house training apply equally to older dogs. The important difference is that some older dogs have to unlearn some toileting habits before learning new ones.

With a crate

Crate training is ideal, although an older dog who is not used to a crate will need to be conditioned to the idea of using it. In these circumstances I would suggest a sturdy plastic crate that comes apart in the middle, leaving the bottom looking much like a typical dog's bed. Get the older dog used to this bed, and after several days reassemble the crate, keep the door open, and toss a little food or favourite toys in. Serve meals in it if you like, but do not close the door. Get your dog used to spending time in it with the door open. This works fastest when the crate is in your own bedroom at night.

■ **Provide your dog** *with toys, water, and a chew to keep her occupied.*

■ **Dogs should** *be introduced gradually to a crate.*

Adult dogs can control their bowels and bladder far longer than pups can, so they can be crated for longer periods of time. Crate your dog when you're not around to watch him (but not all day!). When he's in a crate, make sure he has amusements to keep him occupied, for example a chew toy with cheese spread in the hollow middle. Take him out as you would a pup, at least four times a day, but you can eliminate the hourly garden visits. Always give your "Do it" command as he is toileting, followed by praise.

Without a crate

If you are not using a crate, your older dog should be tethered to you and not allowed to roam the house freely until after he has relieved himself outdoors. If he starts to urinate or defecate in the house, correct him with a sharp "No!" then immediately take him outside. Of course, praise him with your most impressive "Good boy" when he performs where you want him to.

■ **Do not scold** *your dog if he messes; simply be more vigilant in the future.*

The key to success is to limit the chances of a dog messing where you do not want him to mess. Be consistent. And remember that accidents will happen. Keep your cool. If they are happening frequently, it's your fault because you are not keeping close enough tabs on the dog. Be consistent and patient.

Incontinence, where urine leaks out because the muscle that controls the bladder has become slack, is not uncommon in older dogs. Your veterinary surgeon can also give you advice about professional dog trainers in your area.

Any adult dog can learn the essence of house training within two weeks. If training is taking you longer, contact your veterinary surgeon to make sure there are no medical problems.

There will be lapses

IT IS FASCINATING how fast a creature so young can learn to toilet the way we want him to, but remember, he is a puppy at heart until well after he reaches physical maturity at about one year of age. Expect lapses, especially in these circumstances:

1. Sexual maturity.

2. Sudden household activity, such as a party.

3. Changes in who is his primary leader.

4. Emotional turmoil in the family.

5. The arrival of another pet.

■ **Your dog will quickly** *accustom himself to following a daily routine with regular toilet, meal, and exercise times.*

Routine helps

Dogs have great biological clocks that work best when you set up and follow a daily routine. Feeding times are important. What goes in at a certain time comes out at a certain time. It couldn't be much simpler!

Use your dog's love of routine to your advantage by associating toileting with a really powerful reward, such as going for a stimulating walk. Try to ensure that your timetable includes time for you to take your dog into your garden for him to relieve himself, back in the house if he does not, back out for a second try and, only after success, a long, rewarding walk. If you are training your dog to eliminate in the street, follow the same routine: out to the gutter, a maximum five-minute hang around, then back inside, and out again for another try. Only after successful toileting in the gutter do you wind him up with praise and an active, exciting walk.

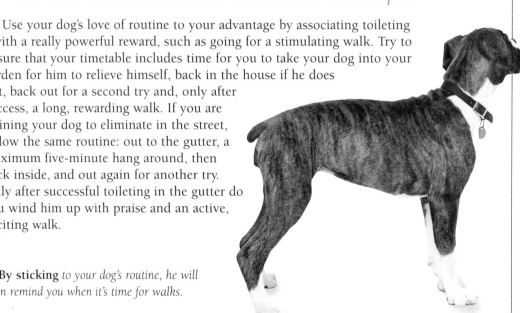

■ **By sticking** *to your dog's routine, he will soon remind you when it's time for walks.*

Messing at night

Some dogs become house trained during the day but mess at night. If your dog is over five months old and behaving like this, he has probably developed a habit of messing at night. It is very unlikely that physiologically he needs to relieve himself. In these circumstances, he should sleep in your bedroom with you, in a bed he cannot get out of (such as a crate). When he needs to relieve himself he will whine. In a daze, get up and take him outside. Next night, when he whines again, lie there in bed, cursing under your breath for 10 minutes, then take him out. No fuss. Out and in. Just keep it simple. The next night, wait 20 minutes. Over a two-week period you will train his body to wait until morning. You will also be making it clear that outside is the place to go – even at night. When training is complete, he returns to wherever you want him to sleep.

Loss of training can mean:
- *Your dog was never fully trained.*
- *Sex-related urine-marking.*
- *Submissive urination.*
- *Fear, stress, or anxiety.*
- *High excitement.*
- *A medical problem.*

■ **Dogs occasionally forget**
their toilet-training with sex-related urine-marking.

Submissive urinating

You want to know what makes a veterinary surgeon feel miserable? He looks at a dog, the dog looks at him, and then piddles. When that happens I know that dog probably has been frightened at the vet's or has really low self-esteem.

Dogs urinate when they are frightened but, more frequently, females in particular urinate as a sign of submission. Do not mistake this for a lapse in house training.

Submissive urination is a natural way a low-ranking dog appeases a high-ranking one. This is why urinating when excited is more a puppy than an adult problem. Most pups look upon us big humans as naturally high-rankers. If your pup piddles when he sees you, do not reprimand him or show anger. Do not even stroke his head or reach down and touch him. These are the actions of high-rankers. Instead, ignore him and walk away, either to an area where there is newspaper on plastic sheeting, or out the back door where he can relieve himself.

■ **Remember** *that a crate can be used to toilet train both puppies and older dogs.*

Most pups outgrow submissive urinating as they mature and build confidence. Curiously, these pups are the easiest to obedience train because they concentrate so intently on you, but it is absolutely imperative to avoid scolding or anger during training.

If your dog urinates submissively, keep plastic sheeting and an absorbent towel inside the front door, so you are prepared for mishaps during the training time necessary to bolster your dog's self confidence.

■ **Give careful consideration** *to paper training as your dog will require retraining to relieve herself outside.*

A simple summary

✓ House training is simple if you are consistent and conscientious. It's going to take some early effort on your part, but your effort will be well-rewarded when you have a dog who is reliably house trained.

✓ Puppies will need to relieve themselves after eating, playing, waking up, or becoming excited.

✓ A crate is an excellent tool for house training. Just make sure your puppy always views his crate as a positive place, and that he doesn't spend too much time crated.

✓ Do not punish accidents. This will only teach your puppy to fear your arrival, and will not help with house training. Interrupt them if you see them happening; otherwise, clean them up when the pup is elsewhere.

✓ If necessary, you can train a pup to use papers indoors, but you will then have to retrain the dog to go outside when he is an adult.

✓ House train an adult dog in the same way you would a puppy, with a regular schedule and unsupervised time in his crate.

✓ You can teach your dog to eliminate on cue by using the same command phrase every time as the dog goes, and then praising him when he's finished.

✓ Some dogs experience submissive urination – this is not a house training problem, but one of lack of confidence.

■ **The excitement of play** *encourages puppies to relieve themselves afterwards.*

Chapter 12

Simple Canine Etiquette

WHEN YOUR DOG RESPECTS YOU as a leader and when she knows her name, she is ready for simple obedience training. This is easiest with puppies, because they naturally look up to you as a strong leader. Older dogs take longer to accept a new person as their leader, but through your confident and consistent behaviour a dog learns to respect you.

Teaching good manners, to come, stay, sit, and lie down, is surprisingly simple. Most dogs willingly carry out these activities because they want to please their leaders and because it is in their interest to do so.

In this chapter...

✓ How to begin

✓ Coming to you

✓ Delighted to sit

✓ Content to stay

✓ Willing to lie down

DOGS WANT TO PLEASE THEIR OWNERS, WHICH MAKES TRAINING ENJOYABLE

How to begin

YOU ARE GOING to use word and hand signals, and you promise to be consistent with them. You have chosen suitable rewards, and your puppy knows you have them. You understand that eye contact and body language are important. You know that timing is vital. You are not going to ask your dog to do something you cannot make sure she will do. What next?

Keep lessons short

A minute or two is perfect for a pup. Five minutes is too long. Older dogs have greater powers of concentration, but dogs with even the best mental stamina cannot concentrate on training for more than about 15 minutes at a time. Pups are capable of concentrating on training several times during the day.

Keep lessons enjoyable

Is your puppy tired or frightened or cold? If she is not enjoying herself, forget about training. The opposite applies, too. Is she so full of joy that first she needs to run 144 figure-8s? Let her. Give her a chance to burn off a little of that puppy energy. Once it's out of her system, she will concentrate more on what you are doing.

Start as you mean to continue

Plan ahead. You will be using specific words as commands, and will use hand or body signals with those words. Make sure everyone in the family is using the same words and signals. Write them down. Here are some examples, but you can use what you like.

■ **To teach your dog** to come to you, hold your arms out wide and say "Come."

"Come"

"Steady"

■ **When slowing** *your dog down, say "Steady."*

"Finished"

■ **On releasing** *your dog from a command, call "Finished."*

SPARKY'S WORDS AND SIGNALS

SPARKY'S ACTION	YOUR WORD COMMAND	YOUR HAND OR BODY SIGNAL
Pay attention to you	Sparky	One hand raised with palm up
Come to you	Come	Both arms held out wide
Sit	Sit	Hand points to the floor and moves down
Stay there	Stay	Show flat palm of hand straight out
Lie down	Down	Hand sweeps down and out
Being a good dog	Good girl or Good boy	Thumbs up
Stop what she's doing	No	Hands cross over each other
Not quite right	Wrong	(signal not necessary)
Released from a command	Finished	Both hands rise
Walk with you	Walk	(signal not necessary)
Wait with you	Wait	(signal not necessary)
Relax, slow down	Steady	(signal not necessary)

YOUR DOG'S WORDS AND SIGNALS

As I said, these are simply examples. With your family, decide what words and signals you want to use. Then write them down. Here is the form to fill in. Photocopy it, put up a copy in the kitchen, and give copies to everyone in the family. Then stick to it.

DOG'S ACTION	YOUR WORD COMMAND	YOUR HAND OR BODY SIGNAL
Pay attention to you	_____	_____
Come to you	_____	_____
Sit	_____	_____
Stay there	_____	_____
Lie down	_____	_____
Being a good dog	_____	_____
Stop what she's doing	_____	_____
Not quite right	_____	_____
Released from a command	_____	_____
Walk with you	_____	_____
Wait with you	_____	_____
Relax, slow down	_____	_____

Train when your dog's mind is alert

An ideal time to train is just before a meal. With pups that means you have three or four ready-made training opportunities each day. As your pup matures and you're feeding her fewer meals each day, train her shortly after she wakes up and after she has emptied her bladder and bowels.

At first, always combine food rewards with praise. Eventually, only give the most powerful reward, food, intermittently. Giving rewards intermittently, rather than constantly, is the most effective way of reinforcing learning.

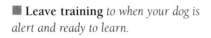

■ **Leave training** *to when your dog is alert and ready to learn.*

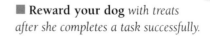

■ **Reward your dog** *with treats after she completes a task successfully.*

Avoid distractions

The easiest place to begin training is inside your own home. This applies to simple obedience such as come-sit-stay-down, but also to leash training, or walking beside you. A hallway is an almost ideal place to begin training because it is such a boring place to be.

Once your dog reliably responds in that location, move on to a slightly more distracting environment, the back yard for example. Only when your dog reliably responds to training in those locations should you advance to even more distracting surroundings, such as the street or a park.

Train in small increments. Avoid leaps from one skill level to a much higher one. Forget about trying to train several dogs at once. It is virtually impossible. If you have two pups, keep one out of earshot while you train, reward, or discipline the other.

■ **Start training** your puppy *inside the home where she is in a familiar environment.*

Always finish with fun

Always finish formal training sessions on a high note. These short episodes each day should be fun for both of you. If your pup just can't seem to get something right, go back to something she really knows how to do well and end the session with that exercise. Then play with your pup.

However, don't save the most powerful reward for the end of the session. If you do, you are unwittingly training your dog to want the session to end so she can get hold of the potent reward.

Don't make training unnecessarily difficult for your dog. If you have long hair, pull it back from your face. If it's sunny outside, forget the sunglasses. To respond best, your dog needs to be able to see your eyes.

■ **After a training session**, *play with your dog so that she associates learning with fun.*

195

Don't get flustered

Avoid persistently repeating commands. It only confuses your dog. If training is not going well, stop. Think about what you are doing. The problem is with you, not with your dog.

I don't mean that to sound harsh, but virtually all dogs have the capacity to learn basic obedience in a short period of time – within days for some and a maximum of a few weeks for dogs that need some retraining. Don't be bashful about asking for help. Front office staff at veterinary clinics are probably your best bet for sound advice on finding a good local trainer. You can also look for members of the Association of Professional Dog Trainers (APDT) and the Association of Professional Behaviour Counsellors (APBC) both of which endorse positive motivation training methods.

■ **If your puppy** *does not respond well to training, seek advice from a recommended trainer.*

PUPPY CLASSES

Puppy classes are like pre-school for kids, an ideal environment for early learning and moulding behaviour. But just like pre-school, some puppy classes are better than others.

When choosing a puppy class, look for the following:
✓ There is a restricted puppy age group, preferably under 16 weeks old.
✓ The pup's entire human family is encouraged to attend.
✓ Free play takes place among small groups of pups.
✓ Classes last about an hour, go on for about six weeks and cover a set curriculum.
✓ Your vet or the owner of a well-behaved dog recommends the class.
✓ The instructor is a member of APDT or APBC.

You can ask to attend one class without your pup before you enrol, to make sure you like what you see. When attending a puppy class, look for the following:
✓ Classes are closely supervised, including free play.
✓ Children attending classes are closely supervised.
✓ Brash pups are not allowed to intimidate shy ones.
✓ Bold puppies are selected for their own play group.
✓ All classes end on a positive note for pups and their people.
✓ Students are sent home with homework to do before the next class.

Coming to you

THIS IS THE EASIEST *command for a pup to learn. Use meal times as excellent opportunities to teach your dog to come.*

THE LESSON

1. Crouch down a short distance away from your puppy, show her the food bowl, say her name and, as she begins to move toward her meal, give the command "Come".

2. As she approaches, say "Good girl" enthusiastically.

3. Give her the meal.

4. Between meals, do the same exercise a few times each day, using a food tidbit to entice your dog to come.

5. Graduate to standing upright and getting her attention by calling her name, then say "Come" as she starts to approach. Stroke her as her reward.

Within only a few days she will come to you willingly when she hears her name and the word "Come".

"COME"

■ **Teaching your dog** *to come to you, is the easiest command for her to learn.*

■ **Once your dog** *has come to you, reward her with the bowl of food.*

INTERNET

www.apdt.com

The website for the Association of Professional Dog Trainers lists all members by region.

www.apbc.co.uk

Website for members of the Association of Professional Behavioural Counsellors.

Variations on training "Come"

Older, strong-willed, or shy dogs may not come so willingly. To make sure your dog always complies with your instructions, use a **houseline** *or a lead to ensure you can always get your dog's attention.*

Don't use the lead like a fishing line, to reel in your dog. Like a smallmouth bass, she will put up the most amazing resistance. Give a quick tug on the lead to get your dog's attention, then draw her to you with the reward, not tension on the leash. Make sure the reward is something your dog truly finds rewarding. Take your cue from her.

NYLON CORD LONGLINE

■ **Do not** *"reel in" your dog on the lead; she will only resist.*

AVOID THESE MISTAKES WHILE TRAINING

1. Never say "Come" unless you are sure your dog will obey. If you cannot ensure she will comply, she's learned that she does not have to obey you all the time.

2. Never use the word "Come" to call your dog from something exciting to something less interesting. The call to come should always be met with enthusiasm if you want your dog to come reliably.

3. Never use the word "Come" to call your dog to discipline. She's no fool, and will soon learn that "Come" means something bad is about to happen and will run the other way.

Delighted to sit

Puppies learn to sit on command just as quickly as they learn to come to you. When teaching "Sit", concentrate on your dog's head. Control her head and her body will do what you want it to. It's really that simple.

THE LESSON

1. Stand up facing your dog and, with her food bowl or a food treat in your hand, ask her to "Come". (Depending on your dog, you may have her on her houseline to make sure she responds.) Be calm. She is probably hungry and you don't want to overexcite her.

"COME"

2. When she reaches you, raise your hand holding her food or treat up just enough to clear the dog's head, then back from the nose to the eyes or ears. Make sure she is watching her reward. As her head follows the food above, her rump will naturally go down. As you see her bending her hind legs, give the command "Sit".

"SIT"

3. When she assumes a sitting position, say "Good girl" and give the food immediately.

"GOOD GIRL"

4. Once she is obediently sitting as she faces you, graduate to standing beside her while giving the command "Sit". Initially always give a food reward, but eventually give them intermittently. Finally, words of praise alone will be sufficient.

Variations on training "Sit"

Most dogs naturally sit when they want to keep an eye on something above them. Some do not. If your dog does not sit for a food reward, hold her collar in one hand and use your other hand to tuck her hindquarters into a sitting position. Give the command "Sit" as you do this, and instantly reward her with a food treat and a hearty "Good girl".

When your dog has learned to sit like a pro, you can start to give the "Sit" command when you are walking with her and you stop, or when she is playing and you want her rapt attention.

■ **If your dog** *refuses to sit, tuck her hindquarters into this position with your hand.*

AVOID THESE MISTAKES WHILE TRAINING

1 Avoid over-excitement. It's hard for a dog, especially a puppy, to sit still when she's very excited. If meals are so exciting that your dog cannot concentrate on your commands, do not use the meal as a reward. Train her on a fuller stomach, using less stimulating but still interesting rewards such as a toy.

2 Never give a command without being able to make sure your dog complies. If you do so, you are actively training your dog to disregard that command.

Content to stay

WITH "COME" AND "SIT" *under her collar, your puppy has actually learned to follow a sequence of commands. The next stage is to add a third command, "Stay" or "Wait". This will be vital for her safety in the future. "Stay" is simply a prolonged variation of "Sit". After you have trained your dog to sit for a food reward, then sit for simple verbal praise, graduate to "Stay", reinforcing the command with your chosen hand signal.*

THE LESSON

1. Make sure your dog is looking up at your face. Don't stand too close; you don't want her looking up vertically.

2. After she sits, show her the palm of your hand while you command, "Stay".

3. Keep the duration of the "Sit-stay" short, then calmly give a small food reward.

4. Gradually increase the duration of the "Stay", also graduating to the command word alone without the food treat.

5. Over a period of a week, repeat the exercise, gradually backing up until you are giving the command at a distance. Complete the "Stay" by introducing your release word "Finished". Reward her when the exercise is finished.

Variations on training "Stay"

■ **Praise your dog** *after each command but do not overdo it or you will over-excite her.*

Try training with your dog sitting at the base of a wall. That keeps her from sliding backwards. If your dog does not respond properly or gets up when she should be staying, avoid the word "No". Save that for more serious crimes.

Introduce a neutral word when she does not get it right. Personally, I like "Wrong". If, for example she rolls on her back or starts to get up, say "Wrong", stand up, and induce her back into a sit position.

AVOID THESE MISTAKES WHILE TRAINING

1. Avoid an abundance of praise after releasing your dog from "Stay". Too much praise on your part excites your dog and teaches her to jump around and be exuberant at the end of a training session. Keep your praise muted.

2. Never try "Stay" training when circumstances make it difficult for your dog to concentrate on what you are doing. If she is worried about the presence of other dogs or is more interested in investigating other activities, her mind is elsewhere and she is not learning. During each short training session, you want her rapt attention.

Willing to lie down

"Lie down" requires a little more work on your part and understanding on your dog's part. All of the commands so far have anticipated willing behaviour by your dog. Now you will be asking her to do something she naturally does, but may be reluctant to do on command. That's because lying down is a submissive gesture between dogs.

THE LESSON

1. With your pup in a sit position, kneel to her right, holding her collar with your left hand and a food treat in your right hand.

2. Put the food treat in front of your pup's nose. Make a fist around the treat so the dog cannot grab it out of your hand. Then, using a sweeping action, move your treat-holding hand forward and downward in an arc. As your pup lies down to keep track of the now-floor-level food treat, give the command, "Down". Keep the treat clenched in your hand so she cannot grab it.

3. Continue moving the food along the floor until she is completely lying down. Praise her with "Good girl" and give her the treat.

4. Once she understands "Down", prolong it with "Stay", rewarding her good response initially with food and praise, then food interspersed with praise, and finally with verbal praise alone.

5. Release her from her "Down-stay" with the release word "Finished".

Variations on training "Down"

If your pup creeps forward on her haunches rather than lying down, kneel beside her and, while she is sitting, put the palms of your hands under her forelegs, lift her gently into a begging position, then lower into a lying position. Instantly reward her with praise and treats.

If she refuses to stay down, using both hands apply gentle pressure to her withers. Reward her for lying down, then release her with the word "Finished".

AVOID THESE MISTAKES WHILE TRAINING

1. Do not try to make your dog stay down for more than a few seconds at first. Work up to a whole minute very gradually.

2. Don't bore your dog with too frequent or too long periods of training. A few minutes two or three times a day is just about right for most pups. Take advantage of feeding and exercise times for more natural training situations.

Be patient

You are teaching your dog a completely new language. Think about the last time you tried to learn a foreign language. I'm sure there were times when you felt frustrated because it sounded like gibberish. So be patient and reasonable with your dog. Remember how long it takes you to learn a new language. That way you will appreciate your dog's amazing abilities.

Come, sit, down, and stay are the most important lessons your dog will ever learn. Everything else you teach her will be based on this, and these behaviors form the basis of canine good manners.

A simple summary

✓ Keep all your dog's lessons short and enjoyable.

✓ Use your pup's hunger before mealtimes to your advantage, by offering training treats. However, if your pooch is the pickier type, find a toy or a game she really likes to use as a training reward.

✓ Avoid distractions while training, and be sure to finish each training session on a high note.

✓ Be sure everyone in your family is using the same words and signals, and using them consistently. Make a list of the commands you are using to teach your dog, and post it where everyone can see it.

✓ "Come", "Sit", "Down", and "Stay" are easily taught, and form the basics for further training.

Chapter 13

Walking the Dog

AHAPPY, TAIL-WAGGING pet walking securely by your side, not pulling on his lead, is one of the great joys of living with a dog. One way or another, most of us manage to teach our dogs to come, sit, and stay. Walking comfortably on the lead is another matter. Teaching your dog to walk by your side is not as simple as the basic canine etiquette we covered in Chapter 12, because good training depends on your being able to walk and chew gum at the same time, as it were.

In this chapter...

✔ Plan ahead

✔ Train indoors first

✔ Walking without a leash

✔ Walking on the leash

✔ Moving outdoors

✔ A few more obedience suggestions

A DOG THAT DOES NOT PULL ON THE LEAD MAKES THE PERFECT WALKING COMPANION

Plan ahead

When you walk, which foot do you naturally lead with? This is important, because you should consistently keep your dog on this side when training him to walk with you. His cue to walk is seeing your lead leg, the one closest to him, moving forward. If your feet are dyslexic, train them first before using them in coordination with your dog.

Use the right equipment. Your dog must be used to his collar before you start training him to heel. If he does not yet accept it, go back to basics and put it on him just before play, activity, and feeding, so that he associates his collar with the joys of life. Use a collar with a flat buckle and metal ring for the lead. Choose a lightweight standard leash for training. Leave fashion accessories for later. Make sure he reliably understands basic obedience: "Sit", "Come", and "Stay". He must understand "Sit" because this is always the take-off point for heeling.

■ **Start with** *a lightweight lead when you are training your puppy.*

■ **Dogs are** *traditionally trained to walk on their owners left side.*

Trivia...

Traditionally, dogs are trained to walk at your left side. The tradition evolved out of gundog training. The dog walks to the left, while the handler carries his shotgun and shoots from the right. The dog is always at the handler's heel which, of course, is why walking at your side is called heeling. If you plan to participate in any type of dog training classes in future, it's better to begin with your dog at your left side.

Train indoors first

KEEP IT SIMPLE. *Both you and your dog have to concentrate that little bit more on this one. Always start by letting your dog play vigorously to burn up excess energy, and then practise training in your home first. Familiarize him to the feel of the lead by attaching it to his collar and using it when training him to come to you.*

Train where there are no distractions. A hallway with a long wall is perfect. One client of mine had the great idea of training in his living room by moving his sofa a few feet away from the wall and training along behind it, and eventually anticlockwise and clockwise around it. From the hall, move on to the garden. Again, let your pup look, smell, and listen to life for a few minutes before you start training.

Always keep the first sessions short, beginning with a few seconds and a few feet forward. Repeat this twice a day, increasing both time and distance. It is amazing how fast your dog will learn to walk beside you as long as you are patient, consistent, and not too ambitious.

On or off leash does not matter

■ **Play with** *your dog to release his excess energy before you begin a training session.*

It really does not matter whether you start training to heel on or off the lead. It is not an issue of right or wrong, but rather what feels best for you and your dog. (It may, however, be an issue for your local police officer. Make sure walking your dog off the lead is legal in your area before you try it. Also make sure you are in a safe area in case your dog decides to run after something rather than heel.)

What is important is that training should be fun, a real tail wagger. If you are in a bad mood, wait until you are feeling more positive before you begin training. I will start with training off the lead, give you a few variations, then show you how to train with a lead.

Walking without a leash

USE FOOD TREATS *and praise in the following sequence:*

1. Position your pup in a sit to your left (if that is the side you have chosen) and, holding his collar with your left hand, say his name to get his attention. Let him smell the food treat in your clenched fist.

2. As you step forward with your left foot and he follows the scent of the treat, let go of his collar and give the command "Heel" (or "Walk" if you prefer).

3. After only a few steps give the command "Wait", get down to his level (to prevent jumping up) and give him the food reward. If it is necessary, use your free left arm, extended under his belly, to prevent him from moving forward out of the "Wait" position.

End of lesson. If both of you are still alert, repeat the sequence, but do not overdo it. With each lesson extend the distance you move in a straight line. When your pup is consistently responding to "Walk" and "Wait" in a straight line, introduce swings to the left and right.

Simple to the right

1. Walk forward with your pup at your left. Keeping your right hand with the food treat low in front of the pup's nose, give the command "Heel" as you turn to the right.

2. Your pup has to speed up because he has farther to go when turning right. After a few steps in the new direction, give the command "Wait", stop, and reward good behaviour with the food treat and words of praise.

More difficult to the left

1. Left turns are, at first, more awkward for both of you. With your pup walking forward on your left, give the command "Steady" as you move your right hand holding the food treat in front of you and to the left.

2. Your pup will slow down (and soon learns that "Steady" means "slow down") as his nose leads the rest of his body to the left. You may need to guide a left turn with your hand on his collar. Once he has turned left and taken a few steps, give the command "Wait", stop, and reward his good behaviour with the food treat and praise.

Problem solving

Most pups respond well to this training, but here are some common problems and how to overcome or avoid them:

Food is no fun

It is important to "addict" your pup to the food treat you are using. Dried liver treats work so well because they are smelly. Yeast-based vitamin and mineral tablets such as Pet-tabs are excellent because they are smelly and nutritious. If your pup simply is not interested in food, find a toy, usually a squeaky one, that triggers intense interest and use it as the reward for compliance.

Jumping up

If your puppy jumps up to get at the treat, you are holding it too high. Hold your hand lower, and at the same time use your free left hand on your dog's collar to prevent jumping. If your pup is an obsessive foodie, try training for a few minutes after meals (but after your pup has emptied his bowels and bladder).

No concentration

If your puppy is having a hard time paying attention, you probably have chosen the wrong time or place for training. Try again when he is better prepared. If, during training, he is distracted from what you are teaching him, use your left hand on his collar to bring him back to the correct heel position, get his attention with the food treat, and continue. If a distraction is overwhelming, command him to do something you know he will do, for instance a sit, reward him with verbal praise, and continue later when the distraction is no longer there.

Walking on the leash

WHEN A PUPPY *willingly follows you off the lead, it is easy to graduate to heeling on a lead. Use a lead with a bolt-snap of appropriate weight for your dog. If you have not introduced the lead before, let your pup look at it and smell it.*

1. Attach the lead to your puppy's well-fitted, comfortable collar. With your puppy on your left, hold the end of the lead and the food treat in your right hand. Your left hand holds the slack in the lead. Avoid tension on the lead at this point. Command your pup to sit.

INTERNET

www.petopia.com

Petopia offers a wide variety of collars, harnesses, halters, and leads for sale.

2. Start walking forward (with your left foot), and as your puppy gets up to move, give the command "Heel". Let him feel only the slightest tension on the lead. If he surges forward, slide your hand down the lead, give a slight jerk, and the command "Steady".

3. After only a few steps give the command "Wait", get down to his level (to prevent jumping up), and give him the food reward. Verbally reward him, then go through the same training sequence again.

4. Once he is heeling on his lead in a straight line, graduate to turns. Guide him to the right with the food in your left hand, and as he turns in that direction, give the command "Heel".

"HEEL"

5. Teach left turns by increasing your speed at first rather than having your puppy decrease his. With the lead in your right hand, slide your left hand down the slack to your puppy's collar. Guide his nose to the left with the treat in your right hand. When he has learned to turn left at his regular speed, repeat the maneuver with you walking at your regular speed and him slowing down. As he slows down, give the command "Steady" (or "Slow" if your prefer).

A simple variation

1. After your pup has used up excess energy in play, attach the lead to his collar and lure him to your left side with a food treat. When he comes reward him with praise and the food treat.

2. Hold the lead against your body so that the length remains constant and loose but not so loose that it reaches the ground. Get your puppy's attention by saying his name, then step forward. Usually your pup will naturally move forward with you. Keep the lead slack. It's just "There".

3. Keep an eye on the slackness in the lead. If it looks like it's about to go taut, stop. Remember to continue to hold the lead against your body so that the length is always constant. This brings your pup to a halt too.

4. Use a food treat to encourage your pup back to your side. Wait until he is calm and inactive before setting off again. If he goes behind or across in front, stop once more and begin afresh by luring him back to your left side. Do not reposition yourself to help your pup out. You want him to learn to position himself with you, not the reverse.

5. Repeat this exercise, all the time talking positively to your puppy until, after a week or so, he is walking by your side without pulling on his lead. Be patient. Walking with you requires concentration from both of you. Do not expect a dog to have as much concentration as you do.

More problem solving

As hard as you try, a dog will be dynamically inventive, creating variations you had not expected. Here are a few more you might have to contend with:

Climbing the leash

If your boisterous pup tries to climb his lead, say "No!", move away, give the command "Sit" and go back to the beginning of the exercise.

Chewing the leash

If your happy-go-lucky buddy thinks it's more fun to chew the lead than to walk attached to it, invest in an unpleasant tasting but safe chew deterrent such as Bitter Apple spray. Spray the parts of the lead likely to be chewed. Deterrent spray can be used on other chewable articles in the house. Trainers call this *aversion therapy*.

Collapsing in a heap

Some pups collapse because they are overly submissive. Others do it simply because it's fun. Submissive pups need active encouragement to stand on all fours. Be gentle and patient. Use a favourite squeaky toy as encouragement, and plenty of praise to build confidence. Jokers need to be reminded there is a time for play and a time for concentration. If your puppy collapses in fits of fun when you put his lead on, get him into a sit and get his full attention before proceeding with lead training.

Gregarious pulling

Avoid shouting. Avoid anger. Do not lose your concentration if your puppy acts like a kite out of control when you put his lead on. Walking on the lead is one of the most important necessities for a happy relationship between you and your dog. Do not take chances. If lead training is not going well, ask your veterinary surgeon to suggest a professional trainer.

■ **To stop** your puppy from chewing the lead, spray it with a safe but foul-tasting liquid.

Moving outdoors

GRADUATE TO REAL-WORLD *walking exercises after you have trained your dog to heel in the quiet of your home and garden. When your dog hears the word "Heel", he should know that it means "Walk close and pay constant attention to me". Start training in quiet public places and keep it simple. Then move on to where there are more distractions and obstacles. Continue using food treats but use these ever more intermittently. Eventually you will only need a few in your pocket for the most distracting of situations.*

Even if you naturally walk at a steady rate, vary the speed of your walk to give your dog the stimulation of the unexpected and variety. Remember, a wagging tail means your puppy is not bored. If he gets distracted – and he will – you must get excited, get enthusiastic, get theatrical, whatever it takes to get his attention back on you.

Practical accessories

There are some simple pieces of equipment you can use to help your dog walk calmly by your side. Let's take a look at them.

Head halter

■ **When placing** *the head halter over your dog's head, give him a reward.*

For some curious reason, we have used head halters for centuries to control animals such as horses, but we've rarely used them with dogs. Think what it would be like to lead a horse with a lead attached to a collar. Seem dumb? There is really no difference with a dog.

On a halter, the lead clips to a ring on the halter that is under the dog's jaws. If a dog pulls forward, his own momentum pulls his head down (and his jaws shut). This is a "no fun" position for any dog. Common sense tells him to stop pulling. As he does so, he gets an instant reward: his head is back up where he wants it to be.

■ **Fasten the head halter** *behind your dog's neck, and make sure it is not too tight.*

Head halters such as the Halti, developed by a professional trainer and a university faculty veterinary surgeon, are ideal for any dog but especially for rambunctious, bold or independent individuals. The strap around the muzzle delivers a subtle psychological message to dogs with thuggish tendencies that you are a powerful, high-ranking leader.

■ **Choose body harnesses** *over collars for dogs with thick necks or soft windpipes.*

Body harness

An alternative to a standard collar is a body harness. Use a body harness rather than a collar on breeds with thick necks and small heads, such as Pugs and Bulldogs, and on breeds with soft windpipes, such as Yorkshire Terriers and Chihuahuas.

Choke chain

Choke chains are still commonly used by disciplinarian trainers. As a dog pulls forwards, the chain around his neck tightens until it hurts or he cannot breathe. So he learns not to pull on his lead. That is the theory. In practice, many dogs still pull, even with choke chains. A choke is not a method of training. It is a form of discipline. And if you put the choke chain on the wrong way, it tightens but then does not loosen up when a dog stops pulling.

There are no situations where you should use a choke chain. There are circumstances where a *half-check collar* is acceptable.

■ **Do not use** *a choke chain; a half-check collar is a better alternative.*

A few more obedience suggestions

NOW THAT YOU *and your dog have learned "Come", "Sit", "Stay", "Down", "Walk", "Steady", and "Wait", here are a few more lessons that I find simple for dogs to learn and really practical to use.*

Leave it

I mentioned that I live surrounded by take-out restaurants. Whether you live as I do with discarded burgers and fries, or in the remotest part of the country with decomposing animals or their droppings, you will want your dog to understand what you mean when you say "Leave it".

1. A little aversion therapy goes with this command. Put your dog in a sit-stay and get down on your haunches. Hold a food treat in one hand and make a fist (thumb and forefinger up) with the other. As the dog reaches for the treat, pop him under the jaw with enough pressure to close his jaws but not so much that it hurts (or knocks him off his front feet). As you do so, say, "Leave it".

2. Offer the treat again and repeat the exercise. Continue doing so until he hesitates or turns away. When he does so, verbally praise him but of course do not give the food reward. Most dogs learn "Leave it" very quickly.

Male dogs always sniff first before urine-marking. Teaching the "Leave it" command works as well to stop leg lifting where you do not want legs lifted as it does to halt scavenging for decomposing goodies.

■ **Teach your male dog** *not to sniff around and scent mark with the command "Leave it".*

215

Off

As I write, old Lexington has forgotten I'm in the library. I can see through to the living room, where she has got up on the sofa and is in a deep (deaf) sleep. She understands the "Off" command. In fact, she never, ever gets on the sofa when anyone is at home. For years we would come home to a warm sofa, not knowing which of our dogs had gone where dogs are not allowed to go. It was only when Lexy went deaf and did not hear us come in that we learned who the comfort-seeker was. She knows she is not allowed on the sofa (when people are around), but no one in the family has the heart, at her age, to use this command to get her off.

1. If your dog is on the sofa (couch, bed, table, television) without your permission, take him by the collar, say "Off", lead him down to the floor, then praise him.

2. If your dog is a persistent offender, or if there is even a hint of a snarl from him, leave his lead (or a houseline) attached to his collar while he is indoors. When you see him on something he should not be on, give a slight jerk on the lead, aiming in the downward direction you want him to go. When his feet hit the ground, command him to sit, then praise him.

Get out of here (aka Go to bed)

There will be times – plenty of times – when you do want your dog to disappear. Several staff members at my veterinary clinic bring their dogs to work. Two elderly Boxers, a middle-aged Spinone and a young Legato Romagnolo (honest!) in a reception area can be a bit much, so this command, "Go to bed", is one that all these dogs learned early on.

■ **If your dog** *persistently sits where he should not and snarls when he is removed, keep him on a lead indoors.*

1. "Go to bed" is really just an extension of a down-stay. Standing near your dog's bed, call him by name.

2. When he comes to you, say "Go to bed" as you lead him to his bed. At the bed, command "Down-stay".

This takes a little practice, and you must be consistent in enforcing it, but it is a great command for your dog to learn. Use it when you are busy, or even when you have guests over who are not quite the dog lovers you and your family are.

A simple summary

✓ Training a dog to walk comfortably beside you is more complex than teaching sit or down, but is essential to a good relationship.

✓ Begin training indoors to minimize distractions.

✓ You can train on or off the lead, it doesn't matter.

✓ Use a food treat to lure your dog to walk beside you, and keep your walks short and straight at first.

■ **Once your** dog has mastered walking with you indoors take him to more distracting locations.

✓ With your dog on lead, you can still use food as a lure, but also use a constant length of lead to help keep the pup from forging ahead of you.

✓ When you are doing well indoors, move outdoors to progressively more distracting locations.

✓ "Leave it", "Off", and "Go to bed" are other useful obedience exercises that will help make your dog more of a pleasure to live with.

■ **Use food** treats to reward your dog when training him to walk beside you.

Chapter 14

Life as a Dog

DOGS ARE NOT PERFECT, but in vital ways they are, well, nicer than us. Dogs do not plan devious forms of retribution and revenge. They do these things honestly and simply, because they are excited or bored. Dogs do not know what guilt is. If you come home to canine destruction and your dog cowers, she does so not because of guilt but because she is reading your body language.

In this chapter...

✓ Mental, physical, and social activities are vital

✓ Have a plan

✓ Simple retraining rules

✓ HELP! Where to get it

✓ Boredom problems

✓ Excitement problems

DOGS ENJOY THE SIMPLE LIFE

Mental, physical, and social activities are vital

Let us be fair, and frank. We keep dogs for our benefit, not theirs. We want them to adapt to our lifestyle rather than live according to theirs. We want them to live in an environment that we find pleasurable.

Then we get annoyed when our dogs, denied their natural outlets for social interactions with other dogs, denied their need to burn up energy, denied the opportunity to use their brains, howl or bark for companionship, jump on us with excitement, or dig to China. These are not dog problems. They are our problems. We provide ourselves with mental, physical, and social activity. Do the same for your dog, but in dog terms. Here are some ideas.

■ **Dogs dig to** *burn up energy or to find buried bones; find an alternative outlet for your dog to use up her excess energy.*

Mental activity

Training, training, training (how much simpler can it be?). "Come", "Sit", "Stay", "Down", "Heel", and later "Fetch" provide your dog with daily mental stimulation. "Fetch" is terrific for sedentary owners. A *kong* is a great fetch toy, because it bounces in so many different directions when you throw it.

Fetch training is quite easy, especially with pups. Begin by throwing a soft toy only a short distance. Let your pup chew on it or do whatever she wants, then get her attention with a "Come". As she returns, show her a food reward. As she opens her mouth to get the reward, say, "Drop it".

■ **Keep your dog** *active so that she doesn't find her own games.*

Make sure your dog has mental stimulation when you are absent by providing stimulating toys. Cheese spread or peanut butter in the hollow of a sterilized bone is excellent. So too are plastic balls or cubes that drop food rewards as they are nosed around the floor.

Physical activity

This is really simple. Jogging, cycling, and swimming – all are excellent. Choose the activity best suited for the size, breed, and age of your dog. (Sending your dog out alone in the back garden is not exercise. Just forget about that now.) If you're jogging, the best pace for your dog is a brisk trot. If you're cycling, buy a product specifically made to attach your dog's lead to your bicycle, so that you can keep both hands on the handlebars. Again, cycle so your dog trots rather than runs. Swimming is the favoured exercise for spaniels and retrievers, although places to swim are limited in urban areas. Only let your dog in a swimming pool that has steps for easy entry and exit. I am lucky that I have hundreds of acres of off-lead park within a ten-minute walk of where I live. This provides ideal exercise opportunity for my dogs and satisfies their third need, social activity.

Before starting any activity program, check with your veterinary surgeon about its suitability for your dog, especially if she is small, mature, or overweight. And remember, dogs do not sweat the way we do. Never exercise your dog in hot sunny weather. Always carry water, for your dog as well as for you. Collapsible water bowls are available from pet supply stores.

Finally, no pounding exercise for puppies please. Wait until adolescence, usually 12 to 15 months, before embarking on a serious exercise programme. Those young bones need time to finish growing.

■ **One of the** *easiest games to play with puppies is "Fetch".*

■ **Make sure that** *your dog interacts socially with other dogs from a young age.*

Social activity

Right now, while Inca is a little nobody, her twice daily park visits are teaching her good manners in her social interactions with other dogs. It still amazes and impresses me how urban dogs that have never met each other meet in a park for the first time, sniff ears and bottoms, then more often than not engage in active social play. Right now Inca chases any dog to play with.

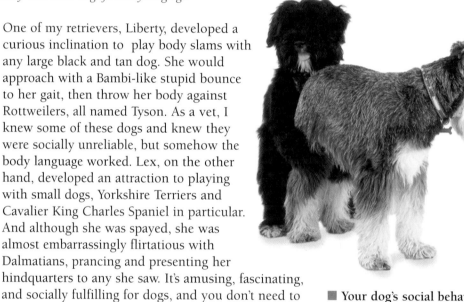

One of my retrievers, Liberty, developed a curious inclination to play body slams with any large black and tan dog. She would approach with a Bambi-like stupid bounce to her gait, then throw her body against Rottweilers, all named Tyson. As a vet, I knew some of these dogs and knew they were socially unreliable, but somehow the body language worked. Lex, on the other hand, developed an attraction to playing with small dogs, Yorkshire Terriers and Cavalier King Charles Spaniel in particular. And although she was spayed, she was almost embarrassingly flirtatious with Dalmatians, prancing and presenting her hindquarters to any she saw. It's amusing, fascinating, and socially fulfilling for dogs, and you don't need to understand it all to enjoy watching.

■ **Your dog's social behaviour** *could look embarrassingly flirtatious.*

Be prepared for unwanted activities

Every dog – every single dog – will develop habits you do not want her to have. Most, fortunately, are minor and easy to live with, but some are antisocial enough that they need to be changed. In some ways you can anticipate whether serious problems will develop.

IS YOUR DOG ANTISOCIAL?

Read through this list. If your answers are mostly in the left column, it's much less likely that your dog will develop serious problems. If the majority of your answers are in the right column, it's time to start working now to head off potential problems.

1. Where did you get your dog?	Breeder/friend	Ad/shelter/pet store
2. How old was your dog when you acquired him or her?	Under 18 weeks	Over 18 weeks
3. Has your dog been neutered or will he/she be neutered?	Yes	No
4. Have you previously owned a dog?	Yes	No
5. When is your dog fed?	At set times	On demand
6. Does your dog eat after you have finished?	Yes	No
7. When does your dog relieve herself?	At set times	No set times
8. Where does your dog sleep?	Her own bed	A family member's bed
9. How often is your dog groomed?	Frequently	Infrequently
10. How does your dog react to grooming?	Willingly	Unwillingly
11. When is your dog exercised?	Set times	On demand
12. How long is exercise time?	More than 1 hour a day	Less than 1 hour a day
13. Do you have off-lead control?	Yes	No
14. Where are the dog's toys kept?	In a toy box	On the floor
15. How often does your dog play with other dogs?	Frequently	Infrequently
16. How often does your dog meet or play with other people?	Frequently	Infrequently
17. How long is your dog left at home alone?	Less than 4 hours	More than 4 hours
18. How often does your dog have special playtime with you?	Frequently	Infrequently

■ **Train your dog** *from when she is a puppy to avoid any unwanted behaviour.*

Have a plan

KNOW WHAT YOU are going to do when problems develop. First, minimize the chance of an unacceptable behaviour happening again. For example, if your dog raided the rubbish bin, simply move the rubbish bin where it cannot be raided. Or cover it with a secure lid. End of problem. If your dog is finding dessert in the cat litter box, make the box inaccessible to her. If she is drinking from the toilet, close the lid. (This might involve a little guy training – more difficult than dog training.) If she is destructive when left alone, keep her in her crate with a wonderful chew toy filled with peanut butter.

A little compromise is useful

Some problems are more likely to occur in one dog rather than another. Problems can be exaggerated by breed, poor breeding, poor early socialization, or being abused or abandoned before becoming part of your family.

For example, you might have chosen a Fox Terrier for her appealing looks, then been appalled by her desire to convert your garden into a moonscape. But you must remember that terriers were bred to dig! Do not try and overcome this "problem". Instead, keep things simple by redirecting her natural desires. Train her to dig only in an approved digging area.

Eliminate the cause

Does your dog trash the house when she is left alone? If she does, chances are she is bored or anxious because you are gone. Try to understand the reason for her behaviour. There always is one — and it is not revenge on you for being left alone.

■ **If your puppy** is teething, provide her with chew toys to avoid her from finding a substitute chew.

INTERNET

www.wonderpuppy.net/
canwehelp/index.html

This site, called Can We Help You Keep Your Pet?, offers links to a wide variety of pages that deal with common canine (and feline) problems, such as aggression, housetraining, barking, and destructiveness.

Take away hidden rewards

This is easy when the rewards are obvious. If your dog begs at the table and the weakest link in the family (I hate to say it, but usually a husband) gives her a tidbit, the reward is obvious. Control the tidbit giver and the begging will stop. Sometimes, however, the reward is not so obvious. If your dog trembles when she sees another dog and you pick her up, you are not reassuring her – you are rewarding her for trembling!

Switch to another reward

If your dog is chewing a shoe, train your family not to leave their shoes around, but leave her a chew toy to chew. If she jumps up to say hello, train her to sit when you come home and reward her for sitting, rather than disciplining her for jumping. If she barks when she hears a noise, train her to fetch and carry. It's tough to bark when you have a toy in your mouth.

■ **Bitter Apple spray** *is excellent to prevent your dog from chewing.*

Try automatic correction

Ideally, create circumstances where a dog learns to stop doing something by herself, without your obvious involvement. Remember the Bitter Apple spray on the lead to prevent chewing? That is "self-correction". Use Bitter Apple spray, Tabasco sauce, or other safe but disagreeable tastes to prevent chewing where you do not want chewing. Use noise the same way. Inexpensive vibration-sensitive alarms for windows, available from most hardware stores, can be put on the bed or sofa if you do not want your dog sleeping on the furniture in your absence. (For your neighbours' sake, use alarms that turn off very quickly.) If you are at home and see your dog doing something you do not want her to do, a squirt from your every ready water pistol or a clunk on the floor from the fizzy drink can filled with a few coins, combined with a verbal "No!" from you, works wonders.

Be creative and, as always, a little dramatic, when you are making these corrections. They should seem to come from nowhere, so that your dog will believe they happen even when you're not around. It is a natural way dogs learn from the situation, rather than from your obvious intervention.

■ **If your dog** *is a comfort-seeker, place a vibration-sensitive alarm on chairs to prevent her from sitting on them.*

Simple retraining rules

THERE IS NO END *to the creativity of the dog's mind. Although bad habits vary, almost all of them can be diminished or corrected by following this simple program.*

Go back to basic obedience. Make sure your dog understands all the basic commands.

There is no such thing as a free lunch. Make sure your dog does something for you, such as sitting or lying down, before she receives any kind of reward, even a verbal "Hello".

Avoid problems. Make sure you can enforce obedience commands.

■ **Provide your dog** *with an acceptable outlet for natural behaviour and ensure that her energy is used up with exercise.*

Satisfy your dog's natural needs by creating acceptable outlets for natural behaviours.

Eliminate the satisfaction your dog gets from her unacceptable behaviour. Sometimes this will involve mild corrections.

Persevere. Do not expect miracles overnight. Typically, it takes about three weeks of diligent, consistent retraining to overcome most common behaviour problems. If you are unsure or if aggression is involved, get professional help.

HELP! Where to get it

BEFORE WE GO ANY FURTHER, *a word about professional help. I am quite sure that never before in the history of our relationship with dogs has there been so much good professional advice available for dog owners.*

Do not think that professionals will view you as a failure if you ask for advice and help. They will not. In my mind, asking for advice is the surest sign of your commitment to your dog, your family, and your neighbours. There is a variety of help available.

■ **Use a water** *pistol to correct your dog's behaviour in the short term; it forces her to concentrate on something else.*

Puppy socialization classes

Puppy classes provide a secure foundation for future behaviour and for overcoming behaviour problems. Open to owners and pups under 16 weeks old (some puppy trainers go up to six months), these weekly classes enable pups to socialize with other pups and with people. Good trainers bring a mellow older dog to the classes, a dog that quietly mutters "Get lost!" to any pup that gets too rambunctious.

Obedience classes

Good dog trainers use positive methods to teach you to train your dog in basic obedience. These classes are open to older dogs, but also to puppies who have not attended socialization classes. Your veterinary receptionist is in a good position to know who the best trainers are. Alternatively, contact one of the trainers' groups listed in Appendix A at the end of the book.

> ### Trivia...
> The vet who developed the concept of puppy classes is Ian Dunbar, a British vet who lives and works in the United States. He calls them *puppy parties*.

Advanced training groups

While basic training is all that is needed for most dogs, advanced training in areas such as agility, tracking, or canine sports provides an outlet for the natural energy of dogs, especially breeds originally used in these activities. Contacts are listed in Appendix A.

Residential training

Although sending your dog off for training is useful for specific or specialized work such as gun dog training, personally, I feel it has little value as a way of overcoming a household behaviour problem. Virtually all common behaviour problems develop because of us – either our honest mistakes with our dogs or our unwarranted expectations of what dogs can do. Therefore, I do not recommend this option.

Personal trainers

There is nothing better than one-to-one training. If you can afford one, a personal trainer for you and your dog is ideal. Ask your veterinary surgeon for advice on who to use. Private dog trainers are available in virtually all urban and suburban areas.

■ **Remember that** *treats should only be given when your dog has done something good for you.*

Veterinary help

The quality of veterinary advice for behaviour problems has improved enormously in the last decade. In the 1980s the best veterinary schools introduced compulsory core curriculum courses in the management of canine behaviour problems. By the mid 1990s pharmaceutical companies were providing veterinary surgeons with medications to use in conjunction with retraining programmes for dogs suffering from conditions such as separation anxiety.

Your veterinary clinic should therefore be your first port of call if you have any questions about your dog's behaviour. Be sure to ask your veterinary surgeon if he or she has experience in dealing with canine behaviour problems.

Natural but unwanted problems

I am going to divide unwanted behaviours into three categories: boredom problems, excitement problems, and aggression problems. This is a pragmatic division, covering the most common problems we have with our dogs. Aggression is so important that I am devoting the entire next chapter to it.

Boredom problems

Dogs do not carry out premeditated crimes against the family. Instead, boredom leads to anxiety, which leads to creativity, which produces mayhem. Separation anxiety is especially common in rescued dogs or those that have become overly dependent on their owners.

■ **Dogs bark or howl** *out of frustration if they are separated from you; provide toys and chews to occupy her when you are out.*

All of the following are signs of boredom:

✓ Chewing doors, wallpaper, rugs, clothing, household linen, car interiors, even themselves. Labrador Retrievers and Doberman Pinschers are particularly prone to excessively licking their forelegs when they are bored, leading to skin problems that need veterinary attention.

✓ Digging in the carpets, in the dirt, or in your bed can be a sign of boredom. Do not mistake boredom digging from digging to bury something or digging to create a cool pit to lie in.

✓ Howling and barking, when left alone, rather than when the dog hears a noise. Wolf cubs howl to make contact with mother. Dogs bark out of frustration when they're separated from you.

✓ Fence jumping or rhythmically pacing back and forth in a garden along the fence, or in the house from one window to another. Sometimes pacing is combined with howling, digging, or even urinating.

■ **Rhythmic and repeated** *jumping is often a sign of separation anxiety.*

Preventing boredom

Prevention is always easier and better than trying to overcome a problem.

1. Before leaving home, make sure your dog has had physical, mental, and social activity. Exhausted dogs are less likely to bark, dig, and destroy.

2. Feed your dog before you leave. A dog naturally rests when her stomach is full.

3. Before you leave, get out a favourite toy, rub it in your hands to leave your scent on it, and give it to her.

4. Always leave quietly. Draw the curtains if necessary and leave a radio or television on to mask distracting noises from outdoors.

5. Never leave your dog at home alone all day.

6. If you must leave your dog at home alone, get a friend to visit to take your dog out for play and exercise. Or get a professional dog walker or drop your dog at a dog day care centre.

■ **Feed your dog** *before you go out; it will help her to sleep while you are away.*

Cures for boredom

Keep it simple. The cure for boredom is to eliminate the cause! In addition, if your male dog is barking, digging, destroying, or escaping because he is looking for sex, consider neutering him.

■ **Make sure** *your dog has plenty of different stimulating toys and receives enough play and exercise, as a bored dog is an unhappy dog.*

Chewing

As I mentioned, apply taste deterrents to objects you do not want chewed. Use the crate constructively if your young dog is simply going through her irritating "chew everything" phase, which lasts until about eight or nine months of age. And provide exciting chew toys at all times to dogs of all ages. Dogs need to chew something.

Digging

If you have an instinctive digger, redirect her energy away from the flower beds or lawn to an acceptable area. Restrict her to a safe area of the garden and give her a sand pit to dig in.

■ **Place chew toys** *inside the crate to curb your dog's chewing if she is going through the "chew-everything" stage.*

Howling and barking

The best way to turn off barking is to train your dog to bark on command. Here's how:

1. Attach your dog's lead to a fence, stand a few feet away and tease her with a toy. When she barks out of frustration, give the command "Speak" the moment she barks, then give the toy as a reward.
2. When she consistently barks to the word "Speak" for the toy, switch to verbal rewards: "Speak", "Woof!", and "Good girl".
3. Once she understands "Speak", give the command "Quiet" when she is barking and reward her with the toy as soon as she stops. Be patient. This takes time.
4. When she consistently stops barking when you say "Quiet", move a short distance away and repeat the exercise, returning to her initially with a reward.
5. Eventually switch to verbal rewards at a distance when she responds to your "Quiet" command.
6. When this is completed, set up mock departures, giving the "Quiet" command before you leave. Stand outside the door. If she barks, make a noise, for example by dropping an aluminium pan. You want to startle her into stopping her barking. Return and praise her for being quiet.

This exercise takes time and patience on your part. If you can stick to it, I think you are a marvellous and dedicated dog owner.

■ **To stop your** *dog from barking randomly, train her to bark on command.*

Jumping

For fence jumpers, create obstacles. Tin cans strung on a rope about 30 cm from the fence and 1 metre off the ground make a nice, noisy deterrent. Chicken wire on the ground at take-off distance from the fence works well, but make sure the gauge of the wire is too small for your dog's foot to slip through. Chicken wire is also an excellent deterrent to digging.

Excitement problems

DOGS SHOW THAT THEY *are excited in different ways. Some bark.*
Others pull on the lead. Many jump, wanting to lick your face. Terriers
often nip with excitement, while Bull Terriers in particular have a
tendency to chase their tails.

Preventing excitement

Active exercise and good basic obedience training are at the root of
preventing over-excited behaviour. Planning can also make a big
difference. If your dog jumps on visitors to greet them, make sure she is
on a lead or in another room when visitors come into your home.

■ **Overcome**
over-excitement
with prevention
training and an
active lifestyle.

Pulling on the leash

Think about it: you sit around all day doing nothing, then see
the lead come out. You are about to be released from jail for a
half-hour of activity. Wouldn't you get excited? Be realistic,
the real cure is more activity. But if your dog has developed the
common habit of pulling on her lead, try the following:

1. Do not turn this into a match of strength. Your dog will win.
   Instead, go back to basics until you are sure your dog follows
   basic obedience signals.
2. Proceed to basic heel retraining but now, with her
   on her lead at your left, slide your left hand
   down the lead to near her collar and if she
   pulls, pull back firmly and
3. command her to sit.
   Start again, giving the "Heel" command. If she pulls,
4. give another yank and command "Sit".
   Repeat this exercise until she walks quietly without
5. pulling. Reward her with a food treat.
   Graduate to more distracting environments
   and circumstances.

■ **Keep your dog** *on*
the lead indoors if she
jumps up to greet visitors.

Jumping up

It is better to use a positive command, "Sit", than a negative one, "Off". If your dog
thinks she is a canine missile, aiming her tongue at your mouth each time you come

home, just ignore the flamboyant greeting. Avoid eye contact and go about your business until all four of her feet are back on the ground. Do not raise your voice, wave your aims, or in any other way increase her excitement. Only when she is quiet should you give the command "Sit" and reward her with a quiet "Hello". Praise calm obedience.

Nipping

Terriers in particular tend to tug on clothes, or your body parts, when excited. Overcome this unpleasant habit by training your dog to carry a toy in her mouth. If she is preoccupied with one job, it's difficult to carry out another. Integrate toy carrying with basic "Sit-stay" obedience.

Barking

Again, toy-carrying is a wonderful way to muffle barking. To control barking itself, follow the procedure for controlling boredom barking.

■ **Bored dogs,** *especially Doberman Pinchers, are prone to excessive licking of their forelegs.*

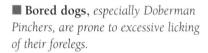

A simple summary

✓ Dogs are simple, straightforward creatures. They have needs that arise from the fact that they are dogs, not people, and these needs must be met.

✓ Dogs need rewarding mental, physical, and social activity to be content.

✓ Dogs can quickly develop undesirable habits, so it's best to be prepared to recognize and correct them early on.

✓ Plenty of good professional help is available to prevent and/or solve doggie problems.

✓ Bored dogs cause more problems than active, engaged, stimulated ones.

Chapter 15

Understanding Juvenile Delinquency

CANINE JUVENILE DELINQUENCY can be avoided through good early socialization and responsible parenting. I know I sound like a 1960s liberal, but the facts are overwhelming. A well-raised dog avoids a life of crime.

Cambridge University scientists had owners of Cocker Spaniels fill out self-assessment questionnaires about their own personalities and found a direct relationship between aggression problems in Cockers and push-over personalities in owners. It's not simple to alter your personality, but you can ensure your pup has as full and as stimulating an early life as possible.

In this chapter...

✓ Why dogs bite and show aggression

✓ Selective breeding problems

✓ Different types of aggression

✓ Food and toy aggression

✓ Neutering

Why dogs bite and show aggression

DOGS DO NOT BITE *just for the heck of it. There is always a reason that is obvious to the dog, but not always obvious to us. Our problem is we fail to see the warning signs, or if we do see them, we do nothing about them.*

Once it develops, aggressive behaviour never disappears on its own. Dogs quickly become skilled at using aggression in stressful or other situations. We have to do something to contain it, reduce it, then eliminate it. Ask yourself these questions:

■ **Parti-coloured Cocker Spaniels** *like this one are unlikely to show signs of dominant aggression.*

■ **If your dog** *growls at other dogs, he has the potential to become aggressive.*

DOES YOUR DOG...

1. Growl at you, other people, or other animals?
2. Show his teeth to you or other family members?
3. Snap when you try to take a toy, bones, or food away?
4. Cringe and hide behind you when visitors approach?
5. Nip at your ankles when playing exuberantly?
6. Chase after moving objects?
7. Give you a glassy-eyed, hard stare that lasts for minutes?
8. Make you invent excuses for his aggressive behaviour, telling friends that "It's just a phase"?

DO YOU...

9. Not worry because he is a Yorkie, not a Pit Bull, and his pushy behaviour is "cute"?

If you answered "Yes" to any one of these questions, your dog has the potential to become aggressive.

Selective breeding problems

THE POTENTIAL FOR AGGRESSION is greater in some breeds, or lines within breeds, than in others. As a general rule terriers and breeds developed to work with livestock are more likely to show certain forms of aggression than are gundogs. That does not mean gundogs are not aggressive. I see more Golden Retrievers who aggressively guard their food than any other breed.

Early learning is vital

While some dogs are born with a greater tendency to become aggressive, problems only occur in homes that wittingly or unwittingly encourage the development of a dog's aggressive potential.

Early socialization to the human family, to strangers, to other animals, and to a whole range of experiences dramatically reduces the likelihood that a dog will reach his "aggression potential". Let me use the Pit Bull as an example. Because of its genetic tendency toward fighting other animals and the extreme power of its jaw muscles, a Pit Bull is a worrisome breed. Yet in my practice, before they were banned, I saw many well-mannered Pit Bulls, properly socialized to friends and strangers. The instinct to chase and kill anything small is still there, and I would not recommend a Pit Bull as a family dog, but the point is that early learning is the most powerful tool for reducing the risk of aggression in your dog.

Trivia...

While there is no question that early socialization and proper training are the two most important factors in controlling canine aggression, aggression in dogs also has some genetic component. The Cambridge researchers found red or yellow Cockers are more likely to show sudden dominance aggression than are those with two or more coat colours. Aggression can also be passed on in families, which is why you should never get a pup that has aggressive parents.

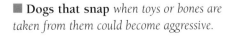

■ **Dogs that snap** *when toys or bones are taken from them could become aggressive.*

It's sometimes a guy thing

There are many different types of aggression, equally shared by males and females, but there is no doubt about what the statistics show:

✓ Aggression is more likely to become a problem in adolescent male dogs.
✓ You and your family are the prime targets.

The reason is the pack hierarchy. When dogs reach sexual and emotional maturity, some of the worries of puppyhood fall away. Some dogs go for higher rank in the pack and challenge people they feel have lower rank, often children. At the same time, sex hormones induce rivalry with other male dogs – what canine behaviourists call inter-male aggression. Most of the dog fight injuries I treat are a result of two male dogs fighting with each other. Again, good socialization is the best way to avoid these problems (as well as hormone control, which I will discuss in more detail shortly).

■ **Fighting between dogs** *is more usual between two males that have not been neutered.*

Read your dog's mind

Pups rarely bite with intent until they are about seven months old, unless they are really frightened. Until that age, they cope with problems by hiding, running away, or doing the "I am not worthy" routine to appease the other dog.

But with sexual maturity, confidence grows. A dog will use body language to express his feelings: hackles up, an intent double-whammy stare, tail raised. If this does not get him what he wants, a growl or teeth-baring follows. And if that is not successful, aggression ensues to sort out the situation.

Most breeds (the German Shepherd is a classic example) are superb at body language. This makes it easy for us to read their minds. Other breeds (the Rottweiler comes to mind) use an abbreviated form of body language. They skip several stages and go from play to aggression very quickly. This makes it more difficult to read their plans, and makes the breed more dangerous to people who are not familiar with it.

■ **Read your dog's body language;** *an unfriendly stare reveals his angry feelings.*

Different types of aggression

WHILE AGGRESSION WAS ONCE *considered a single problem, we know now that there is a whole variety of different forms of aggression, each with its own cause and treatment. It is important – deadly important – for you to understand exactly what is going on when your dog shows aggression to people or animals. Biting you because you touched him where it hurts is perfectly justifiable aggression on your dog's part. Biting you because you tried to push him off the sofa is a crime.*

Aggression is serious business. You should not rely simply on a book to overcome the problem. Professionals know how to help. Get help from your veterinary clinic or local dog training club.

Dominance aggression

This is often directed against you and your family, and is the most common reason why dogs growl at or bite their owners. You might think the growl or bite was sudden, but it was not. Your dog has been assessing your position for some time, and has decided to make a challenge.

DEALING WITH DOMINANCE

If your dog shows signs of dominance, here is what to do. Use this technique if you are certain he has challenged you. It should scare your dog.

1. Avoid physical punishment. It is too provocative and may make matters worse.
2. Use body posture, facial expression, and the tone of your voice to leave him in no doubt that you are the leader of the pack.
3. Attach a lead or houseline to your dog's collar. Use this to move your dog to isolation (one minute) from the family. In this way, you reassert your authority.
4. Do not hold a grudge, but review your relationship with your dog to determine why he thought he could challenge you. For example, remember you eat first, you go first through doorways, you enforce obedience commands. It is the little things in life that teach your dog his place in the pack hierarchy.

239

Dominance aggression between two dogs

This is more likely to occur when both dogs are relatively equal – same sex, age, and size. Dogs of obviously different rank in the pack hierarchy have no problems determining who's in charge, but dogs that see themselves as equals will spar for the top dog position. Some breeds, such as the Dobermann, are more prone to aggression between equals than are others. To overcome this problem, you must first figure out which dog is the higher ranking animal, then treat him as such. Your instinct to comfort the underdog only increases the problem. Remember that dogs live naturally within a pack hierarchy, and feel more secure when it's clear who is in charge. So the highest ranking dog eats first, is petted by you first, and goes out the door first. If aggression is severe and this does not work, get your veterinary surgeon's help. Neutering a dog lowers his rank, and this often cures the problem.

■ **Accept that dogs** *live in a pack hierarchy and do not attempt to overturn the order the dogs have decided on.*

I recommend neutering all dogs with aggression problems, but if, for some reason, that is not possible, neuter the underdog. It may seem unfair, but this is usually enough to stop dominance fighting.

A WORD ABOUT JEALOUSY

Jealousy is as natural in dogs as it is in us. As with us, it can sometimes lead to aggression. A new dog in your home is just cause for jealousy from your resident dog. Make sure each dog has his own personal space. Ignore your resident when the new pup is sleeping, but give lots of attention when the pup is active. Your resident dog will learn to associate the puppy's presence with your increased attention. Make sure there is no eye contact between the dogs when they are fed. Do not let the new dog play with the resident dog's toys. And, at least for the time being, avoid bones. A bone for each will not work if they see each other. Each will want both! And they may fight to get them.

■ **New dogs** *should be given separate toys and bones that do not belong to the resident dog.*

Sex-related aggression

Sex-related aggression is all about sex hormones. That means it may occur year round in males but only twice a year in females, when they are hormonally active. Neutering will take care of this problem for you.

Maternal aggression

This is probably the most fearsome type of aggression in the canine world. Mothers do not mess around. They mean it when they say they will do anything to protect their litter.

Early socialization to a variety of people reduces the likelihood of maternal aggression when a bitch has a litter, but there is a curiosity in canines, different from all other domestic animals. Regardless of whether they are pregnant or not, all females go through a two-month hormonal pregnancy after ovulating. During the later part of this "phantom pregnancy", a female may act strangely about certain items, such as shoes, soft toys, or socks. She might hoard them under the bed or table, and be possessive over them. This is a form of maternal aggression, showing itself as possessiveness. The problem can be avoided through early neutering.

Male to male aggression

More common and more problematic is sex-related male to male aggression. This is more likely to occur in dogs that were allowed to play rough games as pups without correction. To reduce the risks of this type of aggression, do not let your puppy do any of the following:

1. Bite other dogs hard.

2. Put his paws on another dog's back.

3. Mount and thrust on any part of another dog.

Tolerant older family dogs often let pups get away with these activities. (I am amazed how Lex just cringes when Inca climbs on her neck and chews her ears. But when Inca chewed too hard, even this most tolerant of old dogs showed her teeth and growled.) If a pup gets away with too much with a dog he knows, he will try the same with dogs he doesn't know.

If you have a male dog, expect an occasional aggressive incident directed towards him. If you sense a problem from another male dog, the best policy is avoidance. Play with your dog so he concentrates on you, not the provocateur.

There is never any harm in carrying an ever-ready water pistol for squirting another dog that comes too close. If a fight breaks out, keep your arms and legs out of the melee to avoid heat-of-the-moment bites.

Fearful aggression

■ **Fearful dogs** *are likely to demonstrate signs of aggression towards strangers.*

Fear is the most common reason dogs bite strangers. Fear biting is most likely to occur in dogs that did not have the opportunity to meet lots of people as pups – again, under-socialized dogs. It occurs most frequently in dogs who mutter under their breath, "I am not worthy".

Signs of fear

Look for submissive body language. Shy or fearful pups start off life by hiding behind you, running away from what they see as threats, or by rolling over to appease when they are frightened. Submissive urinators can turn into fear biters. The problem is most acute in breeds prone to emotional stress, such as Border Collies. In stressful situations these dogs learn to use aggression to make the "threat" go away.

■ **Revealing the stomach** is *submissive body language.*

Watch your pup for signs of fearful body postures – growling, baring teeth, lowering the head and body – and work on problems before they develop into fear biting.

Allow the fearful pup time to make his own decisions, to be brave enough to come forward on his own to receive a suitable reward. This means you need to interject yourself on his behalf, to protect him from well-meaning people who reach down to stroke him or pick him up. Shy pups need extra attention to boost their meagre self-confidence.

Predatory aggression

Your dog may look like an angel, but he is closer to his roots than you might imagine. Dogs chase moving things. That is what they evolved to do. All dogs chase, but certain breeds — terriers, herders, **sighthounds**, and **scenthounds**, in particular — are genetically superprimed for chasing.

> **DEFINITION**
>
> **Sighthounds** *are breeds that hunt by chasing a moving prey animal, tracking it by sight. Lean, leggy breeds such as Greyhounds, Whippets, and Salukis are sighthounds.* **Scenthounds** *hunt by tracking the scent of their prey. Bloodhounds, Basset Hounds, and Foxhounds are scenthounds.*

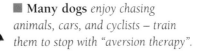

For many, the chase itself is the fun. Others enjoy the pounce at the end of the chase, holding down the small dog that has been caught, grabbing the ankle of the jogger. Still others bite after pouncing, killing cats, savaging livestock. This is a primitive and very basic form of aggression, and it is potentially there within all dogs.

■ Many dogs *enjoy chasing animals, cars, and cyclists – train them to stop with "aversion therapy".*

Heading off the predator instinct

Early socialization and channelling a puppy's desire to chase into chasing toys are the best ways to prevent predatory aggression problems. If your dog chases joggers and bicycles, get friends, armed with water pistols, involved in these activities. When your dog chases them, rather than successfully chasing the object away (which is what your dog thinks happened when the jogger keeps right on jogging), the jogger or vehicle stops and the dog gets an unexpected shot of water in his face. Aversion therapy.

■ Shooting water *into the dog's face is an effective form of aversion therapy.*

243

Territorial aggression

Your dog is most self-confident in his own territory, in your home or garden or car. If he has been well-socialized to visitors in these areas, he will not think of strangers as possible threats. Without this early learning, any visitor means potential danger. Barking sounds the warning, and a show of aggression may follow.

Look at these behaviours from your dog's point of view. The postman comes, makes noise opening the letter box, the dog barks, and the postman leaves. The rubbish collectors come, make noise removing the rubbish, the dog barks, and the rubbish collectors leave. Guarding and barking works!

Trivia...

Although there are many different forms of aggression, one type often occurs in synchrony with another. Predatory aggression often blends with the desire to protect territory.

Dealing with territorial aggression

Prevent (or overcome) this problem by introducing your pup to delivery people, even if it means altering your early morning habits for a while. Have them feed your dog some food treats as they stop by. If your dog is in the garden when delivery people call, leave a favourite toy or food (in a weatherproof box) at your gate, with instructions for it to be given to your dog when the gate is opened. Your dog will still alert you when someone comes to your house, but he will not be compulsively protective of your shared territory.

A car is also territory

Use the same principle in your car. A car is a delightfully small territory, easy to protect. It is your choice how you want you dog to behave in your car. If you do not want him to be aggressive, nip any potential problems in the bud by using aversion therapy and avoiding rewards for delinquent behaviour.

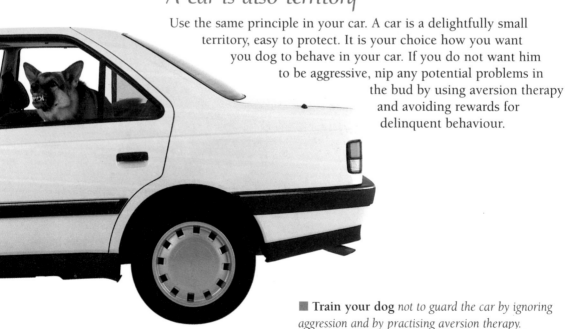

■ **Train your dog** *not to guard the car by ignoring aggression and by practising aversion therapy.*

Food and toy aggression

"IT'S MINE AND YOU CAN'T TOUCH IT!" is not something you should ever let your dog say to you. This habit is more common in dogs that, as pups, had to compete with one another for food.

Teach your pup that being touched while eating is okay, and that hands near the food bowl will not take food away. When you feed him, kneel down beside him and, while he is eating, offer him something even more tasty such as a piece of meat or a liver treat. After he gets used to this, hide the treat in your hand, put your hand in his food bowl and, as he noses your hand, open it up and give the treat. Then let him finish his meal. He will quickly learn to enjoy your presence at mealtimes, rather than feel threatened. Use the same procedure with bones or chew toys he becomes possessive over. And if he ever becomes persistently possessive about a toy, make it disappear – forever.

■ **Avoid possessiveness** *over a toy by exchanging food treats for the item.*

■ **If your dog** *does not willingly give up the toy, confiscate it permanently.*

Health-related aggression

If a dog is ill, expect him to be grumpy. If something hurts, his natural response to pain is to bite. These are natural forms of aggression. Be careful when touching or moving your ill or injured dog.

Aggression and illness

Certain medical conditions are also known to be directly associated with aggression. In one study at the Tufts University Veterinary School, most dogs with underactive thyroid glands also exhibited aggression more often.

The researchers were so impressed with the statistics that they recommended that in any instance of unexpected aggression from a previously reliable dog, the vet look at thyroid function as a possible underlying cause of the change of temperament.

We all know that rabies and aggression go together, but it was only with the advent of magnetic resonance imaging (MRI) scans that vets learned that a variety of older age behaviour changes in dogs, including unexpected biting and aggression, are often associated with brain tumours.

Learned aggression

There are many different forms of natural aggression, but we humans have created one more. Some people like to teach dogs to be aggressive. The best police forces no longer teach aggression, they teach "Retrieve" (as in "Retrieve the bad guy"). But even if you train your dog this way (and believe me, this is a job for professionals only), why keep live cartridges in a weapon? After training your dog to attack (or retrieve) someone, your dog may look upon you as an excellent pack leader, but what about the rest of your family, your neighbours, your friends? Once you have let the genie out of the bottle, it can be hard – really hard – to get it back in. If you want home protection, train your dog to bark fiercely and invest in an electronic burglar alarm.

■ **Avoid encouraging aggressive behaviour,** *as you cannot choose when, or against who, your dog will demonstrate it.*

Neutering

NEUTERING IS A TOUCHY SUBJECT. *When I raise the matter with clients who have delinquent dogs, the wife usually agrees, while her husband sits down, crosses his legs, and disagrees. So let's go over what happens and whether or not* neutering *is an effective way of preventing or treating aggression problems.*

What neutering may do

Neutering is the procedure of choice for preventing unwanted puppies, but it also has effects on the behaviour of male and female dogs.

Male hormones are associated with several dog behaviours. Eliminating (or, to be more accurate, dramatically reducing) male hormones is likely to reduce a male dog's need to frequently mark territory with urine, to be aggressive with other male dogs, and to wander over a large territory preoccupied with sex scents left by other dogs.

Female hormones affect a bitch's personality only during her twice yearly heat cycles. During that time, she urine marks more and wanders more. The hormone of pregnancy, progesterone (which always follows the hormone that stimulates egg release, oestrogen), has a calming effect on behaviour, but also stimulates a possessive or protective attitude toward her pups or her puppy substitutes, such as toys. Neutering eliminates the twice yearly behaviour changes induced by these hormones. In very rare circumstances, however, in naturally dominant females, the absence of the twice yearly calming effect of progesterone can exaggerate a natural dominance.

■ **Do not train** *your dog to be aggressive or you will have problems with friends and neighbours.*

DEFINITION

Neutering *means removing the sex-hormone-producing apparatus from the male or female. In males the testicles are removed. In females the ovaries and uterus are removed.*

INTERNET

www.city.vancouver.bc.
ca/police/structure/
op-support/oas/dogs/
dogsqd.html

For a really interesting overview of how dogs are used by the police, including a history of police K9 units and a look at training procedures, type in this long web address and visit the Vancouver, Canada, Police Department's Dog Squad.

AGGRESSION CAN BE DEADLY

Each year millions of people, often children, are bitten by dogs – usually their own dogs. Some of these bites are fatal. Barbara Woodhouse, the eccentrically famous dog trainer, wrote a book called *No Bad Dogs*. This is mostly, but not completely true. There are some bad dogs, bad genes, bad breeding, bad upbringing. But these are rare. Most of the dogs euthanized because of aggression could have been saved if people understood what was happening before it got so bad that euthanasia became an acceptable option.

VIP   *If your dog shows any signs of aggression, do not wait until the problem gets worse. Talk to your veterinary surgeon immediately. He or she will be able to recommend where you can get help to overcome the problem.*

What neutering will not do

Neutering has no effect on house guarding, on fear biting, on predatory aggression, or territorial aggression. It has no effect on other aspects of a dog's personality, except that dogs pay more attention to people because they are paying less attention to sex-related activities with other dogs.

When to neuter

The evidence is quite conclusive. Just before puberty is an excellent time to carry out this procedure. Neutering a dog who is not yet an adult perpetuates the personality as it is. If you like your pup's personality at six months of age, then, subject to your veterinary surgeon agreeing there is no reason why it should not be done, this is when the pup should be neutered.

■ **If your dog bites** *other animals or people, seek professional help.*

A simple summary

✓ Early socialization and effective training can prevent many aggression problems.

✓ Dogs bite for many reasons, several of which are related to pack hierarchy.

✓ Dog-to-dog aggression is often seen between unneutered males. Neutering is the first step to take to remedy the problem.

✓ Shy dogs may bite out of fear.

✓ Dogs with a strong predatory instinct may be triggered to bite by fast-moving objects.

✓ Dogs may bite to protect territory or possessions.

✓ Neutering controls some forms of aggression.

✓ Don't take any chances with a biting dog. Get professional help as soon as your dog shows any signs of aggression.

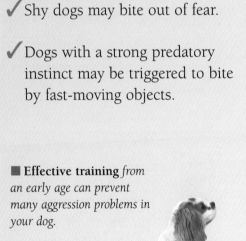

■ **Effective training** *from an early age can prevent many aggression problems in your dog.*

PART FOUR

A HEALTHY DOG IS A HAPPY DOG

HEALTH AND BEAUTY

IT'S UP TO YOU to make sure your dog is in top physical and emotional shape. *Preventing* problems is always simpler, cheaper, and less traumatic than curing them. Keep your dog's body in trim with *routine* maintenance and inspections. Your best partner in this endeavour is your veterinary surgeon. Make sure the two of you are on the same wavelength, so that both of you approach your dog's health with similar objectives.

The first part of prevention is routine parasite and infection control, but *diet* is equally important. A diet should be well-balanced and in reasonable portions. Fat dogs are not healthy, and are at increased risk for many health problems. Learning canine *first aid* is vital if you are to cope with unexpected emergencies.

Chapter 16

Choose the Right Veterinarian

I N THE BEST CIRCUMSTANCES, you and your veterinary surgeon form a team, both contributing to the physical and emotional well-being of your dog and your family. Your choice of veterinary surgeon is a personal one, based partly on convenience and cost, but also on an indefinable feeling of ease or comfort you have with a particular veterinary practice.

Early in my career, the veterinary surgeon's role was to act as a firefighter – to fix a problem once it had happened. I was expected to know and do everything. This is no longer true. Your veterinary surgeon should provide you with the best possible advice on preventing problems, and when serious or complicated problems do occur, he or she should willingly and readily consult with specialists or with faculty from one of the veterinary colleges.

In this chapter...

✓ Can veterinarians do everything?

✓ Visit and ask questions

✓ Costs

253

Can veterinarians do everything?

VETERINARY MEDICINE HAS CHANGED *enormously in the last 30 years. Traditionally, things were very simple: veterinary surgeons were responsible for transportation and livestock. Dogs and cats were pretty much irrelevant. About 50 years ago dogs raced into the picture, and 30 years ago cats started their climb in importance. I like the grand term used by veterinary educators. We were, once upon a time, "omnicompetent". Is your horse lame? I'll fix it. Is your turtle egg-bound? I'll make a hatch door opening and free it. Is your cow's stomach twisted? I'll rotate it. Does your dog have itchy skin? I'll find the cause and correct it. Are your pigs fighting? I'll tell you how to stop it. Is your cat pregnant again? I'll prevent it. Is your parakeet's beak too long? I'll trim it. Veterinary surgeons were expected to know and do everything. It is still a fantasy that many of us, myself included, hold dear.*

Types of veterinarians

The omnicompetent veterinary surgeon is a figment of our professional fantasies. There is simply no such thing as a veterinary surgeon who can do everything. There is just too much information for one person to know.

However, reality means that some veterinary surgeons are obliged to try to be jacks-of-all trades and are pretty good at it. This is the James Herriot fantasy, where a veterinary surgeon may be asked to attend to a calving, then treat a hamster for wet-tail, then discuss the submissive urination of an Irish Setter. These vets are said to be in "mixed" practice. More numerous are veterinary surgeons in "small animal" practice, while others concentrate on "large animal" practices, and still others specialize in certain species or body systems, and are usually called "specialists".

■ **Many veterinary surgeons** *choose a particular area of animal care to work in.*

Mixed practice veterinarians

Throughout rural Britain, the mixed practice veterinary surgeon has often replaced the veterinary surgeon who used to treat farm animals. He sees any animal who needs attention, and often has a preference for the agricultural side of practice.

Many, if not most mixed practices have several veterinary surgeons. At least one veterinary surgeon usually has a particular interest in dogs. If your local veterinary facility is a mixed practice, check out who on the staff is the person with that special interest in dogs. He or she is the person you should try to see with your dog.

Small animal veterinarians

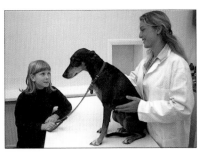

■ **Most small animal** *veterinarians are in urban areas – mixed practices are usually found in rural areas.*

In urban and suburban (and some rural) areas, virtually all veterinary surgeons restrict themselves to companion animals: dogs, cats, birds, rabbits, and other pets. These are the people you are most likely to see with your dog. I fall into this category. Among small animal, or companion animal veterinary surgeons, some of us have chosen to restrict our practice to just dogs, just cats, or some other species. These veterinary surgeons are not necessarily "specialists" in the medical sense of the word, but rather individuals who feel most comfortable with one particular type of animal. Because this is all these vets do, they usually gain extra experience with their chosen species.

Specialists

In the UK, the Royal College of Veterinary Surgeons (RCVS) supervises, examines, and recognizes postgraduate clinical aptitude; it adds a selection of initials after a veterinary surgeon's graduate degree, which is designated as "MRCVS".

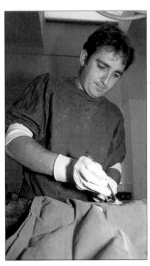

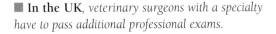

■ **In the UK,** *veterinary surgeons with a specialty have to pass additional professional exams.*

THE SPECIALIST'S ALPHABET

In Britain there are three levels of post-graduate speciality experience recognized by initials after your veterinary surgeon's name: Certificate (Cert.), Diploma (Dip.), and Specialist levels. It takes a least two years to gain a Cert., at least four years to gain a Dip., and at least five years, a halo, and a wealth of authority and respect to become a Specialist.

These levels of postgraduate experience are indicated by lots of letters after a veterinarian's name. The combinations are endless but, for example, in my practice one of my colleages hold a Cert. SAM (Certificate in Small Animal Medicine) and a Cert. Card (Certificate in Cartdiology). With his veterinary degree and the MRCVS (Member of the Royal College of Veterinary Surgeons) after his name, we had to completely redesign our staff board to accomodate his string of initials! (In Britain there is a quiet competition amongst veterinary surgeons to see who would get the highest scrabble score for their qualification letters.)

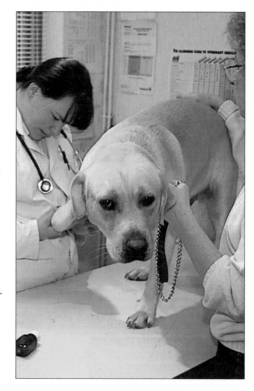

In Europe there are veterinary colleges that grant recognition through examination in speciality areas. If, for example, you see the letters ECVIM after your veterinary surgeon's name, it means he is a member of the European College of Veterinary Internal Medicine. When veterinary surgeons move from one country to another they take their advanced qualifications with them, so you may see any of these letters anywhere.

■ **There are many veterinary** *specialties, from anesthesiology and behaviour to nutrition and dermatology.*

When choosing a veterinary practice, if you see any of the letters I've listed in the box after a veterinary surgeon's name, you should give that practice an extra gold star in your evaluation.

Different kinds of clinics

Big, fancy veterinary facilities do not automatically mean advanced abilities. All veterinary practices should have a bare minimum of examination apparatus, X-ray machine, emergency operating facilities, basic laboratory equipment, and an after-anesthesia recovery room. This minimum is necessary to cope with emergencies. Some veterinary practices will have more.

Usually, the size of the facility is determined by the workload seen at the clinic, and what people in the area are capable of paying for veterinary care.

Location and cost

Location and cost are linked. Urban practices charge more than rural ones because expenses such as property, rent, taxes, and salaries are higher in urban areas. Costs also reflect a veterinary surgeon's investment in facilities. A small animal practice such as mine will have routine equipment, but a specialist practice may invest hundreds of thousands of dollars more in diagnostic and treatment technology. In most, although not all circumstances, a veterinary surgeon's charges reflect costs.

■ **After-anesthesia** *recovery rooms should be found in every veterinary practice, along with equipment to cope with emergencies.*

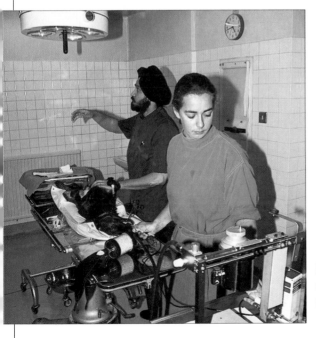

■ **More expensive, specialized equipment** *is found in larger practices; check whether this is reflected in their charges.*

Visit and ask questions

Dog-owning friends and neighbours, people who have had first-hand experience, are your best source of recommendations. Before committing yourself and your dog, arrange to meet with the veterinary surgeon and to see the facilities. Even where space is at a premium, a veterinary surgeon should be willing to show you behind the scenes, the operating area, dog accommodations, and diagnostic facilities. It may appear a little chaotic, but under the chaos the premises should be clean and organized.

My receptionist is responsible for arranging new client visits. She ensures that a new dog owner, preferably with her dog, has a good look around, meets as many of the staff as possible, including me, and has any questions answered.

ETHICS AND VETERINARY CARE

Do you have strong opinions about how animals should be treated? Most of us do, so find out what your veterinary surgeon thinks. Let me give you an example. I will not dock tails. I find it reprehensible, and I use such a strong term intentionally. I will not carry out surgical amputations so that a dog conforms to the traditional standards of the breed – standards no longer necessary when a dog is kept as a pet, rather than for fighting or hunting. One of my veterinary colleagues, ten minutes away and a good friend, thinks I am being ridiculous. If a Boxer or a Schnauzer breeder has a litter of pups, he feels it is only right to dock the pups' tails to the length requested by the owner. People who feel I am introducing my moral judgments into their private decisions will feel more comfortable with my colleague than with me. This may seem to be a minor factor, but it is not.

■ **Not all veterinary surgeons** *will do every procedure, such as docking, if they believe it is morally questionable.*

At some time, you and your veterinary sergeon will be faced with some agonizing, possibly life-and-death decisions to make on your dog's behalf. If you understand each other, where each is coming from, those decisions are far, far easier to make.

Twenty-four-hour emergency care

Emergencies rarely happen at convenient times. Every veterinary surgeon must provide round-the-clock emergency coverage. Find out how this is offered. Is there a special number to call? Does emergency cover rotate through different practices? Is there an emergency and critical care facility used by your veterinary surgeon after hours? If there is, can they access your dog's medical records or speak to your veterinary surgeon when they need to?

■ **Make sure** *your vet provides 24-hour emergency care.*

The comfort factor

Ultimately, your decision should be a comfortable one, in the same way you should feel comfortable with your children's paediatrician. This often means convenience of location, hours, ambience, staff, and recommendations from other dog owners. You are developing an ongoing relationship between your dog, you, and your veterinary surgeon. Each interacts with the other two. You and your dog should both be comfortable with your choice. It's that simple.

Costs

■ **Choose your** *vet on where you and your dog feel most comfortable.*

LET'S START WITH an analogy. You go to see your doctor because you seem to lack energy. He examines you, does some blood tests, and arranges for X-rays and an ultrasound of your abdomen. These suggest that something might be happening in your spleen. An appointment is made for a laparoscopy, to take a biopsy of your spleen and determine exactly what is happening. You are concerned with your health, but pleased that, step by step, your doctor has identified where the problem lies and soon will tell you exactly what the problem is.

DEFINITION

During laparoscopy, a rigid viewing instrument called a laparoscope is used to view the inside of the pelvis and abdomen through small abdominal incisions.
A biopsy is the removal of a small sample of living tissue to use for diagnosis.

Back to your veterinary surgeon. You take your dog in because she is lethargic. Your veterinary surgeon examines her, takes a blood sample, and tells you he will phone you later in the day with the results. On the way out you see the receptionist and pay for the examination and the blood test. That afternoon your veterinary surgeon calls, tells you the blood test has not given him enough clues and says he would like to X-ray your dog's belly because there might be a problem there. You take your dog back for X-rays, and are told that an ultrasound and perhaps an exploratory operation might be needed to make a diagnosis. You see a cash register in your mind, ringing and ringing. Why can't your vet make a diagnosis without all these fancy tests?

How much will you pay?

We accept that, for ourselves, detailed diagnostics are sometimes necessary. We do not stop short because most of us are covered by health insurance. And although veterinary surgeons carry out the same types of tests for considerably less than doctors charge, many dog owners question why a diagnosis takes so long or costs so much.

People think that veterinary surgeons make lots of money because their charges seem so high, but income tax figures show a different story. Veterinary education is a poor investment compared to other professions for future income.

The shock of a bill for thousands of pounds for treating your dog's medical problem is a considerable one. So why not protect yourself the way you do for unexpected house and car expenses by insuring the health of your pet?

Health insurance for dogs

We are lucky that in Britain, health insurance for pets has been available for almost 20 years. More than half my clients have chosen to insure their pets, and I am sure this is one reason dog owners are pleased with the services we provide. You can insure in one of several ways. The first is to take out insurance with an experienced provider such as Pet Protect, Pet Plan, or DBI.

■ **Protect yourself** *against unexpected medical bills by purchasing pet medical insurance*

■ **The veterinary** *practice should be clean and friendly.*

INTERNET

www.petplan. co.uk

You can find details of Pet Plan's insurance policies for home or abroad on this site

The second option is to act as your own insurer. For each of your pets, invest a sum equal to an insurance premium in a secure investment. Insurance company figures show that claims are high in the first year, then drop until dogs are eight years old. Then claims start to climb again as the years advance. If your dog is typical, by the time she is a senior citizen you will have a couple of thousand pounds tucked away for unexpected veterinary bills.

A simple summary

✓ You should feel comfortable with the vet that you choose. That means feeling the clinic is clean and friendly, the vet is competent, and also simply feeling comfortable with the arrangement.

✓ Most vets you will encounter are in small animal practice. This means they take care of a wide variety of pets.

✓ Vets can gain specialist status through continued study. This is an indication of a practitioner who keeps learning.

✓ Visit, see the facilities, and ask questions when you are choosing a vet.

✓ Health insurance for pets is available, or you can set up your own special savings account to pay for health care.

■ **Your vet** *should be competent at handling your dog and administering medication.*

Chapter 17

An Ounce of Prevention

THE ADAGE IS A SIMPLE ONE, but an ounce of prevention really is worth a pound of cure. It's cheaper, too. Plan ahead for the prevention of internal and external parasites, illness, and accident. This is simpler and safer than ever. For example, advances during the last decade mean that older, cruder insecticides to control fleas and ticks have now been replaced with sophisticated biological weapons that devastate the internal and external parasites without affecting your dog's health.

Prevention also includes vaccinations. Many veterinary surgeons now recommend a core series of vaccines, with others added according to the risks in your geographic area and your dog's lifestyle.

In this chapter...

✓ Parasites on the inside

✓ Parasites on the outside

✓ Managing fleas with science

✓ Vaccinating your dog

FORETHOUGHT WILL ENSURE THAT YOUR DOG AGES HEALTHILY

Parasites on the inside

DOGS HAVE INTERNAL PARASITES ranging in size from microscopic single-celled Giardia to grotesquely long tapeworms. Fortunately, there are new, marvellously effective, safe, and convenient worming medications that prevent or eliminate virtually all dog worms. If internal parasites give you the willies, skip the details of this section. Instead simply follow your veterinary surgeon's (and product insert) instructions for worm prevention medications such as Drontal plus, Panacur, Stronghold, or other effective treatments.

■ **Roundworms** *can be passed from mother to puppy through her milk.*

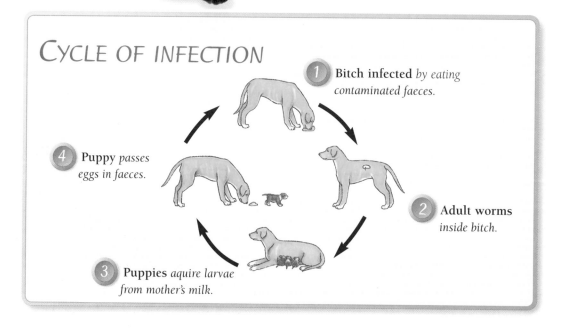

CYCLE OF INFECTION

1 **Bitch infected** *by eating contaminated faeces.*

2 **Adult worms** *inside bitch.*

3 **Puppies** *aquire larvae from mother's milk.*

4 **Puppy** *passes eggs in faeces.*

INTERNAL PARASITE TREATMENT

PARASITE	HOW DOGS ARE INFECTED	DIAGNOSIS	TREATMENT
Roundworms	Mothers pass these worms to their pups before the pups are born. Sometimes contracted from suckling on the mother's contaminated skin.	Severely affected pups are pot-bellied.	Mothers are wormed routinely during pregnancy and pups from 14 days of age, according to veterinary instructions.
Hookworms	One species (*Uncinaria*) occurs in colder climates and is picked up when dogs lick material contaminated by worm eggs. Another species (*Ancylostoma*) occurs in warm climates and is contracted through mother's milk or by larvae burrowing through the skin.	Weight loss, diarrhoea, blood in the droppings or skin inflammation, around the paws or belly.	Mother and pups are wormed, the environment is cleaned, and clinical conditions such as anaemia are addressed.
Whipworms	Worm eggs build up in the environment, where they may survive for years in shaded areas. Eggs are accidentally eaten by dogs, and mature into tiny adult worms, causing severe damage to the intestines.	In severe cases the coat is dull and a dog loses weight and may have abdominal pain and tarry, with dark blood. Diarrhoea often very smelly.	The environment is cleaned and all dogs are wormed.

■ **Whipworms can live** *in the environment for years and may be accidentally ingested by your dog.*

INTERNAL PARASITE TREATMENT

PARASITE	HOW DOGS ARE INFECTED	DIAGNOSIS	TREATMENT
Tapeworms	The most common (*Dipylidium caninum*) is picked up by eating an infected flea. Other tapeworms can be contracted from uncooked organ meats from a variety of livestock, but especially sheep.	Tapeworms rarely cause signs of disease in dogs. The most common sign is dried or crawling tapeworm segments that look like grains of rice in the hair around the anus.	Worm according to your veterinary surgeon's instructions. Avoid access to animal carcasses or uncooked organ meats and infestations.
Giardia	A microscopic, single-celled parasite picked up from contaminated water.	Diarrhoea, possibly with blood and abdominal pain. This is an underdiagnosed cause of diarrhoea in dogs.	Treat all water when hiking and camping. Give Panacur or other veterinary recommended treatment. Clean up all excrement because cysts can be shed in the stool.
Heartworms	Eggs are passed on to a dog by mosquito bites. Eggs mature into large worms that live in the heart.	Coughing and debility do not occur until the disease is well advanced.	Monthly preventives are available. Follow your veterinary surgeon's advice. Dogs that spend more time outdoors are at greater risk. This disease is easier to prevent than it is to treat.

■ **Dogs cleaning contaminated skin** *around their paws or belly can ingest hookworms.*

Public health warning number one: roundworms

Canine roundworm eggs can be passed to people. Children are especially susceptible because they play in dirt (which could be contaminated) and put their hands in their mouths.

The larvae can migrate through our bodies, and can sometimes end up in an eye, causing blurred vision in that eye. More important, roundworms are implicated in childhood allergy and asthma. Foxes, coyotes, and wolves carry the same roundworm.

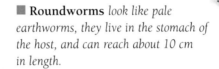

■ **Roundworms** *look like pale earthworms, they live in the stomach of the host, and can reach about 10 cm in length.*

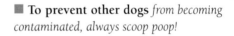

■ **To prevent other dogs** *from becoming contaminated, always scoop poop!*

ROUNDWORMS

1. Worm your puppy routinely with a product approved by your veterinary surgeon.

2. Worm pregnant dogs according to your veterinary surgeon's instructions.

3. Worm your dog after he has been on a course of corticosteroids because his immune system has been compromised.

4. Worm all dogs routinely if you are at risk in your area (your veterinary surgeon will know the local risk factors).

5. Avoid contaminating the environment by removing all dog droppings from the ground immediately.

6. Train your children to wash their hands after playing with young puppies.

Public health warning number two: tapeworms

While most tapeworm infections are not a danger to us, one type of this worm, *Echinococcus multilocularis*, carries the dangerous alveolar hydatid disease. Dogs can get infected when they eat larvae in infected rodents, field mice, or voles, or when they come in contact with the stool of wild animals that are infected. Once the animal becomes infected, the tapeworm matures in his intestine, lays eggs, and the infected animal passes eggs in the stool. These tapeworm eggs, which are directly infectious to other animals, are too tiny to see, and will stick to anything with which they come in contact. Dogs are not usually harmed by the tapeworm, but in people it can cause serious liver damage, and can also spread to other organs.

Trivia...

If your dog is scooting his butt along the carpet or grass, he may be irritated by worms, but it is more likely his anal glands are blocked. The anal sacs contain information-laden (and to us, foul-smelling) liquid. A couple of drops are discharged each time a dog passes a stool. If the sacs become blocked, larger dogs often lick their behinds, while smaller individuals drag their backsides to release the impaction. Clearing them is a job for your vet or a professional groomer.

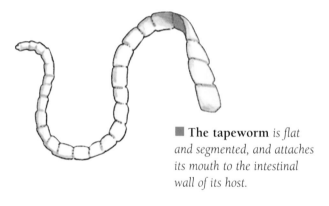

■ **The tapeworm** *is flat and segmented, and attaches its mouth to the intestinal wall of its host.*

ROUNDWORMS

1. Never allow a dog access to animal carcasses.

2. Don't let your dog wander freely where he may be able to catch and eat wild rodents.

3. In areas where hydatid disease occurs, teach children not to play with dogs you do not know.

4. Worm dogs in affected areas routinely (every six weeks) with a wormer such as Droncit, or any other product recommended by your vet.

Parasites on the outside

DOGS CAN SUFFER *from almost as many external parasites as they can from internal ones. Again, there are marvellously effective, safe, and convenient parasite preventives and treatments. If creepy crawlies do not appeal to you, once more, skip the details of this section. Instead simply follow your vet's advice and the product insert instructions for Revolution, Frontline, Program, Advantage, or other effective medication given you.*

EXTERNAL PARASITE TREATMENT

PARASITE	HOW DOGS ARE INFECTED	DIAGNOSIS	TREATMENT
Fleas	Fleas are activated by body heat, larvae "come alive", mature into fleas, then hop on your dog for a blood meal; they spend the rest of their time producing flea eggs. Fleas are picked up from the environment and from other animals.	Fleas cause itchiness in most dogs. Look for fleas or flea "dirt", shiny black specks on the skin, especially over the rump.	Prevent or treat with effective, safe medications. Always treat all dogs and cats in the house, as well as the whole house and garden.
Ticks	Ticks wait in long grass. A shadow, vibration, even a minute change in temperature tells them a meal has arrived. The tick attaches to the dog, burrows its mouth into the skin and sucks its meal until it bloats with blood and drops off. Ticks many carry a range of diseases, including Lyme disease.	Ticks swell enormously and are easily seen when engorged.	Apply alcohol to the tick to kill it, then, using tweezers, twist it at its base at the dog's skin to pull it out. Pulling straight out may leave the mouth parts of the tick behind, and lead to infection. Prevent ticks by using a veterinary recommended preventive product. Do not squeeze ticks.

EXTERNAL PARASITE TREATMENT

PARASITE	HOW DOGS ARE INFECTED	DIAGNOSIS	TREATMENT
Mites	Ear mites are contracted from another dog, usually a pup's mother; they are most active at night. Demodex mites are inherited from mother and cause problems in dogs with faulty immune systems.	Dogs with ear mites produce wax and debris in their itchy ears. Demodex often causes hair loss without itching.	Treat with a veterinary ear drop or lotion. Your veterinary surgeon will dispense a prescription treatment.
	Sarcopic mites (scabies) is acquired from another dog, fox, coyote, or wolf with scabies; the mite tunnels in the skin.	Scabies is intensely itchy, often affecting the ear tips and elbows.	Responds to Stronghold and other veterinary treatments.
	Cheyletiella mites are most commonly a puppy problem, inherited from mother.	These mites cause a thick dandruff over the back, often with no itchiness.	They are easily killed with anti-flea treatments.
Lice	The same size as human lice, dog lice are contracted in unhygienic environments such as puppy mills. The lice leave their eggs, called nits, glued to the dog's hair.	Lice cause itchiness and, if an infestation is intense, like fleas, they cause blood loss and anaemia.	Lice are destroyed by most effective anti-flea treatments.

■ **Comb your dog** *regularly to check if he has fleas.*

Public health warning number three: fleas

Dogs and cats contract tapeworms by swallowing contaminated fleas. So can we! Eliminate this risk to your children by treating your dog (or cat) with an effective flea repellent, such as Revolution, Frontline, or Advantage.

Tea-tree oil in its essential oil form is dangerous to dogs, and potentially lethal to small dogs. In dilute formulations made especially for pets, it is an excellent antibacterial and antifungal preparation but has no effect on fleas or other external parasites.

Cheyletiella mite
Highly contagious, this mite resembles a flake of moving dandruff.

Flea
This tiny insect moves rapidly through the coat, and prefers puppies to adult dogs.

Demodex mite
This mite lives in the hair molecules and is only visible through a microscope.

Louse
This visible parasite feeds on the skin and glues its eggs onto the host's hair.

Harvest mite
This mite is visible in autumn as a red dot.

Tick
Ticks can swell to the size of a small pea when feeding on blood.

Sarcoptes mite
This mite lives around the ear tips and elbows and causes severe itching.

■ **Fleas, lice, and mites** *are often confused for each other because identification is difficult.*

Managing fleas with science

A FEW WORDS about flea powders, flea collars, flea shampoos, flea sprays, and flea dips. Many of them either do not work, or do work but are potentially harmful to you or your dog.

Powders

Flea powders are messy. Some are dangerous. I do not advise using them, but if this is your preferred method of treatment, only use powders containing pyrethrin powder. This is relatively non-toxic to dogs but dangerous to fleas.

Collars

Flea collars also have seen their day. They are worn around a dog's neck, and sensible fleas simply move to a dog's rump. Some dogs have an allergic reaction to a flea collar. If you want to use a collar avoid any containing organophosphate chemicals.

Shampoos

Flea shampoos containing pyrethrins are effective. This is an excellent way to rid your dog of fleas and cleanse and soothe the skin at the same time. Use a shampoo recommended by your veterinary staff. However, remember that flea shampoos offer very little protection against reinfestation.

Sprays

Flea sprays are good, bad, and ugly. I prefer hand pump varieties such as Frontline, with substances toxic to fleas and ticks but not to dogs or us. Take care when using any spray, to avoid the eyes. Use household flea sprays that contain flea growth inhibitor. These sprays prevent flea eggs from turning into fleas (without harming the silverfish under your carpets!)

■ **Before flea spraying** *your dog, comb her coat to untangle the knots.*

■ **Use a pump-action** *flea spray and avoid your dog's eyes.*

■ **Use the flea spray** *under your dog's chin where fleas may hide, keeping it away from the mouth.*

Dips

Forget about old-fashioned flea dips. I am not aware of any that are safe.

Drops and spot-ons

Used correctly, flea "drops" on the skin of the neck are good, safe flea deterrents. They only work when the product makes contact with the skin (and spreads through the thin fatty layer on the surface of the skin). These preparations are not effective if the drop only gets on the hair.

New products that come in tablets or drops, such as Program and Revolution, do not kill fleas. They sterilize fleas that feed on treated dogs. This is a superb way to eliminate fleas on your dog and in your home, as long as your dog has no allergies. If your dog is allergic to flea bites, use a product that repels or kills fleas dead.

ALTERNATIVE WAYS TO CONTROL FLEAS

Fleas leave their eggs and larvae in your carpets. Professional carpet treatment with sodium polyborate, sodium tetraborate, or sodium borate for flea eggs is effective, and usually comes with a one-year guarantee. Do not use laundry-grade borax. According to the American National Animal Poison Control Center it may cause eye, respiratory, and kidney problems.

1. Sticky pads saturated with flea pheromone and left under a light are said to attract fleas (but not larva or eggs) to a sticky end. The results are questionable.

2. There are ultrasonic devices you attach to your dog's collar that emit vibrations said to repel fleas, but these have never been independently tested.

3. In America, nematodes, bugs that eat fleas, are commercially available for your garden. Though effective, they can be difficult to keep alive, especially in hot, dry areas.

4. Feeding garlic or hanging a garlic clove around your dog's neck is a modern myth. It may prevent bites from vampires, but not from fleas. To a flea, garlic simply spices up the meal.

Vaccinating your dog

HERE IS ANOTHER SECTION *you can deal with quite simply. If you are not interested in the gritty details of infectious disease, just follow your veterinary surgeon's advice about when your dog should be inoculated against which infectious diseases. The subject of routine inoculation is, however, a topic of intense discussion. My advice is to read what follows, and then, with your vet, develop an inoculation timetable that is appropriate for where you live and your dog's lifestyle.*

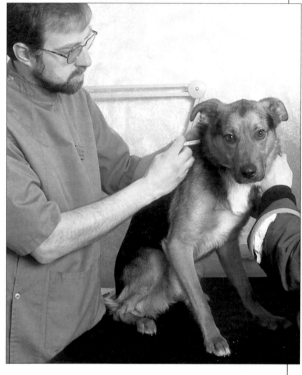

■ **Develop an inoculation** *timetable for your dog with your vet; consider where you live and your dog's lifestyle.*

How vaccines work

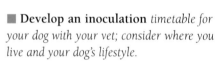

A vaccine contains bacteria or viruses that have been modified so they do not cause disease, but are still able to awaken the body's immune system to manufacture protection against that disease. When a dog is vaccinated against distemper, for example, some of his specialized white blood cells learn to produce anti-distemper antibodies. Antibodies fight off specific infectious diseases.

Trivia...

In the 1960s distemper was the number one infectious killer of dogs. Thanks to effective vaccination, it is now so rare that I have not seen a case for over ten years. That does not, however, mean the disease is eradicated. Dog owners in Finland in the early 1990s made that mistake. Thanks to routine inoculation, distemper was so rare that many, eventually most, dog owners stopped vaccinating against the disease. From out of nowhere it came back with a vengeance, killing dogs that had never been vaccinated, but not affecting those that had been protected with effective distemper vaccine.

How long does protection last?

Right now, no one knows for sure how long vaccination protection lasts because, with the exception of rabies vaccine, manufacturers have never been asked to provide an answer.

When the Canadian government told rabies vaccine manufacturers they wanted a vaccine to last a minimum of two years, most manufacturers discovered that the vaccines they sold with a recommendation for yearly boosters actually gave two years, protection.

A lesson from Finland

The distemper outbreak in Finland, terrible as it was, showed that effective distemper vaccine gives protection for three or more years. While no studies have been carried out with canine parvovirus vaccine, according to one survey of cats vaccinated against feline parvovirus (usually called cat distemper), antibody levels remain high for over two years.

■ **With the exception** *of the rabies vaccine, which lasts two years, it is not known how long vaccine protection lasts.*

INTERNET

www.bsava.com/petzone /vaccineq.html

The British Small Animal Veterinary Association site offers information for veterinarians and general pet care articles. This part of the site looks at vaccinations.

www.doglogic.com/ vaccinemain.html

This page, written by Jean Dodds, DVM, looks at some of the controversies surrounding the traditional annual vaccination schedule.

Are we vaccinating too often?

If no one knows how long protection lasts, the safest option is to revaccinate every year, as some manufacturers and veterinary associations recommend. More enlightened manufacturers and several respected veterinary schools have opted for a different approach, because there is a concern – albeit a vague one – that frequent vaccination might have an unwanted effect on the immune system. This is especially a concern with *multivalent vaccines.*

For example, there is circumstantial evidence out of the University of Pennsylvania's veterinary school that a disease that causes the body's immune system to attack its own red blood cells occurs more frequently in the month following a routine inoculation than it does at other times in a dog's life. (When British veterinary surgeons carried out a similar analysis of this disease, they could not find a similar link.)

■ **Make your veterinary surgeon's** *job easier by handling and examining your dog regularly.*

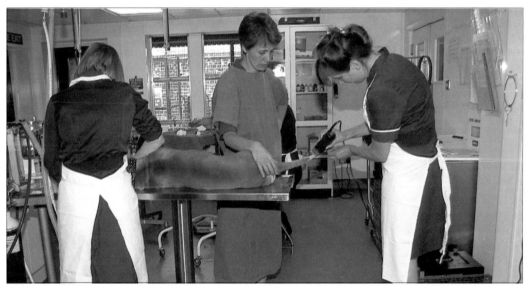

■ **Some vets** *are concerned that vaccinating dogs too often can impair their immune systems.*

Other circumstantial evidence suggests that multivalent vaccines may sometimes stimulate antibodies against a dog's own thyroid gland, the gland in the neck responsible for regulating the dog's metabolism. These concerns will require much more study before anything can be said definitively.

Meanwhile, vaccination is the most important preventive measure you can take to ensure your dog's good health. Here are my recommendations of when you should vaccinate your dog and against what diseases. But this is only one example. Where you live, the risks will be different. Always discuss the vaccination schedule with your vet.

■ **Puppies over three months**
can be vaccinated for rabies.

CORE VACCINATIONS

These are the most important vaccinations all puppies and adult dogs should have. Additional non-core vaccinations will depend on your dog and the area in which you live.

DISEASE	AGE FOR PUPPY SHOTS	ADULT BOOSTERS
Rabies	Only necessary if going abroad. 8 weeks or over if mother in not inoculated. 12 weeks or over if mother is inoculated.	Every two years
Parvovirus	8 weeks, then 10 or 12 weeks, depending on manufacturer's advice.	Booster at 15 months, then every three years.
Distemper, Hepatitis/ Adenovirus	8 weeks, then 10 or 12 weeks depending on manufacturer's advice.	Booster at 15 months, then every three years.

ADDITIONAL NON-CORE VACCINATIONS

These are more inoculations, not routinely given but available for pups and adult dogs at risk.

DISEASE	AGE FOR PUPPY SHOTS	ADULT BOOSTERS
Parainfluenza	8 weeks, then 10 or 12 weeks, depending on manufacturer's advice.	Booster at 15 months, then every two years.
Leptospirosis	8 weeks, then 10 or 12 weeks, depending on manufacturer's advice.	Booster at 15 months, then every year.
Bordetella (Kennel Cough)	At least one week before risk of exposure.	Booster at 9 months if risk continues.

Prevent all types of accidents

One of the major reasons dogs end up in veterinary clinics is injuries caused by accidents. I know I sound like I come from the dark ages when I say, "I remember when...", but the fact is that before there were lead laws I saw dogs with broken bones two or three times a week. Orthopedic surgery was a core element of my work. Avoid road traffic accidents. Control your dog. Do not let him off his lead unless you know it is safe to do so. Make sure he is wearing his ID. If he does get lost, you want to make sure the people who find him know who to contact.

■ **Many broken bones** are caused by road traffic accidents.

Finally, at the risk of irritating you through repetition, be extra vigilant when your bitch is in season. She will be playing by her own game plan, which may well be completely different from yours. Prevent unwanted pregnancies.

■ **Prevent wandering** *by keeping your dog on a lead when outdoors.*

■ **If your bitch** *has not been neutered, prevent unwanted pregnancies by keeping her on a lead outdoors when she is in season.*

A simple summary

✓ Dogs can be plagued by a variety of internal parasites, all of which can be eliminated with medications.

✓ Roundworm and tapeworm can both be passed from dogs to humans.

✓ Dogs also have a variety of external parasites, now much more easily controlled with modern preventives. Avoid poisons, and talk over flea prevention with your veterinary surgeon or groomer.

✓ There is some controversy about how often to vaccinate dogs against a variety of infectious diseases and which vaccines are really necessary. Consult your veterinary surgeon for the best schedule for your area.

Chapter 18

Healthy Eating

HEALTHY EATING MEANS A NUTRITIOUS, well-balanced diet: the simplest way to achieve this goal is to feed your dog premium foods. As dogs progress through the stages of life, their energy needs change. Make sure what you are feeding is appropriate for the age, size, and energy level of your dog.

In this chapter...

✓ Your dog's needs are different

✓ Dry dog food

✓ Wet dog food

✓ Home cooking

✓ All dogs are different

✓ Tackling fat

✓ Speciality diets

A HEALTHY DIET SHOWS IN THE DOG'S APPEARANCE

Your dog's needs are different

LET'S START WITH TASTE BUDS. *We have lots of them. Compared to us, dogs have relatively few. We humans are social eaters. We have been inviting our friends over for a bite to eat since the year one. We are evolutionary nibblers. Dogs, on the other hand, are competitive eaters. They evolved to eat whatever is available, and to eat it quickly.*

Basically, meat

Meat, fat, and bone are the basis of life for dogs, and contain all the essential amino acids, essential fatty acids, vitamins, and minerals they need. And clean water, of course, is the very essence of life. Fibre is also needed to promote good digestion and solid stools.

■ **Dogs survive in** *the wild by being the quickest eaters in their pack, making them naturally competitive over food.*

Some dogs eat grass because they like it, but grass, roots, berries, and vegetables are really only emergency sources of nourishment. Dogs find it difficult to digest these foods, although when they are cooked, more nutrients do become available.

What is really best?

The best dog food manufacturers only use nutrients fit for human consumption in their products. Their premium products are made to fixed formulas, which means the ingredients are always the same. At the next price level down, foods are manufactured to set nutritional and quality standards. While the nutritional value of these foods remains constant, the ingredients vary. This is important to know if you have a dog with a tricky tummy or inflexible taste preferences.

Finding the balance

In the late 1990s, clever manufacturers realized that by carefully balancing the type of fibre in dog food, they could encourage healthy digestion. This has become a fixed feature of the best foods.

In your dog's intestines there is an elaborate ecosystem of bacteria competing with each other for permanent residence. These are essentially the nice guys, responsible for helping to digest food. In fact, these bacteria do even more. Some of them boost your dog's immune system and provide protection from harmful bacteria. The best diets, with carefully balanced fibre content, nourish these bacteria and at the same time inhibit the development of bacteria known to be associated with diarrhoea.

Reading a dog food label

Dog-food makers always provide a guaranteed analysis on the label, usually listing the protein, fat, fibre, and moisture levels. Many dog owners are interested in how much protein there is in prepared dog food, but forget about looking at labels to compare protein levels. It does not work that way.

To compare the levels of anything in food, you have to convert the information you have been given to a "dry-matter" basis – what is left after all the water has been removed. For the mathematically minded, here is how you do it. A typical canned food label might say:

Crude protein	7.5%	Crude fat	5%
Fibre	0.2%	Moisture	80%

This food is 80 percent moisture, so it is 20 percent dry matter. A dry food is typically about 10 percent moisture and 90 percent dry matter.

Calculate the true levels of protein and fat using this formula:

$$7.5 \times 100 \quad = \quad 750 \quad \times \quad 20\% \quad = \quad 37.5\%$$

Label's nutrient percentage (eg crude protein)	Dry matter content percentage	**Dry matter nutrient content**

That means the canned food I just described has 37.5 percent protein, once all the water is removed. This is the only way you can accurately compare basic protein and fat contents of one food with another. If you want to avoid the arithmetic, all pet food manufacturers will gladly give you this information. I only wish they would put it on their labels!

■ **Always supply** *your dog with a clean bowl of fresh water.*

Dry dog food

THE CONVENIENCE OF ALL-IN-ONE *dry food has made it an increasingly popular type of dog food in the UK. This is what I feed Inca. These foods are cooked under pressure then dried. Fat is sprayed on the particles for palatability, but because fat can go rancid, dry foods need a preservative. Heat, humidity, light, and even oxygen can spoil dry dog food.*

MIXED VARIETY   PUPPY VARIETY   HIGH-ENERGY VARIETY

SENIOR DOG VARIETY   LOW-CALORIE VARIETY   STANDARD VARIETY

Perusing preservatives

Substances called *antioxidants* are excellent preservatives. Vitamin C (ascorbic acid) and vitamin E (tocopherol) are commonly used antioxidants. Synthetic antioxidants are also used as preservatives. It sounds better to use a vitamin as a preservative, and many food manufacturers have switched from synthetics to vitamins C and E, but not because there is any evidence that these are better as antioxidants. They switched because of public pressure. Curiously, natural antioxidants do not last as long as synthetic ones.

> **DEFINITION**
>
> *An antioxidant is a substance that destroys free radicals – atoms in the body that destroy cell membranes. Antioxidants, because they destroy free radicals, are good for dogs as well as good for preserving food.*

If you choose a dry food that is "naturally" preserved, buy your food from a retailer with a high inventory turnover and, once opened, store it in a sealed container in a dry, cool location.

Wet dog food

CANNED FOOD, mixed with dry food, remains the most popular method for feeding dogs in Britain, and Ireland. Heat sterilization and vacuum sealing prevent canned and vacuum-packed foods from spoiling, so no preservative is needed. This is what I feed Lex.

Some canned cons

Most canned foods are nutritionally complete by themselves, while others require that dry food be added to balance the nutrients. Canned food is highly palatable, but it provides no exercise for the teeth and gums and is apt to spoil if it is not eaten immediately.

Manufacturers seldom tell us how many calories there are in their foods. As a guideline, assume that a standard can of food contains about 400 calories. A phone call to the manufacturer's help line will give you an exact answer for each product.

STERILIZED BONE

PRESSED KNUCKLE CHEW

BALL

BONE

PRETZEL

SHOE

HAMBURGER

■ **If you feed your dog** *wet food, make sure she has chew toys to exercise her teeth.*

Home cooking

I love my dogs but simply do not have the time, or the inclination, to cook for them. If you are willing to cook for your dog, remember that muscle meat alone is low in vitamins A and D, and in calcium.

Dogs are not simply meat-eaters. A diet consisting solely of muscle meat does not provide a dog with the essentials of life. Dogs are omnivores. They eat a variety of foods. Here is a sample balanced home-made diet for an adult dog:

INTERNET

www.ludin.com.au/~hollow/dogrec~1.html

Hollow's Hound Recipes contains a variety of dishes, from casseroles to cookies, that have been dog-tested.

www.biddeford.com/~seadog/treats.html

Favourite Dog Treat Recipes gives you 101 ways to bake your own dog biscuits.

70 grams chicken
28 grams liver
140 grams uncooked rice
10 grams sterilized bone meal
A pinch of iodized salt
½ teaspoon sunflower
  or corn oil

■ **Meat and** *vegetables provide a dog with virtually all the ingredients required for a nutritious, balanced diet.*

Cook the rice, bone meal, salt, and oil in twice the volume of water. Simmer for 20 minutes, then add the chicken and liver and simmer for another 10 minutes. Cool before feeding. This recipe produces about 800 calories of energy – enough to feed an active 10-kilo dog for a day.

A dry-matter nutritional analysis of this diet shows it has: 17% protein, 31% fat, and 53% carbohydrates.

■ **Avoid feeding** *your dog tofu as it increases mucus production, which can be life-threatening for deep-chested dogs.*

Diet no-nos

Avoid tofu and other bean products as food sources, especially if you have a deep-chested breed such as a Great Dane or any type of setter. These products stimulate mucous production and may increase the risk of stomach bloat, which can be life threatening.

Trivia...

Chocolate? We may need food that appeals more to our brains than it does to our bodies, but dogs do not. In large amounts, chocolate is actually toxic to dogs.

Take care with dairy products, too. Puppies produce an enzyme that digests milk, but by adulthood little of that enzyme is still produced. Cow's milk causes diarrhoea in many dogs.

Bones?

Dogs love bones. And like every veterinary surgeon in the country, I have had to open up dogs' bellies to repair the damage bones have caused. Bones are also perhaps the most common cause of fractured teeth. If you plan to give your dog bones (and gnawing on a bone does massage the gums and scrape the teeth), introduce them to your pup as early as possible so that she learns how to handle them responsibly. Offer only the hardest bones (beef shins and knuckles are good), and don't let your dog become possessive over them.

■ **Chewing bones** *can damage your dog's teeth or result in the swallowing of part of the bone so consider alternatives.*

Cat food?

If you have a cat and a small dog, chances are your dog will tell you she'll die unless she eats cat food. She is lying, but there is logic in her behaviour. Cat food is rich in tasty protein, because cats need more protein in their diets than dogs do. The problem is that too much protein is not healthy for your dog. If you have a cat, make sure Pussy is fed where your dog cannot steal the food.

A vegetarian diet?

A dog is able to survive on a well-balanced vegetarian diet, but this is a path no dog willingly follows. Vegetarianism is a human ethical decision foisted, I feel unfairly, on some dogs. If you think it is important that your dog shares your ethical principles about meat-eating, make sure you get professional advice from a canine nutritionist on how to create a balanced vegetarian diet for your dog. (Never try this with cats. A cat must eat meat to live, and will die if fed a vegetarian diet.)

■ **Think carefully** *before feeding your dog a solely vegetarian diet and always consult your vet first.*

All dogs are different

EACH DOG HAS her own individual energy requirements. These needs change with her age and activity level, even with the seasons of the year. Sex influences the nutritional needs of a dog. While some lose their appetite when they're out looking for sex, others have increased energy demands. Like us, who her parents are also predetermines a dog's metabolic rate. Some individuals, indeed, some breeds, are born with a tendency to be lean or fat.

■ **Sex and the seasons** *influence a dog's diet. Be prepared to vary your dog's food intake throughout her life.*

Needs change with age

Your dog's energy needs change throughout her life. Essentially, her needs increase as she becomes more active, then decrease in her senior years. Here are average calorie requirements for different body weights, lifestyles, and ages. Dogs in cooler climates need slightly more calories per day, depending on how much time they spend outside.

DIFFERENT CALORIE NEEDS FOR DIFFERENT DOGS

Weight (Kg)	2–5	6–10	11–20	21–30	31–40	41–50
Lifestyle	Calories					
Inactive	185–370	420–620	665–1040	1,080–1,410	1,445–1,750	1,780–2,070
Active	210–420	480–705	775–1,180	1,225–1,600	1,640–1,990	2,025–2,350
Working	295–590	675–990	1,065–1,665	1,725–2,255	2,310–2,800	2,850–3,310
Pregnant	220–440	505–740	800–1,250	1,295–1,690	1,735–2,100	2,140–2,480
Senior	150–300	345–505	545–850	885–1,155	1,180–1,430	1,460–1,690

Contrary to what many pet owners think, older dogs do not benefit from less protein in their diet. They do gain from better quality, easier-to-digest protein.

Sex and calories

Sex takes up energy, and not just the act of sex. For male dogs in particular, just looking for sex consumes energy. Sex means more wandering (or vagrancy, if you like), more leg lifting, more territory to mark and defend, and more fighting.

Male and female sex hormones also affect metabolism. When these hormones are reduced, through neutering or advancing years, many dogs (about one third, in my experience) have a tendency to get fat. Weight gain after neutering is extremely simple to prevent.

When your dog is neutered, make sure you know his or her exact weight, and reduce food consumption by 20 percent. Chances are your dog will retain her pre-surgical weight. If she is losing pounds, return her to her former meal size.

Eating during pregnancy

Pregnant dogs require very little increase in food until late in their pregnancy. Increase a mother-to-be's food by 10 percent a week during the last four weeks of her nine-week pregnancy. After she gives birth, her energy requirements explode when she is producing milk for her pups (in part because bitch's milk contains about 40 percent more energy than

■ **A mother's** *food intake increases enormously when she is feeding her pups.*

cow's milk). At the height of lactation she will need three times her daily food intake. Even after her pups reduce their milk consumption, her metabolism is turned up so high that she will continue to need 50 percent more calories than normal just to get back into standard condition.

Active dogs have special energy needs

Does your dog have athletic potential? Any dog does, really, and if yours is allowed to exercise as much as dogs love to exercise, she will burn up more energy than average. The Iams Company studied intensely active dogs and calculated that working dogs that herd, guard, or search need 1.5 to 2.5 times more food energy than pet dogs. Racing dogs need even more. While a pet Husky may typically need 2,000 calories per day, a working Husky in Alaska might need 10,000 calories daily.

■ **Even after a** *bitch stops feeding her puppies, she requires 50 percent more food than normal.*

Tackling fat

I VIRTUALLY NEVER, EVER SEE emacated dogs. Even thin dogs are uncommon. Ideal weight dogs make up only a slight majority of my patients. Almost as many are overweight or obese. My problem is that while owners of obese dogs know they are living with unhealthy fatties, many people do not recognize when a dog is simply overweight. Use this chart to assess your dog's body condition.

BODY CONDITIONS AND SHAPE

EMACIATED
- Ribs showing, no fat cover
- Severe abdominal tuck
- Bones at base of tail raised with no tissue between skin and bone
- No palpable abdominal fat

THIN
- Ribs easily felt with minimal fat cover
- Waist obvious behind ribs
- Bones at base of tail raised, and covered in minimal fat
- Minimal abdominal fat

IDEAL
- Slight fat cover on ribs
- Waist can be seen behind ribs
- Bones at base of tail smooth, covered in thin layer of fat
- Minimal abdominal fat

OVERWEIGHT
- Ribs not easily felt, with moderate fat cover
- Waist hardly discernible
- Bones at base of tail felt under moderate layer of fat
- Moderate abdominal fat

OBESE
- Ribs not felt due to thick fat cover
- No waist, abdomen distended
- Bones at base of tail difficult to feel through fat
- Extensive abdominal fat

■ **Obesity in dogs** is a common Western phenomenon; keep to the recommended amounts of food and do not overdo the treats.

Counting calories

Calorie counting has become second nature to many of us, but it can be extremely difficult to find out the calorie content of dog foods. As a general rule, assume that any food labelled "low calorie" or "lite" has 15 to 25 percent fewer calories than manufacturer's regular brand. However, this does not tell you how many calories the regular brand has.

Starting a diet

To overcome obesity, start by keeping an accurate record of what goes in. I know that sounds too simple, but it can be surprising how many snacks are given to dogs. Feed low-fat, high-fibre foods. This lowers calories while retaining bulk. Increase the dog's exercise if possible, and avoid crash diets: they may only drive your dog's metabolism to be more efficient and store more fat away. (My wife Julia is nodding in firm agreement to this fact.)

During the first weeks of a diet, it is necessary for members of your family to wear blinkers. All dogs practice the mournful brown eyes routine in front of mirrors. They know how effective this manoeuvre is. They wait for you to glimpse it out of the corner of your eye. Be resolute. In theory at least, you are emotionally stronger than your dog.

■ **Do not reward** *your dog's begging for food.*

BORN TO BE FAT

Like us, fat truly does run in families. A dog's body condition is influenced by what you feed, but also by genetic factors. According to surveys carried out at veterinary schools, these breeds are more prone to obesity than others. If you have one of these dogs, be extra vigilant about the amount you feed your dog and about the treats and snacks offered by the weak links in the family:

American Cocker Spaniel • Basset Hound • Beagle • Cairn Terrier • Cavalier King Charles Spaniel • Collie • Dachshund • Labrador Retriever • Norwegian Elkhound • Shetland Sheepdog

Specialty diets

WITH THE VARIETY *of specialty diets now available for dogs, I am happy to argue that it is simpler to ensure a balanced diet for your dog than it is for yourself. There are puppy diets for routine pups, puppy diets for fast-growing breeds, high-energy foods for working dogs, reduced calorie diets for overweight dogs, balanced fibre diets for dogs prone to diarrhoea, extra nutrient diets for dogs susceptible to joint disease, balanced essential fatty acid and selected protein diets for dogs prone to allergic itchy skin problems – and that is just the beginning. Manufacturers such as Iams, Waltham, and Hill's produce ranges of foods, available through veterinary surgeons, to nourish dogs with kidney, bladder, heart, liver, bowel, and skin conditions. These companies also provide veterinary surgeons with a variety of tasty, nourishing convalescing diets for debilitated dogs or for those who have had surgery. The choice is excellent and ever-increasing.*

The "natural diet" for humans is raw meat, worms, roots, berries, and cockroaches (we really do produce an enzyme in our intestines that digests cockroach shells!), but with time we have found that cooked food is often yummier. It is the same with dogs. Raw meat is not really necessary for them or for us, although as carnivores know, fresh sushi or beef carpaccio can be a real treat. Because of the risks of bacterial contamination and, in some regions, parasites, raw meat for your dog is generally more dangerous than cooked meat.

■ **Chicken is** *easily digested and is lower in calories than red meats.*

■ **Rice is** *easily digested and, added to chicken, makes great food for convalescing dogs.*

■ **Make sure all** *bones are removed before feeding fish to your dog.*

A simple summary

✓ A dog's diet should be meat-based, but she needs other ingredients as well.

✓ The best dog foods use quality ingredients that are considered suitable for human food, and mix the food to the same formula every time.

✓ Water in dog food can make it difficult to compare the true nutrient values of different dog foods. To compare dog food label information, you must first convert the numbers to a dry-matter basis.

✓ Each dog has her own calorific requirements, and only you can adjust food intake to keep your dog lean and healthy. Use the manufacturer's suggestions as a guideline, but you must monitor your dog's body condition and feed accordingly.

✓ Antioxidants are used as preservatives, but do not protect the freshness of foods as long as synthetic preservatives do.

✓ Obesity is a major problem with our dogs. The best way to deal with it is to feed a high-quality food in measured portions, and never let your dog get fat in the first place.

✓ A raw diet holds risks of bacterial contamination and parasites.

■ **Light and** *nutritious, scrambled egg is great for puppies and convalescing dogs.*

■ **Sugar-free** *breakfast cereals with milk are a good source of vitamins and provide a tasty light meal.*

Chapter 19

Good Grooming

GROOMING KEEPS YOUR DOG in good physical condition, saves you avoidable veterinary expenses, and strengthens the bond between you and your dog. Start early, when your dog is still an impressionable pup, and use effective rewards.

In this chapter...

✓ Brushing your dog

✓ Hair repair

✓ Washing your dog

✓ A safe manicure

✓ Ear inspections

✓ Eye checks

✓ Mmmmmassage

WELL-GROOMED DOGS ARE A PLEASURE TO BEHOLD

Brushing your dog

THERE IS AN OBVIOUS BENEFIT, *and a not-so-obvious one, to grooming your dog. The obvious is that he looks more attractive and his skin is healthier after grooming. The less obvious is that each time you groom him you are sending a subtle message that says, "I am the natural leader."*

Smooth coats, such as Boxers

This is simple. Using a bristle brush, hound glove, or chamois, first brush against the *lie of the coat,* then with it. Once a week is all your dog needs.

Wiry coats, such as Fox Terriers

Brush as you would a Labrador's coat, but once a month you must also thin the overgrown hair on the back by running a stripping comb through it. A stripping comb cuts out the longest fly-away hairs. Wiry coats should be professionally stripped every three to four months to reduce their density and unkempt appearance. There are also special texturizing shampoos that give body and coarseness to wiry coats. Brush twice a week.

■ **Boxers should** *be groomed with a chamois once a week.*

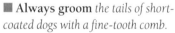

■ **Always groom** *the tails of short-coated dogs with a fine-tooth comb.*

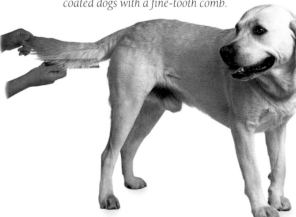

Short coats, such as Labrador Retrievers

The *undercoat* needs the most attention. Use a slicker brush, grooming with the lie of the coat to remove tangles, then against the lie of the coat to remove loose undercoat. Brush with a bristle brush to remove loosened dead hair and remaining debris. Finish with a fine-tooth comb, paying special attention to the thickest hair on the neck and tail. Brush once a week, and twice a week during seasonal shedding.

Trivia...

If you plan on showing a wire-coated dog, seek professional grooming help. Brushing "ruins" the coat in the eyes of dog show judges.

Long silky coats, such as Yorkshire Terriers

Some longhaired breeds, such as the Maltese and Yorkshire Terrier, have no undercoat. This makes them particularly sensitive to irritation from rough grooming. First, tease out tangles with a slicker brush, then use a bristle brush to position the hair properly. Follow this by combing through the hair. Brush daily, carefully removing untidy ends with scissors at least once a month.

■ **Be careful when** *combing the coat of silky-coated breeds because they have no protective undercoat.*

Long dense coats, such as Shetland Sheepdogs

Remove tangles with a slicker brush, then use a pin brush to brush through the densest parts of the coat. After a thorough pin brushing, use a wide-toothed comb all over, paying special attention to the tufts of hair, called feathering, on the legs, chest, hindquarters, and tail. Brush daily and trim away excess hair every month.

■ **When grooming** *dogs with long dense coats, pay special attention to the long tufts of hair that matt easily.*

Trivia...

From what dogs tell me, breeds such as West Highland White Terriers, Bearded Collies, and Schnauzers just love summer buzz cuts. After clipping, they are brighter and friskier. The hairstyle might not conform to the show ring, but clipped hair grows back very quickly. Be careful of sunburn when the dog is no longer protected by his coat.

Clipping breeds such as Poodles

Clipping is necessary every six to eight weeks in breeds with curly coats that simply keep growing, like Poodles and Bichons Frise. My advice is if you want your dog to look good, brush him often but leave fancy clipping to a professional groomer. She has the equipment and experience to clip properly, without irritating your dog's skin and without making your dog look like he has been attacked by a thousand moths. Most groomers can groom, wash, dry, and clip your dog in about four hours.

If you do want to clip your dog yourself, always do so after you've groomed and bathed him.

■ **Breeds such as** *Poodles need clipping every six to eight weeks.*

PROFESSIONAL GROOMING

Select a groomer as carefully as you chose your veterinary surgeon. Recommendations from other dog owners and from the staff at your veterinary clinic are the best place to start. Avoid groomers who want your dog to be tranquillized before they will begin. They do not have the golden touch with dogs.

Be clear in your mind about exactly what you want and expect. Without firm instructions groomers will groom either to breed standards or according to their own preferences. If you want your dog to look a certain way, explain this clearly.

Good groomers are real treasures. If you show your appreciation to your own hairdresser with a "thank you very much" gratuity, why not do the same for your dog's groomer?

Toe hair

Some breeds, including all of the Spaniels, grow an abundance of hair between their toes. This hair acts like a magnet for dirt, debris, and grass seeds (sometimes called foxtails). Once caught in this hair, these foreign bodies easily penetrate

■ **If your dog** *has a lot of hair between his toes, trim it frequently because trapped dirt can cause abscesses.*

the skin, causing abscesses. Use blunt-tipped scissors to cut away excess hair between the toes. Be careful. It is easy to cut the skin by mistake. A professional groomer or your veterinary staff are always available to help.

Shedding hair

All dogs, even dogs with short, smooth coats, shed hair. It is the perfectly normal way they get rid of old hair and make way for new. Dogs that spend a lot of time outdoors have well-defined shedding seasons, usually late spring and late autumn. Dogs that spend a lot of time enjoying the central heating are more likely to shed year round. Dogs need extra attention paid to their grooming during their shedding seasons.

Hair repair

YOU WILL BE AMAZED *at what you will find in your dog's hair. As well as fleas and ticks, hair is a magnet for gum between the toes, paint and tar, knots and tangles, and, if you live where I grew up, fish hooks, and horse manure.*

Gum

It is easiest to cut a wad of gum out of the hair, but if you want to avoid this, apply a little cooking oil as a lubricant and slowly massage the gum loose from the hair.

Burrs

A dab of cooking oil around the burr loosens it up. Spray cooking oil works very well.

■ **Dogs that enjoy** *an outdoor life have well-defined shedding seasons, usually late spring and late autumn.*

Paint and tar

Clip the affected area. Never use paint or tar remover. These are dangerous chemicals, possibly fatal if licked.

Mats and tangles

Dust the area with cornstarch. This acts as a dry lubricant to the knot. Then use a slicker brush, followed by a wide-toothed comb, to gently loosen the knot. If necessary, use scissors to cut the mat into manageable smaller ones.

Fish hooks and barbed tips

Leave the removal of fish hooks to your veterinary surgeon. In an emergency, cut the hook with wire cutters and remove via the smooth cut end.

Other animal scents

Is you live in the country, it's possible your dog may come in one day smelling of fox odours or other strong scents. A tomato juice soak masks the odour of most of these strong scents. There are several other home formulas for removing these scents, using feminine douches or hydrogen peroxide/baking soda combos. Use as soon as possible on your dog.

> ### Trivia...
> The best way to control dog dander, the dry flaky particles that we allergy sufferers may be allergic to, is by routinely shampooing your dog. By routine I mean weekly for breeds such as Cocker Spaniels, and every two weeks for breeds such as Labradors who suffer from fewer skin problems. All dogs produce dander. The best dog to have in a home with allergy sufferers is one with healthy skin who is washed and clipped frequently.

Washing your dog

Dogs love dirt. Little Inca dug a hole in the garden deep enough to lose her head in before she was ten weeks old. Her nose and feet were plastered with sandy mud. Older Lexington cruises her territory looking for fox droppings to roll on. Both of them find dead fish on the beach, kick up sand, and roll in the dunes.

Fortunately, dog hair is naturally self-cleaning – but not so self-cleaning that it only needs washing once or twice a year, as some people will tell you. Most dogs benefit from a bath about once a month. Some longer coats need more frequent attention, while smooth coats need less.

GUIDELINES FOR BATHING YOUR DOG

JUG   SHAMPOOS

TOWELS

COTTON BALLS

■ **Bathing equipment**

1 Brush your dog before bathing to remove knots and tangles.

2 Use a non-slip rubber mat in the tub to give your dog a safe footing.

3 Make sure the water is not too hot. Run it first to get the right temperature.

4 Put balls of cotton in your dog's ears to keep the water out.

5 Remove leather collars, but always have a nylon mesh collar on so you can grab it if your dog decides to make a run for it when he's soaking wet.

6 Use a shampoo made especially for dogs. They are less likely to dry out the dog's skin.

7 Take great care to avoid getting shampoo in the dog's eyes.

8 Use a handheld sprayer to wet and rinse your dog. If your bath is not equipped with one, get an inexpensive rubber one that fits on the tap.

9 Have plenty of towels ready. Your dog will want to shake to rid himself of all that water, and to make sure you get as wet as he is.

10 Don't let a wet dog outside unless the weather is warm and sunny.

■ **Dry your dog's** *face first and have lots of towels ready for his body.*

Shampoos and Conditioners

There is a wide range of shampoos specially formulated for different coat textures and skin conditions. Your veterinarian or groomer, or the dog's breeder, will be able to advise you about what type of shampoo is best for your dog's skin.

For emergency baths, use any type of baby shampoo. Keep it simple! In a pinch, a mild dishwashing detergent such as Fairy Liquid is a good choice.

Herbal

These shampoos contain "natural" ingredients. However, some of these natural ingredients can irritate sensitive skin. I see this with certain shampoos that contain tea tree oil. Westies seem to be particularly allergic.

Oatmeal

These shampoos soothe the skin and are useful to help reduce itching.

■ **Seek professional** *advice before using products that contain tea tree oil on your dog; some breeds are allergic, and as an essential oil it is poisonous.*

Medicated

You'll find a variety of medicated shampoos, containing skin antiseptics and other substances that cleanse or nourish the skin. Use these when recommended by your veterinarian.

Hypoallergenic

Available at your pet supply store or your veterinarian, these are usually perfume and dye free – suitable for dogs known to have allergic skin problems.

Conditioning

These are like the all-in-one shampoos for us: shampoo and conditioner in one. Avoid using this kind of shampoo on wiry coats. It will just soften them.

■ **Oatmeal shampoos** *reduce itchy skin.*

Flea and tick control

Regular bathing does not get rid of fleas. A few fleas might get washed off, but essentially all you are doing is giving the fleas a shampoo. If fleas are a problem in your area, use a flea control product such as Frontline, which is not washed off by routine bathing.

There are also flea and tick shampoos to deal with a sudden infestation. Most of these shampoos contain a pyrethrin insecticide – a natural chemical produced by chrysanthemums. This is a reasonably safe and effective flea repellent. Pyrethrins are broken down in direct sunlight, so in sunny climates their effectiveness is short-lived. Be sure that you also treat the environment indoors and outdoors, or your dog will simply be reinfested.

Enhancers

Colouring shampoos are used mostly on show dogs to enhance white or dark coats.

■ **Regular shampooing** *will not kill fleas.*

Dry

Dry shampoo is a powder that is dusted through the coat, then brushed out. This is a natural way to clean a dog's coat, akin to rolling in sand to massage the skin and clean the fur. It is useful for cleaning a small area rather than the whole dog.

Careful drying

Put a large towel over your dog and let him shake while he's covered by it. Shaking throws off an enormous amount of water, so beware. Chances are he will want to rub himself on the carpet or grass. Try to prevent this until he is drier.

Good towelling removes most water, but for dogs with dense coats a hair dryer works wonders. Use the low temperature setting. Higher temperatures can irritate and damage hair. (There are dryers especially made for dogs. Check in pet equipment catalogues.)

In warm, sunny weather, outdoor drying is just fine. In chilly weather, make sure he is absolutely dry, including behind his ears and on his chest, before letting him outdoors.

■ **Use a low temperature** *hair dryer to dry your dog's coat as heat irritates the skin.*

A safe manicure

EVEN CUTTING THE LIFELESS NAIL *in front of the quick can hurt if the nail is thick and you have to press hard on the nail cutters. If in doubt, ask your groomer or veterinary staff to show you where to clip your dog's nails. Blood-stopping powder is available from pet supply stores shops in case of accidents. Cornstarch works equally well.*

Dogs do not like having their nails trimmed, and with good reason. There is living tissue, filled with sensitive nerves, inside the root of the nail. If you cut too close to the root, this tissue, called the quick, bleeds, and it hurts.

The best time to clip nails is after bathing your dog, when the nails have been softened by warm water. Use a sharp, guillotine-type clipper and replace it twice a year before it gets blunt from use. Scissors-style clippers are more likely to annoy dogs because of the pressure needed to cut the nail. Use an emery board or metal file to smooth the rough edges after clipping, and do not forget to cut the dew claws, the fifth nails or thumbnails that are up on your dog's leg. If your dog is not bothered by the sound or vibration, electric nail grinders are available.

Checking the anal sacs

I got right through veterinary school without once having to do anything to a dog's anal sacs. But as soon as I was in the real world of clinical practice, understanding anal sacs became one of my first priorities. Certain breeds, Dachshunds but not Yorkies, retrievers but not shepherds, spaniels but not sighthounds, are predisposed to anal sac problems. Avoid conditions such as painful abscesses by checking the sacs before bathing, or while grooming your dog.

■ **During grooming** *check to see if your dog's anal sacs need emptying.*

There is a scent sac under the skin on either side of the anus, at three and nine o'clock. If the sacs are full, when you feel the skin on either side of the anus it feels like a single hard grape.

Wearing rubber gloves or any type of clean, disposable glove for protection, squeeze this area, starting at four and eight o'clock and finishing at three and nine o'clock – if you understand what I mean. The malodorous discharge is disgusting to us, but enormously attractive to dogs.

Preventing dog breath

Preventing bad breath is not just a social issue. Bad breath usually means a tooth and gum problem, which is the single most common reason dogs are taken to the veterinary surgeon. It can also indicate more serious internal problems. Brushing your dog's teeth is easiest if your train your dog from puppyhood that this is simply part of life's routine. The supplies you need are:

1. A dog toothbrush, rubber finger brush, or gauze to wrap around your finger.

2. Toothpaste made for dogs or oral hygiene gel.

3. A tasty food treat as a reward.

Brushing the teeth

With your dog in a comfortable position, let him smell the food treat then raise his upper lip and brush the tooth-gum margin of the visible teeth. If he does not squirm, give him the reward.

Repeat this exercise daily, each time increasing the time spent and the area of teeth covered until, after about two weeks of training, you are brushing all the teeth, top and bottom from back to front.

Do not share your toothpaste with your dog. It is not meant to be eaten. We spit after brushing. Dogs swallow. Always use a toothpaste that is safe to swallow. This usually means an edible toothpaste made specifically for dogs.

■ **Remember to** *reward your dog after brushing his teeth.*

305

Ear inspections

Check your dog's ears routinely for odour, inflammation, and wax build-up. Floppy-eared dogs such as Labrador Retrievers, Cocker Spaniels, and Basset Hounds are more prone to ear problems because of the damp, warm climate in their ears — an environment that yeast, ear mites, and bacteria just love.

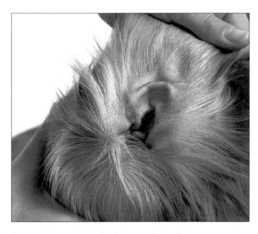

Ear wax

Do not worry about a little nondescript ear wax. Ear wax is a natural form of protection for the ear canal. Only remove it if there is a lot of wax. Use a wax remover made just for the purpose, available from your veterinary surgery, or simply wipe the inside of the ear with a cotton ball moistened with mineral oil. If wax builds up again within a week, take your dog to the veterinary surgery for a checkup.

■ **Inspect your dog's ears** *for inflammation, strong odour, and a build-up of wax.*

Ear hair

Hair growing down the ear canal is a particular nuisance in certain breeds. All wirehaired breeds have ear hair. So too do Poodles, Shih Tzu, Lhasa Apsos, and many Yorkshire Terriers. This hair needs constant, weekly, even daily removal. Finger nails work well. So do tweezers. Grasp a few hairs at a time and pull them out. This is quite easy and not upsetting to your dog. Always give your dog a treat after plucking ear hair.

■ **Remove ear wax** *with a cotton ball moistened with mineral oil.*

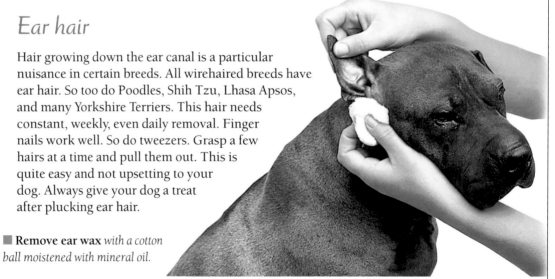

Eye checks

ALTHOUGH THEY ARE *better than we are at seeing even the slightest movement at a distance, dogs' vision is not as good as ours close up. Their eyes, although not as widely placed as a wolf's, are too far apart to give accurate depth of field. As part of your regular grooming routine, always look into your dog's eyes. They should not be runny or red or bloodshot. If anything looks out of the ordinary, contact your veterinary surgeon.*

■ **When grooming your dog,** *check that his eyes are bright and clear.*

Sleepy eyes

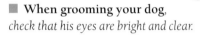

Some breeds, the Yorkshire Terrier is a classic example, develop "sleep" – little balls of dried matter – in the corners of their eyes. This is simply dried mucus, a natural protective secretion that keeps the eyes clean.

Overnight it often forms a small, hard, crusty ball that catches in the hair at the corners of the eyes. Often it is easy to pick off with your fingernail, but if it is firmly stuck, soften it with a cotton ball dipped in body-temperature water. If the eyes and the skin around them do not look normal, contact your veterinary surgeon.

Trivia…

Conjunctivitis is an inflammation of the eye's protective mucous membrane. It may involve redness, swelling, and a watery or mucoid discharge. If infected, the discharge becomes yellow-green. Allergic conjunctivitis and sneezing appears to be increasing in dogs.

■ **Remove "sleepy dust"** *with a cotton ball moistened in warm water.*

Mmmmmassage

DOGS LOVE THIS. *So will you. Massaging your dog relaxes his muscles, stimulates circulation and helps mobility and flexibility, but it also does more. Massaging your dog helps to build trust between you and makes you aware of even the most minute changes in his physical condition. It is the ideal way to carry out routine inspections.*

Never massage an injured, inflamed, or bruised area. Unwittingly, you may make the condition worse.

Giving a massage

1. Start by stroking gently in one direction. Slow stroking helps relax your dog. Gradually slow the pace until your dog is completely relaxed.
2. Once your dog is relaxed, apply circular pressure with the palm of your hand all over his body. Then gently pick up and release rolls of skin.
3. If your dog is happy and content, follow by gently stretching his limbs forwards and backwards, holding each stretch for six to ten seconds.

INTERNET

www.mushing.com/68 massa.html

This page offers a short lesson in basic massage techniques. It was written for mushing dogs, but the principles can be applied to any breed.

■ **Develop your bond** *with your dog, and help him to relax with a massage.*

A simple summary

✓ Grooming is a good way to keep your dog in good health and strengthen the bond between you.

✓ Regular grooming is also an opportunity to give your dog a thorough physical exam. This way, you can spot little problems before they become big ones.

✓ Different coat types require different brushing techniques. Talk to a groomer, your dog's breeder, or your veterinary surgeon about how to groom your dog.

✓ Choose a shampoo specifically made for dogs, ideally one that best suits your particular dog.

■ **Grooming enables** *you to notice quickly any abnormalities on your dog's skin and coat.*

✓ Regular nail clipping is important, but you must learn how to do it and get the proper tool. When you bring your dog in to the vet for his very first check-up, ask your veterinary surgeon to show you how to clip his nails.

✓ Dogs' teeth should be brushed regularly. But never use a toothpaste made for humans.

✓ Ears and eyes should also be checked regularly.

■ **Depending on** *coat type, your dog will require a specific brush and grooming technique.*

Chapter 20

Routine Physicals

Now that you have set up routines for keeping your dog well groomed, you can extend your care to include simple health checks. Train yourself to observe your dog. Use almost all of your senses – sight, smell, hearing, and touch – to monitor your dog's physical state and notice changes in routines. Any change in daily habits is a potential clue to problems in body function.

In this chapter...

✓ Watch carefully

✓ Training for the exam

✓ Your dog's temperature

✓ Your dog's eyes, ears, nose, and mouth

✓ The body, skin, and coat exam

✓ Ear and eye medicines

PLENTY OF EXERCISE ENSURES YOUR DOG'S GENERAL HEALTH

Watch carefully

I FIND OUT as much about your dog's health from what you tell me as I do from physically examining her. In fact, I depend on you to send me in the right direction when I make a diagnosis. I can get there eventually by myself, but when you give me information based on your careful observations, I get there faster and with fewer diagnostic aids.

What to watch for

Here is a simple list of procedures for you to follow when observing your dog. Go through this list before each visit to your veterinary surgeon. Write down any changes from what is normal for your dog, so you do not forget to tell your veterinary surgeon.

1. Observe your dog's behaviour and responses to you.
2. Watch her breathing and panting.
3. Listen to the sounds she makes.
4. Watch how she moves.
5. Be aware of any different smells or odours, both on her and on anything that comes from her. That means her saliva, urine, faeces, and any other discharges.
6. Monitor any changes in her toilet habits.
7. Monitor any changes in her eating or drinking habits.
8. Monitor changes in her weight.

Any unexpected increase or decrease in weight can be a subtle but important indication that there is a medical problem. These changes are difficult to assess just by looking at your dog. Get into the habit of weighing your dog routinely.

For most dogs, this is best done by standing on the scales with your dog in your arms, then subtracting your own weight. Large breeds are best weighed at your veterinary surgeon's office on walk-on scales.

■ **If your dog** *shows signs of constant panting, take her to the vet immediately.*

Changes, breathing, and noises

Dogs experience the full range of behaviour changes we have when we are not well. Watch for any of the following:

- ✓ Increased resting or sleeping.
- ✓ Irritability.
- ✓ Reduced interest in playing.
- ✓ Reduced interest in you.
- ✓ Decreased alertness.
- ✓ Tiring easily.
- ✓ Clinging.
- ✓ Unusual odours.
- ✓ Hiding.
- ✓ Apprehension.
- ✓ Resentment at being touched.
- ✓ Overexcitement.
- ✓ Disorientation.
- ✓ Breathing rhythms that are not relaxed and routine.

■ **If irritability** *is uncommon for your dog, it may be a sign of illness.*

Any of the following changes warrants an immediate visit to your veterinary surgeon:

- ✓ Gasping.
- ✓ Wheezing.
- ✓ Coughing.
- ✓ Choking.
- ✓ Rapid or shallow breathing.
- ✓ Laboured breathing.
- ✓ Unremitting panting.
- ✓ Unusually slow breathing.

Listen for unusual sounds. Groans, yelps, and cries are obvious signs of distress, but listen too for grunts when the dog is standing up or lying down, or even barking when there is no reason for barking. Shivering when it is not cold may mean fear, but dogs also shiver when they are in pain.

■ **Unwillingness** *to involve herself with the family and apprehension can be signs that your dog is not well.*

General appearance and movement

Your dog's general appearance is a fine indicator of her health. Her coat should retain its natural rich appearance. Dullness and lack of sheen are often outward signs of an internal problem. If you notice any of the following, call your veterinary surgeon:

✓ Difficulty getting up or down.
✓ Slowness walking.
✓ Staggering, falling over.
✓ Walking in circles.
✓ Difficulty finding a comfortable position.
✓ Overreacting to light, sound, or touch.
✓ Holding one side of the head down.
✓ Restlessness.
✓ Bloated belly.
✓ Unusual chest movements.
✓ Muscle spasms.
✓ Any body swelling.

The bowels and toilet habits

"Habits" is the significant word here. Dogs develop routine eating, drinking, and toileting habits. Any change in these habits may be important. Watch for and note down for your veterinary surgeon any changes in eating, drinking, and the following:

Urinating

A healthy dog never smells of urine. If yours does, contact your veterinary surgeon. Also look for:

✓ Greater or lesser quantities of urine.
✓ Urinating more or less frequently.
✓ Urinating with difficulty or straining.
✓ Wetting while lying down (incontinence).
✓ Lighter or darker urine.
✓ Blood in urine.

■ **If you dog is** *drinking and urinating more, or less, call the vet.*

Defecating

A healthy dog passes stools almost like clockwork. If your dog's routine has changed and you have not changed her diet, contact your veterinary surgeon for advice. Also look for:

- ✓ More or less frequent defecation.
- ✓ Looser or firmer stools than normal.
- ✓ Normal stool covered in jelly-like mucus.
- ✓ Defecating with difficulty or unsuccessfully.
- ✓ Blood in the faeces.
- ✓ Leaving any residual faeces or other matter around the anus.

Training for the exam

WHEN YOU FLEX your dog's joints or lift her tail or look straight in her eyes, you are behaving, in her view, like a dominant leader. This is fine. In any human-dog relationship we want our dogs to look upon us as natural leaders, to accept our instructions without resentment. If you have any relationship problems with your dog, any questions over which of you is boss, you may find your dog resenting and resisting your attempts to examine her. If you are already firmly acknowledged as leader, a physical examination may be simply boring for your dog.

Training your dog to be fully examined means that you will be able to make some of your own diagnoses and carry out some treatments at home. From a veterinary surgeon's perspective it means your dog will not resent having a full physical examination. Of course, it is easier and faster to make a diagnosis on a dog that willingly allows herself to be examined.

■ **Your dog should** *accept you examining her and lifting her tail; it is a sign of your dominance over her.*

315

What should she accept?

Train your dog, while she is robust and healthy, to allow the following procedures. During training do not try to do all of these procedures in a single session. Examine one area then reward your dog with praise, petting, and treats. The next training session, examine one more area and reward your dog. Do a little bit every day, and eventually she will be your veterinary surgeon's dream.

- ✓ Temperature taking.
- ✓ Eye, ear, nose, and mouth examination.
- ✓ Head and neck examination.
- ✓ Body, limbs, and feet examination.
- ✓ Tail and anus inspection.
- ✓ Skin and coat inspection.

■ **Once in** *a while, take your dog's temperature to accustom her to this proceedure.*

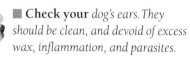

■ **Check your** *dog's ears. They should be clean, and devoid of excess wax, inflammation, and parasites.*

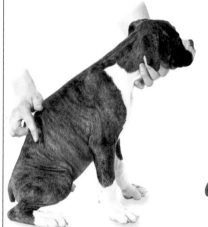

■ **Inspect your** *dog's skin and coat regularly to check for any abnormalities.*

■ **Check your** *dog's mouth from a young age so that she is happy with you examining her.*

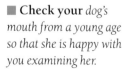

INTERNET

www.pogopet.com

The Pogopet site has a variety of health-related features, including Ask the Vet and Symptom Centres that help explain why your pet may not be feeling well. There are also sections on how to fully examine your dog. Pogopet information can be customized for your particular pets.

Your dog's temperature

YOUR DOG'S NORMAL TEMPERATURE *is not the same as yours. There is a normal range in dogs, generally speaking between 100.5°F (38.1°C) and 102.5°F (39.2°C). Exercise, or even the nervous excitement of visiting the veterinary clinic, can slightly increase a dog's temperature.*

Using a thermometer

If you're using a glass, mercury-filled thermometer, shake it down and lubricate it with a water soluble substance such as K-Y Jelly. Insert the thermometer about 2.5cm into your dog's rectum and hold it in position for 90 seconds. Remove it, wipe it clean, and then read it. Disinfect the thermometer after each use.

Digital thermometers are simple to use and easier to read. There are expensive high-tech thermometers, for example one that is inserted in the ear, but for accuracy a high quality digital thermometer is ideal. Fever strips made for humans do not work, even on hairless breeds. They are not accurate enough on dog skin.

Never try to take a dog's temperature orally. Nor should you try to take your dog's temperature if she deeply resents it. In that case, leave it to your vet.

WHAT YOUR DOG'S TEMPERATURE TELLS YOU

°F	°C	SITUATION	REQUIRED ACTION
106+	41+	heat stroke	cool down immediately, get emergency veterinary attention
105	40.6	dangerous	cool down immediately, seek same-day veterinary attention
104	40.0	high fever	seek same-day veterinary attention
103	39.4	moderate fever	telephone vet for advice
102	38.9	normal	
101	38.3	normal	
100	37.8	normal	
99	37.2	sub-normal	seek same day veterinary attention
98-	36.7-	hypothermia	keep dog warm, get emergency veterinary attention

Your dog's eyes, ears, nose, and mouth

START ROUTINE PHYSICAL EXAMINATIONS at the head, where most injuries will be clearly visible. Remember to reward your dog after each examination with play or a small food treat and next time she will be happy to sit while you look at her.

Having her head examined

1. Check your dog's eyes for redness, discharge, cloudiness, or obvious injuries. Dilated pupils in bright light mean fear, pain, excitement, or shock.
2. Look in the ears for inflammation, discharge, excess wax, or physical damage. Check the skin on the ear flaps, especially the tips of the ears – a happy home for some skin parasites such as burrowing sarcoptic mange mites.
3. The nose should be gloriously cool and slightly wet. There should definitely be no sign of discharge from either nostril.
4. Examine the lips, especially the lip folds in breeds such as spaniels, for smell or inflammation. Look at the gums on both sides. There should be no inflammation or unpleasant odour.
5. If your dog has folds on her face (as do Pugs and Shar-Pei, for example), gently open the folds to check for redness, inflammation, or an unpleasant odour.

■ **When checking** *your dog's eyes look for cloudiness, redness, or any obvious injury.*

■ **The skin on** *your dog's ear flaps should also be checked in an ear examination.*

If you know your dog has had a blow to the head, always get immediate veterinary attention, even when you see no external signs of injury. Inside the skull, the brain is like a large, hard bowl of jelly. The skull offers great protection but concussion – bruising to the brain when the "jelly" is knocked against the inside of the skull – is a common and potentially lethal result of head injuries.

Check the teeth

With age, a dog's teeth lose their brilliant Hollywood whiteness of youth. You may see a little staining, but there should be no tartar on the teeth. Open your dog's mouth. The tongue should be a healthy pink and the roof of the mouth delightfully corrugated and free from debris.

If your dog is pawing at her mouth, always check the inside. When chewing sticks in particular, it is easy for a twig to get caught between the teeth, especially at the back. You may need to use the flat end of a spoon to push a stick or a large splinter out from between the teeth.

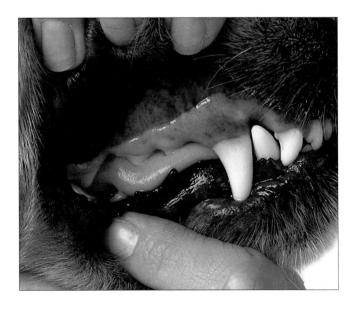

■ **Your dog's gums** *should be free from inflammation and bad odour. Checking her teeth takes some care and trust on both sides!*

The body, skin, and coat exam

START AT THE FRONT *and work your way to the back. Follow the step-by-step procedure I'm about to describe, running your hands over your dog's body to feel for swelling, heat, stickiness, or resentment, which usually means pain.*

The exam

1. Run your hands over your dog's head, cheeks, jaws, and throat.
2. Gently turn her head left, right, up, and down. Resistance could mean pain.
3. Feel down your dog's neck, then over her back, sides, and chest. Any stickiness might indicate a site of skin infection or a penetrating injury, for example, from a bite.
4. Frequently part the hair to examine the skin, which should look "quiet" – that is, without inflammation or much flaking dander.
5. Run your hands over the hips, around the groin and down each limb, feeling the joints and particularly examining for swelling or excess heat. Examine both hind legs or both forelegs together. The muscles and joints should feel perfectly symmetrical. If, for example, one leg feels less muscular than the other, it means there might be pain leading to less use of the less well-muscled limb.
6. Feel along the length of the tail and gently lift it to inspect the anus, which should be perfectly clean and odour free. There should be no discharge from a female dog's vulva and little or no discharge from a male dog's sheath. A male dog's testicles should be symmetrical.
7. Flex each limb. When all is fine, your dog puts her leg down immediately. If she has joint pain, she puts her leg down more tentatively (because it hurt when you flexed it).
8. Move on to examining the feet, checking the pads for damage, the space between the pads for debris, and the nails for length.

■ **Feel down your** *dog's back and check for any stickiness, which could be the sign of an injury.*

■ **Check your** *dog's genitals for any inflammation or discharge; seek veterinary advice if there are any abnormalities.*

■ **Carefully flex** *each of your dog's limbs to check for pain as part of your dog's body examination.*

Special problems in boys

In later life, testicular tumours often occur in only one testicle. A lack of symmetry, rather than clinical illness, is usually the first sign of this problem. Young males often produce an excess of a substance in the penis's *sheath* called smegma. It may actually drip out, especially when a dog is lying down. If this is happening with your young dog, contact your veterinary surgeon for advice.

Giving a pill is simple

The simplest way to give medicine to your dog is by hiding it in food. Try hiding a tablet in a little meatball or sandwiched in bread, especially with a little peanut butter. If your vet says it is OK, try hiding the pill in a little cheese (some medicines should not be given with dairy products). A few manufacturers provide a variety of dog medications in tasty, chewable form.

If none of these methods is possible, for example when food is not allowed with the medication or when your dog is a master at eating all the peanut butter and spitting out the pill, you will have to stick the pill in the dog's mouth and make sure she swallows. This is what to do:

Easy dog

1. Command your dog to sit, then open her mouth with one hand and, holding her head upwards, drop the tablet behind the hump of her tongue.
2. Holding her head up slightly, close her mouth and massage her throat. When she swallows and licks her lips, you know the pill has gone down. Always praise her for good behaviour.

Boisterous dog

1. Hold your dog between your legs with your knees behind her shoulders. Open her mouth by lifting her snout with one hand and lowering her lower jaw with the other. Do not try this if you think your dog may bite you.
2. Drop the pill as far back as possible on her tongue, then close her jaws and massage her throat until she swallows.

If giving pills is futile, your vet may be able to give you medication in liquid form that can be squirted into the side of your dog's mouth.

Ear and eye medicines

NO SENSIBLE DOG enjoys having ear ointment squirted down her ear or getting drops in her eyes. Make these procedures as non-threatening and as comfortable as possible by keeping it simple as you do the following.

■ **By accustoming your dog** *to being examined, she will become an easy patient to diagnose.*

INSTILLING EAR DROPS

1. Clean away excess wax from under the ear flap, especially from around the hole at the bottom, which is the opening to the ear canal. Use a cotton ball with warm water for this.

2. Whenever possible, roll the tube of ointment or drops in your hands to warm up cold medication. Turn it upside down to ensure that when you squeeze the medicine in the ear, you do not first squeeze in an "explosion" of air.

3. Insert the nozzle of the medicine into the ear canal, pointing the tip of the nozzle towards the tip of the nose, and squeeze the bottle.

4. Drop the ear flap back in position and, without letting your dog shake her head, gently massage the area immediately below the ear canal opening. This lubricates the canal with medication.

APPLYING EYE DROPS OR OINTMENT

1. Using a cotton ball soaked in warm water or eye wash solution, remove any sticky discharge from the eye and surrounding skin.

2. While gently holding your dog with one hand, bring the drops or ointment towards the eye from behind her head. You do not want to frighten her.

3. Squeeze out the drops or ointment from above. Ointment flows freely when the tube is first warmed well in your hands.

4. After applying ointment, hold the eye closed for a few seconds. Your dog's body temperature warms the ointment to allow it to disperse, and the greasy appearance will soon disappear.

A simple summary

✓ Carefully observing your dog regularly will enable you to catch health problems at an early stage.

✓ Watch what comes out as carefully as you watch what goes into your dog. Any change in toilet habits might indicate a problem.

✓ Training your dog to be physically examined will make life easier for you, your dog, and your veterinary surgeon.

✓ A dog's normal temperature is between 100.5° and 102.5° F.

✓ It's not so difficult to give your dog medications if you approach the task gently but firmly.

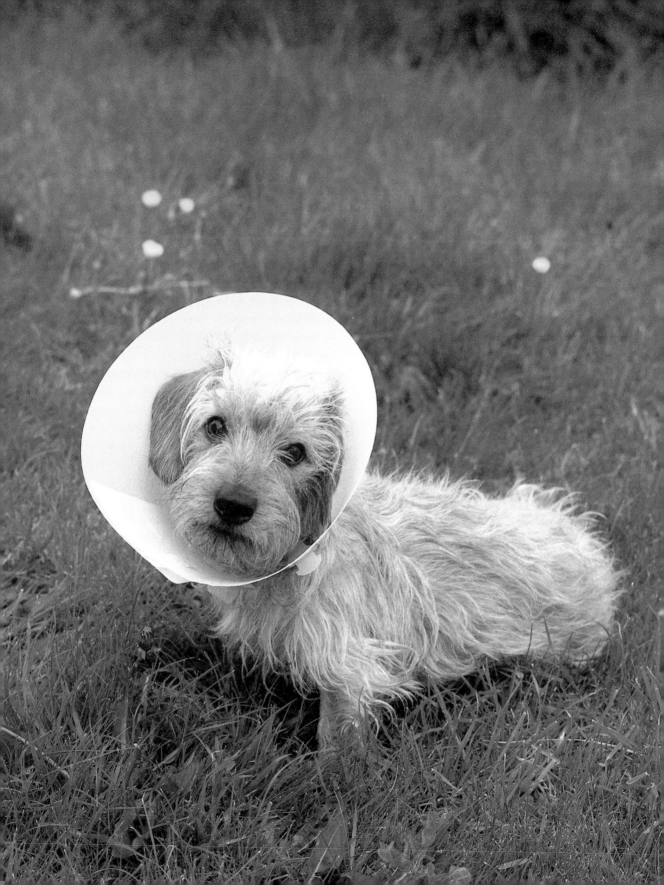

Chapter 21

Saving Your Dog's Life

I HOPE YOU NEVER NEED to use life-saving first aid skills on your dog. The likelihood is low, just as it is unlikely that you will ever be called on to stop bleeding or give artificial respiration or heart massage to another person. But it's still a good idea to know what to do – just in case.

Life-saving first aid is simpler than you think. First you must assess the dangers (making sure you do not put yourself in danger), then restrain your dog, check his heart and breathing, look for signs of shock, and if all of these systems are in order, then administer first aid for physical injuries such as cuts or broken bones.

In this chapter...

✓ **What to do first**

✓ **Serious injuries**

✓ **What is CPR?**

✓ **Bleeding**

KNOWLEDGE OF FIRST AID MAY SAVE YOUR DOG'S LIFE ONE DAY

What to do first

IN ANY FIRST AID situation your dog depends on you to remain calm and to assess the priorities. Is your dog in continuing or immediate danger? Are you in the same danger, or at risk of being bitten because of what has happened? Your first objectives are to:

- *Save your dog's life* • *Prevent any further injuries*
- *Reduce pain and distress* • *Get your dog safely to a vet*

The principles of first aid for your dog are the same as they are for people, but with two differences. First, there are no emergency ambulance or medical services for pets. You will have to give emergency first aid, and then transport your dog to the nearest veterinary hospital. Second, because of fear or pain, your dog may bite you. Preventing this from happening is the opening act of giving first aid to your dog.

Restrain your dog

After determining that you are not in danger, approach your dog calmly. Talk to him reassuringly. (If you do not know the dog, reduce his fear by avoiding direct eye contact.) Check his expression to determine how frightened he is. If you can, loop a lead around his neck. Use your belt, scarf, tie, or any other available item as an emergency collar and lead.

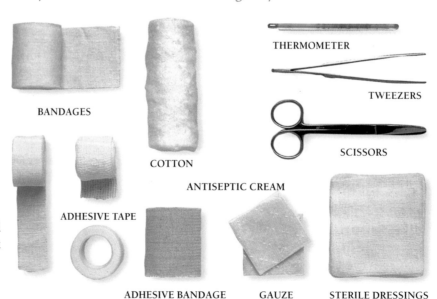

THERMOMETER

TWEEZERS

BANDAGES

SCISSORS

COTTON

ANTISEPTIC CREAM

■ First-aid equipment

ADHESIVE TAPE

ADHESIVE BANDAGE   GAUZE   STERILE DRESSINGS

An emergency muzzle

Muzzle an injured dog if he looks frightened or has obvious painful injuries. A necktie, gauze bandage, even a torn strip of cotton sheet makes a soft and effective muzzle. This should be 50 to 75cm long.

1. Wrap your makeshift muzzle around the dog's nose.
2. Tie it once under the dog's chin, then bring the end back behind the head.
3. Tie the muzzle again behind the head, down on the neck and well back from the dog's ears. Make sure you tie an easy-to-release bow.
4. If your dog's face is too flat to wrap a muzzle around his nose, wrap a towel around his neck. When you grip the towel he cannot twist his head to bite. The towel can be pinned closed while you examine him.

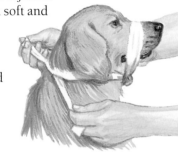

■ **If you do** *not have a gauze bandage, a necktie or torn sheet can be used as a temporary muzzle.*

Do not muzzle a dog with breathing difficulties.

Holding your dog

Your dog should be held safely and reassuringly while you do an emergency examination. If your dog is large, wrap one arm around his neck and support him against your body. This leaves your other hand free to examine him or support him under his abdomen. If your dog is smaller, hold him with one hand gently but firmly by his *muzzle.* Use the elbow of your free arm to press his body against yours, while using your free hand to examine him. Now you are ready to assess his injuries. There is a logical list of priorities.

DEFINITION

As I'm sure you've noticed, I've just used the same word – muzzle – to mean two different things. A muzzle is anything used to hold your dog's mouth closed. It's also the long, flat top of the nose and mouth, from behind the nostrils to the forehead.

Monitor his breathing

Large dogs normally breathe in and out about 10 times a minute, while the smallest dogs may breathe 30 times a minute. Breathing rates increase with pain, shock, lung, and heart problems. Breathing and panting are different. Panting increases with exercise, anxiety, and pain. It is the natural way for your dog to eliminate excess heat. Calculate breathing, not panting, by timing chest movements for 15 seconds and multiplying by four. Of course, if your dog is unconscious and there is no breathing, artificial respiration will be necessary. I'll get to that in a few pages.

■ **Check your** *dog's breathing, if he is in pain, shock, or has heart or lung problems, the rate of breaths will increase.*

Check his heart rate

Your dog's pulse varies from as slow as 50 beats a minute in large breeds up to 160 beats a minute in small dogs. A puppy's heart may beat up to 200 times a minute.

Your dog's heart rate will increase with fever, pain, heart conditions, and in the first stages of shock. To monitor the heart of a large dog, press the fingers of your hand firmly against the left side of his chest, just behind the elbow. On smaller dogs, grasp the chest on both sides, just behind the elbows, and squeeze gently until you feel heart beats. This may be difficult to do on fat dogs.

■ **Make sure you** *know your dog's normal heart rate as it varies between breeds from 50 to 200 beats per minute. If he is in shock the rate will be higher.*

Alternatively, feel the pulse by placing your fingers inside the hind leg where it meets the body. A large artery, the femoral artery, passes through here close to the surface of the skin. Move your fingers around until you pick up the pulse. Count for 15 seconds then multiply by four to calculate the heart rate. Naturally, if your dog is unconscious and the heart is not beating, heart massage becomes your priority. We'll cover that later.

■ **Your dog may** *look normal but be in a state of early shock. He may fall unconscious in late shock.*

Look for signs of shock

Shock is a hidden danger in all injuries and can be an unsuspected killer. A dog may initially appear to be normal externally. But if your dog has been injured, for example in a car accident, even if he runs back to you apparently unharmed, always have him examined by a veterinary surgeon for signs of shock.

Treating for shock takes precedence over first aid for other injuries, such as broken bones. The colour of your dog's gums gives a firm clue. Normal gums are a healthy pink. During shock they become dull pink or even white.

In healthy dogs when you press your finger against the gums, the gums whiten but immediately turn pink again when you remove your finger. The more advanced the state of shock, the longer it takes for the capillaries in the gums (the microscopic blood vessels) to refill and for colour to return. (This is called capillary refill time.) If you have a dog such as a Shar-Pei with naturally black gums, check for shock by gently parting and examining the inner lining of the vagina or by retracting the prepuce and examining the colour of the penis.

Signs of shock

The signs of early shock are:
- ✓ Faster than normal breathing;
- ✓ Faster than normal heart rate;
- ✓ Pale gums;
- ✓ Anxiety or restlessness;
- ✓ Lethargy and weakness;
- ✓ Normal or subnormal rectal temperature;
- ✓ Slow capillary refill time to the gums (more than two seconds).

The signs of late shock are:
- ✓ Shallow, irregular breathing;
- ✓ Irregular heart beat;
- ✓ Very pale or blue gums;
- ✓ Extreme weakness or unconsciousness;
- ✓ Very cool body temperature – less than 98°F (36.7°C);
- ✓ Very slow capillary refill time to the gums (more than four seconds).

Treating shock

If your dog shows signs of shock, do not let him wander around or give him anything to eat or drink. Do the following:

1. Stop any bleeding and give heart massage or artificial respiration as necessary.
2. Wrap him in a blanket to prevent further heat loss.
3. Use pillows or towels to elevate his hindquarters, enabling more blood to travel to the brain.
4. Keep his neck extended (to maximize blood flow to the brain) and transport to your nearest veterinary surgeon immediately.

■ **If your dog** is suffering from shock, wrap him in a blanket to prevent heat loss.

Serious injuries

WHEN THERE ARE POTENTIALLY *serious injuries, do not waste time cleaning wounds. Give life-saving first aid, then get your dog to a veterinary surgeon as quickly as possible.*

When lifting and transporting an injured dog, avoid bending or twisting him, which might cause further injuries. Wrap small dogs in a bulky blanket. An ironing board or removable shelf makes a useful temporary stretcher for bigger dogs. Secure your dog to this stretcher with neckties, torn sheeting, or rope.

What is CPR?

Every living cell in your dog's body needs oxygen to survive. Oxygen is breathed into the lungs, picked up by red blood cells, and pumped by the heart around the body. Brain cells have an enormous need for oxygen, which is why 20 percent of the blood pumped by the heart goes to such a relatively small organ. If brain cells are deprived of oxygen, even for a few minutes, they are damaged or die.

In emergencies, heart massage can restart a stopped heart while artificial respiration puts oxygen into your dog's lungs, to be carried to his brain until he starts breathing again on his own. The combination of heart massage and artificial respiration is called cardiopulmonary resuscitation, or CPR.

> **INTERNET**
>
> **www.napcc.aspca.org**
>
> *This is the site of the American National Animal Poison Control Center. It includes advice on how to avoid poisoning, and what to do if your pet is poisoned.*

CPR MAY BE NEEDED IN THESE CIRCUMSTANCES

✓ Blood loss
✓ Concussion
✓ Electrocution
✓ Near-drowning
✓ Shock

✓ Choking
✓ Diabetic coma
✓ Heart failure
✓ Poisoning
✓ Smoke inhalation

When to give artificial respiration

Only give artificial respiration if your dog has stopped breathing. Check the gums. If they are pink it usually means that oxygen is being carried around the body. If they're blue or white, artificial respiration may be necessary. If your dog's size makes it difficult to determine if he is breathing, place a little piece of tissue in front of a nostril and see if it moves.

How to give artificial respiration

1. Place the dog on his side, clear any debris from his nose and mouth, and pull his tongue forward.

2. Close his mouth, and with his neck in a straight line, place your mouth over his nose and blow in until you see his chest expand. (If you find this offensive, use your hand to form an airtight cylinder between your mouth and your dog's nose. Blow through this. This doesn't work as well, but it's better than nothing.)

3. Take your mouth away. His lungs will naturally deflate. Repeat this procedure 10 to 20 times a minute until he breathes on his own.

4. Check the pulse every 15 seconds to make sure the heart is still beating. If it stops, add heart massage.

5. Get emergency veterinary help as soon as possible.

When to give heart massage

Only give heart massage if your dog's heart is not beating. Check the eyes; they dilate when the heart stops. Feel for a heartbeat or pulse. Check the gums. When you press your finger against pink gums, if they turn white and then return to pink, the heart is still beating. If there is no pulse and the gums do not refill with blood, the heart has stopped.

■ **If you think** *that your dog's heart has stopped beating, check his pupils – they dilate when the heart stops.*

Heart massage for small dogs

1. Place your dog on his side, if possible with his head lower than the rest of his body.
2. Grasp his chest, behind his elbows, between your fingers and thumb. Support his back with your other hand.
3. Squeeze firmly, compressing the rib cage, squeezing up towards the neck. Repeat this action using quick, firm pumps 120 times a minute.
4. After 15 seconds of heart massage, give artificial respiration for 10 seconds.
5. Continue alternating until a pulse returns, then give artificial respiration alone.
6. Get immediate emergency veterinary attention.

Heart massage for medium and large dogs

1. Place your dog on his right side, if possible with his head lower than the rest of his body.
2. Put the heel of one hand on his chest just behind his left elbow, and the heel of the other hand on top of your first hand.
3. Press downward and forward 100 times a minute, pushing toward the neck. (This is energy-draining work when applied to a large dog.) Do not worry if you crack a rib. The circumstances are literally life and death.
4. After 15 seconds of heart massage, give artificial respiration for 10 seconds.
5. Continue alternating until a pulse returns, then give artificial respiration alone.
6. Get immediate emergency veterinary attention.

If two people are present, one gives heart massage for five seconds, then the other gives a breath of artificial respiration. Continue this alternating procedure until the heart resumes beating and it is safe for one person to leave to arrange transportation to the vet.

Bleeding

HEAVY BLEEDING OR SLOW, continuous lighter bleeding will lead to dangerous clinical shock. While internal bleeding is difficult to control, external bleeding can often be controlled by applying pressure.

INTERNET

www.doctordog.com/dog
book/dogch01.html

Doctor Dog's Emergency Section offers illustrated advice on what to do in a variety of emergencies, from burns to electrocution to shock.

Spurting blood means that an artery has been damaged. This is more difficult to stop because the blood pressure is higher in arteries (carrying blood from the heart) than in veins (carrying blood back to the heart). Watch for signs of shock: pale or white gums, rapid breathing, weak, rapid pulse, cold legs or paws, and general weakness.

■ **Add pressure** *and absorbent materials to a bleeding area to prevent blood loss.*

Controlling bleeding

1. If there is a first aid kit handy, apply pressure with a non-stick gauze pad. If this is not available, use any clean, absorbent material such as paper towels, a pad of toilet paper or facial tissue or a clean washcloth.
2. Apply pressure directly on the wound for at least two minutes, adding more absorbent material if necessary.
3. Keep the bleeding area higher than the heart, if possible, but do not elevate a leg if there is a possible fracture.
4. Do not remove the blood-soaked material. It helps with clotting. Leave removal to your veterinary surgeon.
5. Get immediate veterinary attention.

■ **To help clotting,** *do not remove blood-soaked material but bandage the area and take the dog to the vet.*

333

THE PROBLEM WITH TOURNIQUETS

Applied properly, a tourniquet will stop bleeding. But applied improperly it is a very dangerous item. A tourniquet cuts off the blood supply and can lead to the loss of the entire limb. Only use a tourniquet on a leg if there is profuse and devastating bleeding. Wrap a tie or strip of torn sheet above the bleeding wound and tie it with a releasable knot. Slip a pen, pencil, or stick into the knot and twist until the bleeding stops. Hold or tie this down in place while you get immediate veterinary attention. It should be applied for no more than ten minutes. Loosen every few minutes while you transport the dog to the veterinary surgeon.

■ **For snake bites,** *apply an ice pack to the affected area and seek veterinary attention.*

If your dog is bitten by a venomous snake, do not use a tourniquet. It will only increase inflammation. Instead, immobilize the bitten area and apply an ice pack to reduce the size of local blood vessels while you get immediate veterinary attention.

Bleeding nails

A torn nail causes profuse bleeding, but is rarely life threatening. Apply a styptic stick to the torn end to stop bleeding. If this is not available, wrap the area in clean, absorbent material and apply pressure for at least two minutes. Bandage the absorbent material in place and leave for two hours before removing. If bleeding recurs, see your veterinary surgeon.

■ **If you think** *your dog is injured or ill, check his breathing and heart rate.*

YOUR DOG'S FIRST AID KIT

Keep a separate first aid kit for your dog, stocked with items for accidents or emergencies. Always have your veterinary surgeon's telephone number listed by your telephone or programmed into its memory. A standard first aid kit should contain these items:

✓ Thermometer;
✓ Tweezers (for removing ticks and other items);
✓ Rubbing alcohol;
✓ Scissors;
✓ Syrup of ipacec to induce vomiting;
✓ Antiseptic cream (for cleaning wounds);
✓ Sterile water bottle (for flushing eyes or other areas);
✓ Roll of gauze bandage (doubles as an emergency muzzle);
✓ Roll of cotton;
✓ Sterile dressings and bandages appropriate for the size of your dog;
✓ Styptic powder.

■ **Always check for** *shock after an accident, as this could kill your dog.*

A simple summary

✓ Shock is an unexpected killer. A dog may look fine after an accident, then die a few hours later of clinical shock. That's why treating for shock takes precedence over first aid for other injuries.

✓ Even your own friendly dog may bite when in pain. Be cautious if your dog has been injured, and use a makeshift muzzle if possible.

✓ Check breathing and heart beat to determine if mouth-to-muzzle respiration or CPR is necessary.

✓ Try to control any heavy bleeding, but be wary of using a tourniquet. Direct pressure on the wound is usually enough to stop the bleeding.

✓ Have a canine first aid kit stocked and handy.

PART FIVE

YOUR DOG MAY LIVE FOR MORE THAN 12 YEARS

YOUR PARTNER FOR LIFE

YOUR DOG IS AMAZINGLY ADAPTABLE, but sometimes she will need a little help to cope with the changes in your life. Make sure she gets it, and she'll be your steadfast *partner* for years. Just keep things simple and you'll both be fine.

An active life involved in physical and mental *activity* is what your dog yearns for. But time marches on. Dogs are living longer than ever before, partly because of good food and effective preventive medicine, but also because we are willing and able to see our friends through the natural problems that a long life brings. With good *planning* and advanced veterinary care you can minimize the problems that aging brings. There is no cure for old age, but the magnificent bonus of living with dogs is that each new canine personality brings unexpected joys into our lives.

Chapter 22

Your Adaptable Friend

PERHAPS THE GREATEST ATTRIBUTE OF DOGS is their immutability. We change. Our human friendships ebb and flow. But our dogs provide us with the security of always being there, always giving and receiving the same unchanging rewards. Dogs definitely like to keep things simple. Your dog values continuity. She thrives best in an unchanging world. For your sake and for hers, ensure your dog is able to adapt to change.

In this chapter...

✓ Home changes

✓ On the road

✓ Boarding and kennels

✓ Disasters and emergencies

✓ Breeding your dog

✓ The first weeks of a pup's life

DOGS DON'T LIKE CHANGE, SO HELP YOUR DOG ADAPT TO YOUR EVER-CHANGING LIFE

Home changes

DURING THE LIFETIME of any dog, there will be changes in her home life. Moving to a new home may provide your dog with more space, but it is just as likely to result in less. People and pets come and go, and nothing worries dog owners more than the arrival of a new baby. How will your dog react now that she is no longer a baby substitute?

■ **New pets in** the house should disrupt a dog's life as little as possible.

A new baby in the house

If you lavish your dog with all your time and affection, if you play with her, pet her, cuddle her, fawn over her, then yes, you may have jealousy and anxiety problems when your new baby comes home – if only because you will not have the time to continue your former relationship. Plan ahead by cooling the intensity of your relationship. If the dog's sleeping arrangements must change, change them well before the baby arrives.

■ **Train your dog** to wear a muzzle when she is around young children and babies.

When your baby comes home, let the dog smell the new smells but try not to change any more of her routines. Set aside time to give her the attention she deserves. If you do, sibling rivalry is less likely to develop.

Once your baby is old enough to be on the floor, take no chances. Never leave your baby and dog together unattended. If your dog has even a remote tendency to snap, train yours to wear a muzzle in the presence of your baby. Risk is avoidable. Avoid it! You will be able to observe when the two are both mature enough to be left together.

A new dog or cat

Deep down inside, dogs are instinctive chasers. Deep down inside they are also unapologetic sissies. Control the introduction with a cat and you can bring out the sissy in your dog rather than the chaser. Do this by avoiding a situation that allows her to chase.

When bringing a new cat (or dog) into your home, restrict your new pet to one room while leaving the resident to go where she wishes. If your newcomer is a kitten or pup, let your resident sniff it while it is sleeping. If your kitten awakens, hisses, and spits, perfect.

You want your dog to respect your cat – something cats are outrageously good at teaching dogs to do. If it is a puppy, as best possible, let your resident make all the first moves. If your dog shows any inclination to chase your cat or chase other dogs, especially if you have a sighthound such as a Whippet or a terrier such as a Fox Terrier, keep it simple by nipping it in the bud – get in touch directly with your veterinary clinic or a professional dog trainer for immediate behaviour advice.

Do not introduce a new pet to a resident by putting them nose to nose and explaining that they will become each other's best friends.

■ **Introduce new pets**
slowly to your resident dog.

Lex found little Inca a real nuisance until Lex realized it was in her interest to hang around Inca because when puppy got fed, Lex got extra snacks. Your resident learns to enjoy the presence of the newcomer because there are hidden rewards. This is called *positive reinforcement.*

People changes

Dogs are more fickle than we really want them to be. Some individuals develop deep emotional attachments to certain people, but the majority of dogs are very laid back in their emotional relationships with us. In a dog's mind, anyone who provides food, affection, security, and mental and physical activity is easy to love.

Dogs do adapt to people changes. I see it happen routinely when circumstances mean that a dog moves to a new household. I am not the only veterinary surgeon who has been approached by a well-meaning client to put down their dog because they can no longer care for her and, they claim, the dog "can't live without me." Nonsense! It simply isn't true. The idea is a human fantasy.

Dogs cope with people changes best when they already look upon all members of the household as equal. My wife Julia, Tamara, our daughter still at home, and I all take turns caring for Inca when Ben (her "real" owner) is not around. The result is a young pup perfectly adapted to people changes.

DEFINITION

Positive reinforcement *is a term taken from behavioural psychology. It is a reward given immediately following a behaviour, which is intended to increase the likelihood that the behaviour will occur again.*

On the road

I HAVE ALWAYS FANTASIZED about going backpacking with my Golden Retrievers, but never managed to. Even so, travel with your dog has never been easier. You have a choice of books that list accommodations throughout the country that accept dogs. Check out where the local veterinary clinics are, too. These may be good locations to board your dog for half a day if you have to go off without her.

Safe travel

When travelling, make sure your dog is safe and secure. She should be behind the dog barrier in your car, ideally in her comfortable crate, or on a back seat equipped with a harness that attaches to the seat belt anchor and also allows her to lie down.

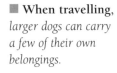

■ **When travelling,** *larger dogs can carry a few of their own belongings.*

Never, ever leave your dog in your car in warm weather or direct sunshine. Heatstroke in hot cars is one of the most common avoidable causes of death in dogs.

Your dog's ambition when you are driving is to hang her head out the window. Do not let her. Open the window just enough to let her nose inhale the excitement of speed. Whole heads hanging out the window risk being injured. Eye injuries from dust and debris are common.

Stop every two hours to let her exercise, and remember your plastic bags when travelling. Clean up after your dog. Carry a water bowl and bottle of water. Collapsible or inflatable food and water bowls are perfect when you're travelling with your dog. If motion sickness is a problem, discuss medication with your veterinary surgeon. If you travel frequently, most travel problems can be overcome pretty quickly with a well-planned programme.

Travel in the European Union

Dogs travelling from the USA and Canada must continue to endure six months quarantine before entering the UK, but if your budget and time are both endless, you can move with your dog to anywhere in the EU without the need for quarantine, have your dog microchipped, vaccinated against rabies, and blood tested, then, six months later, enter Britain without quarantine.

INTERNET

www.takeyourpet.com

This site lists thousands of pet-friendly lodgings and local resources in many American cities.

Trivia...

In the European Union (EU), the Pet Travel Scheme allows dogs to move between the member countries and to rabies-free countries such as Japan, Australia, and New Zealand, and back again, without quarantine, as long as the dog's paperwork is in order. She must be identified with a microchip, vaccinated against rabies, and a month later have a blood sample analysed to show the vaccine has worked.

■ **Place your dog** *in a comfortable crate in the boot of your estate for everyone's safety.*

Trivia...

I am involved with training hearing dogs for deaf people. At any given time we have about 150 dogs in our kennels. We always house two compatible dogs together and, as well as hearing training, all dogs are invited to participate in other activities, such as agility. We learn who needs what to maintain good mental health during their four months of kennelling. Although you will probably never kennel your dog for months at a time, learning what she needs to be content will be useful even if you're only gone a few days.

■ **Large dogs can** *wear special dog harnesses that attach to seat belts in the back seat of cars.*

DOGS ALOFT

Your travel plans may include a trip by air. Make sure your dog's travelling crate is secure, the right size for your dog, and meets the airline's regulations. Your veterinary surgeon and the company will give you accurate guidelines. Your dog should have two forms of ID: her tag and preferably also a microchip.

When flying, avoid hot sunny weather. It is rare, but each year there are fatal accidents when, because of runway delays, dogs suffer heatstroke in the holds of airplanes. Whenever possible book direct flights. Avoid tranquillizers. Giving one may make you feel better, but increases your dog's risk of accidents. Some airlines allow toy-size dogs to accompany you in the passenger cabin.

For more information write to the Air Transport Association. They will send you a free booklet, "Air Travel for Your Dog or Cat."

> 1301 Pennsylvania Ave, NW, Suite 1100, Washington DC 20004-1707, USA.
> www.air-transport.org

■ **Small dogs are** *permitted to travel inside the plane cabin in a dog carrier.*

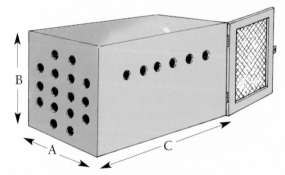

■ **Make sure** *the travel crate is the right size for your dog. It should be twice as wide as she is (A), slightly taller (B), and longer than the length from her nose to tail (C).*

Boarding and kennels

IF YOU JUST CAN'T take your dog along, you may want to consider boarding her in a kennel. I do not have any problems with the idea of boarding my own dog, as long as the kennels are clean and comfortable and the staff are understanding and creative.

What to look for

When choosing a kennel, always visit, inspect, and ask questions. The most conscientious kennel owners provide "home away from home" facilities, including comfortable beds, tasty food, frequent contact with kennel staff, and supervised activities with other dogs. Remember to plan ahead. The best kennels are booked up months before busy seasons, especially Christmas and the New Year.

Contact Michael Oultran at the Boarding Kennel Advisory Bureau for his personal list of kennels (and catteries). His address is: Michael Oultran, Boarding Kennel Advisory Bureau, Little Oultran, Northwich, Cheshire CW8 4RJ. Tel 01606 891 303.

Moving

While cats hate to move to a new home, most dogs actually love the chance to investigate a new territory and transplant their activities from the old environment to the new. Plan as you would for any trip.

Rather than giving her the run of the entire new home, restrict her to a few rooms initially. This reduces the possibility of her marking the territory with her urine. Before she is left alone in the garden, ensure it is escape-proof.

If you want your dog to toilet in a specific area in the new garden, bag a little earth from her previous toileting area and spread it in the new area. Your dog may find it curious to find her own scent, but she will be much more likely to toilet where things smell familiar.

INTERNET

www.petspyjamas.co.uk
www.pogopet.co.uk

The first site lists holiday locations that accept pets while the second gives details of the Pet Travel Scheme.

Disasters and emergencies

ALL OF US, *at one time or another, will be faced with what we consider to be an emergency. It may be, as in my parent's circumstances, an evacuation out of the path of a hurricane in Florida, USA. More commonly it will involve your need to go somewhere immediately, perhaps because of a family emergency. What do you do with your dog?*

Have a plan

As with so much else in life, spending a few minutes planning ahead saves anxiety or heartache later. If you live where natural disasters such as flooding, snow storms, or hurricanes are possible, ask your veterinary sugeon if he can help suggest a disaster plan for your dog. You can also find out if your local kennels can help during an emergency.

Take your dog's medicines, records, and ID

Your dog should always wear identification, but in emergency situations this becomes even more important. Make sure her ID gives up-to-date information, including the telephone number and e-mail address where you can be contacted.

Keep a file that includes vaccination information, microchip or tattoo numbers, medication and feeding instructions, a picture of your dog, and your veterinary surgeon's name and telephone number. Make copies of this information – one for yourself and one to give to a friend in case your records are lost.

■ **Keep a muzzle** *in your first aid box, as even the gentlest of dogs may bite when injured.*

Keep dog supplies at home

If you live where planning for natural disasters is sensible, do not forget about your dog. Store food, water, and medicine to last several days. Make sure medicines in particular are rotated, so they do not go out-of-date. Keep a lead, first aid kit, and, if you have not included it in the kit, material to use as a muzzle, with your emergency supplies. (Even the gentlest of dogs may bite when confronted with the traumas of some emergencies.)

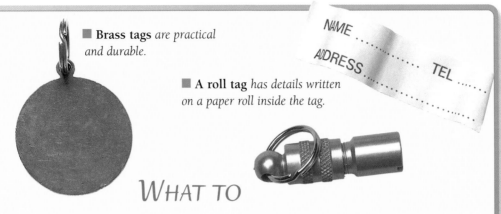

■ **Brass tags** *are practical and durable.*

■ **A roll tag** *has details written on a paper roll inside the tag.*

WHAT TO DO IF YOUR DOG IS MISSING

The panic and feelings of guilt are just terrible when your dog gets lost. Most of us have experienced it at one time or other. I lost Liberty, one of my Golden Retrievers, in the park when I concentrated too much on talking with my mother and not enough on what Libby was up to. A search party searched in vain for her, inside and outside the park. Fortunately, that evening she returned to the park and nonchalantly lay down under a tree, where we found her. It can happen to you too. Here is what you should do:

1. Do not panic. Think sensibly about what your dog may do if she is separated from you.
2. Begin searching immediately, asking people if they have seen your dog.
3. Contact the police, local dog shelters, your veterinary surgeon, and all local veterinary surgeons, giving them a description of your dog and her ID number. Give these people at least two contact numbers for you, ideally your home phone and your mobile phone or e-mail address, if you have them. Keep a phone number list of everyone you contact.
4. Photocopy and post flyers where your dog went missing, with LOST and REWARD in large letters. A reward is always an effective inducement. Include a picture of your dog on the flyers.
5. When she is safely returned, always contact your phone list to give them the good news and to thank them for their help.

■ **Ensure that your** *dog always wears secure and visible identification.*

Breeding your dog

THIS IS A HEARTS *and minds issue. Most of us, who love and respect our dogs deeply, have conflicting feelings about what we should do. I am not the only one who asks myself, is it really fair, am I being true to my heartfelt feelings about the rights of dogs, when I make family planning decisions on their behalf?*

■ **Breeding from** *your dog is a huge decision to make; consider all the pros and cons.*

The pros

The pros of breeding are self-evident. First and perhaps most important to our hearts, we feel that we perpetuate our dogs. The relatively short life of a dog (the typical life span is just over 12 years) is the cause of the greatest sadness we have as dog owners. With purebred dogs in particular, breeding creates a continuity, almost an immortality. Second, and again appealing to our hearts, breeding is "natural." Our hearts tell us that a dog's natural objective is to survive and multiply. This is a beautiful ideal, and I hold it in my mind each time a new dog enters my home. My family will face this dilemma again when Inca is older and we must decide whether or not to let her have pups.

The cons

Most of the arguments against breeding come from the mind, rather than the heart. Be realistic. It might be "natural" to let our dogs breed, but is it "natural" that we keep them as companions at all? In a "natural" environment would there ever be as great a congregation of unrelated dogs as there is in any city park in the morning? Is it "natural" to help runts survive, to intervene in survival of the fittest, which is what we did when we created miniature or dwarfed breeds?

■ **Most dog breeds** *would not exist if we had not intervened and selectively bred dogs over the years.*

To my mind we cannot equate our dogs (or cats) to wild animals that fend for themselves. Dogs and humans have formed an integrated ecosystem – one that has been extraordinarily successful for dogs, enabling them to spread throughout the world and increase in numbers beyond that of all other canids, because we make breeding decisions for them. Breeding dogs is also time-consuming, expensive, and, occasionally, heartbreaking. It requires a great deal of knowledge. Your decision on whether to breed from your dog should be based on your dog and his or her potential partner's inherited good health and temperament, and your ability to make sure you can find caring, responsible homes for the resulting litter.

■ **Most dog-owners** *adore puppies, but consider how difficult it can be to find homes for them all.*

There's an argument from the heart that you must consider, as well. In the United Kingdom there are far more dogs than there are homes for them. Sad, lonely dogs live out their lives in shelters or are euthanized, simply because there is no one to take them home. Are you really sure you want to add more puppies to the world?

Mating, pregnancy, and whelping

Breeding dogs is a serious undertaking. If you plan to breed yours, this small chapter is absolutely not enough information for you to even begin.

You must speak with experienced breeders and your veterinary surgeon, and read a lot more. However, this little explanation of how it happens will help you understand just how much work and time is involved.

The females of most breeds (but not the Basenji) have two *oestrus periods* per year. The level of sex hormones in males is uniform throughout the year – although as with us, there is some evidence that male dogs also experience a little lusty hormonal flush of spring fever.

HERE IS WHAT HAPPENS IN BOTH SEXES:

MALE	FEMALE	PREGNANT FEMALE
Very interested in sex	**PRO-OESTRUS** Lasts 7 to 14 days. The vulva swells. Bloody, then clear vaginal discharge. Increased wandering and restlessness. Will not accept mating.	
Extremely interested in sex	**OESTRUS** Lasts 4 to 7 days. Discharge stops. Eggs are released (ovulation). Pregnancy is possible. Bitch will accept mating.	**PREGNANCY** Multiple eggs are fertilized. Lasts 58 to 65 days. No visible signs for three weeks.
Interested in sex	**DIESTRUS** Lasts 6 to 10 weeks. Hormonal changes continue. Period of "false" pregnancy. Uterus wall thickens. Enlarged mammary glands. Milk production. Mothering toys. No interest in sex.	**VISIBLE PREGNANCY** Activity diminishes. Teats enlarge and become pink. Belly swells. Birth occurs.
Still interested in sex	**ANESTRUS** Lasts 15 weeks. No hormonal activity. No milk production. No interest in sex.	**LACTATION** Lasts 6 to 9 weeks. Body condition deteriorates. Maternal behaviour evolves. Mother encourages weaning.

Breeding your bitch

■ **Your bitch will** *show she is ready to mate by standing with her tail to one side.*

If you plan to breed your bitch, do the following:

1. Ensure you have good homes for the litter before you breed.
2. During pro-oestrus and oestrus, exercise your bitch only on her lead to eliminate any risk of mismating.

3. Have both dog and bitch examined by vets and certified healthy and free from known inherited diseases.

4. Have both dog and bitch examined by vets and certified healthy and free from brucellosis, a sexually transmitted disease.

5. Make sure both dogs are registered with a kennel club and that all the paperwork is in order. Find out what you will need to do to register the pups.

6. Take your bitch to the stud dog. Some fellows have difficulty performing away from home.

7. Arrange for two matings around the twelfth day of oestrus, one or two days apart.

8. Visit your vet three weeks later to confirm the pregnancy.

■ **After mounting** *the bitch, the dog will release his semen within a minute.*

■ **After the semen** *is released, the penis expands to lodge itself inside the vagina; this is known as the "tie."*

Whelping

Your expectant mother will lose her appetite about a day before she gives birth. She becomes restless and seeks out the place she has chosen for giving birth (it's not always the nice whelping box you have prepared at great expense). Shortly before labour begins, her first water bag breaks (there is

■ **If your bitch** *struggles, you may have to steady her so that she does not hurt the dog.*

one for each pup), leaving a puddle that looks much like urine. Contractions begin slowly, then build, with the first pup delivered within two hours of the onset of labour. Each subsequent pup is delivered in intervals of ten to 75 minutes. That's what happens during a normal, uneventful whelping. But it's not always that simple. Always let your vet know when labour has started so that he or she is prepared for an emergency visit.

Get advice if contractions have not begun within two hours of the water breaking or if a pup does not emerge after 15 minutes of strong contractions.

Small litters often produce larger pups that have a more difficult passage through the birth canal. Large litters usually come out like popping peas from a pod. *Caesarean section* is common in very small breeds, such as the Yorkshire Terrier, or breeds such as the Bulldog, which have very large puppy skulls.

DEFINITION

Caesarean section, *usually called simply c-section, is surgical intervention to open the womb to deliver the puppies. It must be done in a veterinary hospital.*

The first weeks of a pup's life

I AM STILL AWESTRUCK at how a bitch that previously seemed totally clueless and dependent on her human family just takes over when she has pups. She really makes it look simple. She provides nourishment, warmth, and protection. Pups huddle together for warmth – the beginning of their enjoyment of physical contact.

Extra feeding

Large litters may need supplementary feeding. After birth your veterinary surgeon will give you advice according to your bitch's unique circumstances. Keep track of each puppy's daily weight gain. The weakest pups and the least pushy get relegated by others to the least productive teats.

The earlier you intervene to help the weakest, the better the head start. You can do this by moving the more vigorous pups to the front teats and the weaker ones to the back (which tend to have more milk).

Mother will provide all the nourishment her pups need until they are three weeks old, when weaning onto solid food such as milky porridge, dry puppy food soaked in warm water, or canned puppy food, begins. Contact your veterinary surgeon about the specific needs of your new litter.

■ **When contractions** *begin your dog will start to pant. She will become tense and her temperature will drop.*

■ **Your bitch will stand** *and circle while she has contractions. Let her find the most comfortable position in which to give birth.*

■ **The new mother** *will immediately clean the pups to dry and warm them, chew off the umbilical cord, and stimulate breathing.*

WHEN SHOULD YOUR DOG BE SPAYED?

Some people think a bitch should have one litter, or if not a litter, at least one oestrus cycle before being spayed. I disagree. We have a lifelong need to nurture, but dogs do not. They are programmed to disengage pretty quickly from motherhood, even to look upon their young as competitors. Projecting your feelings about the constancy of human parenthood onto dogs is making them human in a questionable and even dubious manner.

As for having a heat cycle before spaying, all the veterinary evidence, both medical and behavioural, indicates that this gives no advantages to the dog but creates potential health and behaviour disadvantages. For anatomical reasons, some bitches with poorly developed vulvas should have a first season. Your veterinary surgeon will tell you if your bitch has this need. If not, consider spaying her before her first season.

A simple summary

✓ Dogs are generally quite pragmatic about handling changes in their lives, but do be prepared to guide your dog through any change in your circumstances. Do this with training and with love.

✓ Have a disaster kit prepared, and know what you will do should an emergency strike.

✓ A new cat or dog should be introduced to the resident pet carefully. Do not leave them alone unsupervised until you are positive nothing bad will happen.

✓ Travelling with your pet requires some forethought, but can be enjoyable for all.

✓ Dogs and babies should not be left alone unattended.

✓ Breeding dogs should not be taken lightly. It is a serious matter, and is best left to those who have definite plans to improve the health and temperament of the breed.

✓ It is not true that female dogs need to have a litter, or even a heat season, before they are spayed.

Chapter 23

Simply Fun

THE LUCKIEST DOGS are those with owners who understand that life can be boring for a dog if all it involves is eating, sleeping, petting, and a half hour of outdoor activity each day. Many dogs lead exceedingly dull lives because they are not given a chance to do what dogs were meant to do – work. Yes, I know, it may not be very practical to let your dog herd sheep, drive cattle, chase off wolves, or go to war, but there are some delectable alternatives. Dogs really enjoy organized obedience, work, and agility events. These are challenging for you too, because of the teamwork involved. Another sociable pastime is showing your dog at dog shows sanctioned by the organization your dog is registered with.

In this chapter...

✓ Dog shows

✓ Canine sports

✓ Dogs with missions

CHALLENGE YOUR DOG PHYSICALLY AND MENTALLY

Dog shows

A DOG SHOW sometimes seems like a beauty contest, and of course, beauty is in the eye of the beholder. You and your dog compete against other dogs and their owners to be Best of Breed, Best in Group, or Best in Show in the eyes of the judges. Because judgment is so subjective, dog shows can be very emotional events for their owners. Dogs, on the other hand, usually find a day at a dog show a surprisingly enjoyable event, what with all the different smells and sights. It is the natural born show-offs that are most likely to win at these events.

Who puts on dog shows?

Official dog shows are sanctioned by a registration organization such as The Kennel Club (KC), a national kennel club such as the Swedish Kennel Club (SKC) or the pan-European Fédération Cynologique Internationale (FCI). At any of these shows, you can only enter a dog that is registered with the organization.

■ **Official dog shows** *are put on by clubs that are part of a large governing body.*

How does the judging work?

An official dog show is really a conformation and personality competition. There is a written breed standard for each breed, and your dog is judged by how well he measures up to this written breed standard. Breed clubs, not their registration organization, set the standards. The breed standard will describe the ideal dog, with often minute details about the colour and texture of the coat, body size and shape, position of the ears and tail, eye colour and shape, style of movement, and much more.

■ **The dogs are** *all judged by how closely they conform to a written breed standard.*

Dogs are usually divided and judged by sex. Puppies are judged in their own classes, and in some breeds judging is also divided according to coat colour. Judges choose winners in each class, then the best male and female from among these winners. These two now compete against established champions.

The winner, a single dog, competes against the winners from the other breeds within their group (remember, I talked in Chapter 4 about how breeds are divided into groups). Finally, the winners from each group compete against each other for Best in Show – top dog status. For example, the KC has seven groups, so there are always seven finalists for the top honour.

What it takes to win

Winning show dogs are real exhibitionists. They exude an aura of confidence in the show ring. Judges look for this personality characteristic, and it too must conform to the breed standard, which contains words such as "benevolent", "bold", "sweet", "gentle", or "dignified."

Be realistic about your ambitions for your dog. Buying what a breeder calls a show-quality adult dog should mean you have a dog suitable for showing.

■ **Your attitude** *when showing your dog should be "beauty is in the eye of the beholder."*

There is a great difference however between show-quality characteristics and show-winning potential. This is true whether you bought a top show dog or a top hunting dog or a top any other kind of dog. Buying a show-quality puppy is even less likely to be a guarantee of success.

Unofficial dog shows

Unofficial dog shows are not recognized by a major registration organization. These local shows take place wherever there are dog owners, and I must admit, I like their relaxed atmosphere. The competitors are always a mix of random-breds, crossbreds, and purebreds. The pride people feel in their dogs is as great as you see in official shows. At some of these events, your dog is judged for the waggiest tail, shiniest coat, sparkliest eyes, or "the dog the judge would most like to take home." Other events are run just like official dog shows, but the atmosphere is more relaxed and any dog can enter.

Just as at official dog shows, ribbons and rosettes are awarded. Families, often parents and children together, are just as proud when their dog wins an unofficial ribbon. In fact, some people get quite serious, questioning the judge's decision. I have been a local show judge. I know! "Look at that tail! It can sweep a coffee table clean in two seconds flat! Doesn't that deserve a prize?" The pleasure I get from these shows is seeing how marvellously some people prepare their dogs.

Canine sports

GIVE A DOG *a choice and he'll probably choose the sporting life. In canine sports events, your dog's mental and physical abilities are rewarded. By getting involved in canine sports, you give your dog the opportunity to think, to use his senses, his reflexes, his dexterity, and his strength. If you have an opportunity to attend obedience, working, or agility trials, you will see what I mean. These competitors are the most satisfied of all dogs, simply because they are given the opportunity to do what dogs do best.*

Canine sports offer you a chance to get closer to your dog, as well. When the two of you train together, getting in shape and learning new skills, you'll be amazed at how much better you understand your dog, and your dog understands you.

Obedience trials

In obedience trials, a dog and his handler work through a series of obedience exercises such as heeling, coming when called, staying where left, and in more advanced classes, retrieving.

Top dogs are physically fit but also glorious entertainers. Eyes glued to their owners, they react instantly to hand or word signals. The teamwork is magnificent to watch, as is the enjoyment a dog gets out of this activity.

■ **In field trials** *dogs must be under supreme control.*

Winners are invariably bright, responsive, happy dogs that have an envious ability to concentrate 100 percent on what their handlers are asking them to do. While some breeds, for example Border Collies and Golden Retrievers, excel at obedience, any dog can do well. All major kennel clubs sanction their own obedience trials.

Canine freestyle

This is a little like professional ballroom dancing with your dog. In traditional obedience trials you and your dog carry out a series of set obedience exercises. In freestyle, first, you dress yourself in what you consider to be an interesting costume. Then, to music, you and your dog carry out an intricately choreographed series of moves that combine obedience exercises, tricks, and agility.

Working trials

In these events, dogs use the abilities they were originally bred for. Terriers run through underground tunnels to corner vermin, Newfoundlands and Portuguese Water Dogs do water work, Coonhounds, German Shepherds and other working breeds apprehend bad guys, and so on. Scenthounds also have their own working trial events, where Beagles, Bloodhounds, and even Dachshunds competitively follow scent trails. Some of these sports are organized by the national kennel clubs, and some are set up by breed clubs that want to perpetuate the original working purpose of their breed. Although many participants are family dogs, the winners in these events usually come from lines specifically bred for working ability. Many of the following sports are also based on dogs' natural abilities.

■ **In working trials** *Bloodhounds compete with other scenthounds in following a scent trail.*

DEFINITION

How does a dog point*? With all his body. When a hunting dog is on point, his body is tense and stiff. His back is straight, one front leg is lifted off the ground, his tail is straight out, and his neck is extended so that he is indicating the game with his nose. The idea is for the dog to hold still so as not to disturb the game, while the hunter sneaks up to shoot.*

Field work

These trials test a hunting dog's abilities. Retrievers retrieve under a variety of circumstances. Spaniels flush game and retrieve. Pointing breeds compete to search for and find a bird, then hold a classic *point* while the handler fires a shotgun.

The size, shape, and appearance of dogs in field trials can be considerably different from the looks of their show ring cousins. While working Cocker Spaniels are simply leaner, more lightly coated, and more reactive than their show relatives, lithe, light-boned, hard-muscled but still ever-smiling field trial Labrador Retrievers look radically different from their heavier, more barrel-chested show dog associates.

■ **During field work** *competitions pointers compete to find a bird.*

Lure coursing

In coursing events, sighthounds such as Whippets and Salukis enthusiastically chase artificial lures at awesome speed. It still amazes me how a breed such as a Whippet, bashful and retiring at the veterinary clinic, turns into a prick-eared, muscle-quivering mass of concentrated energy when given the opportunity to run.

Tracking and trailing

In tracking competitions, dogs follow a scent along a track laid by a human. The track can get very complicated, and some types of tracking even cross urban areas. This type of sport requires the ultimate trust of your dog, since only the dog knows where the track goes.

■ **Sheepdogs continue** *to work on farms and trials enable dogs to show the variety of manoeuvres they know.*

Herding

Perhaps the most common working dogs throughout the world remain working sheepdogs. There are trials for real working sheepdogs all over the world in which individuals compete against one another to perform a set series of herding manoeuvres. (As well, in North America and Europe there are events that test a herding dog's ability to move ducks.)

Trivia...

Most national kennel clubs, including The Kennel Club, also sponsor canine sporting events. Contact them for rules and information about how to get started. You'll find the addresses in Appendix A of this book.

Sledding

Sled racing over a well-maintained snow course is increasingly popular in North America and Scandinavia. The sport is governed by The International Sled Dog Racing Association. If snow is not available, dogs compete pulling a sled on wheels, called a gig. There are also long-distance sled dog events such as the Iditarod in Alaska, although there is a question in my mind about the physical conditions these dogs must endure. Foot and paw damage is not uncommon. That said, there is no doubt that sled dogs such as Huskies and Malamutes revel in the challenge of sledding events.

■ **Malamutes and other** *Arctic breeds compete in sled-pulling races across the snowy landscapes of North America and Scandinavia.*

Agility

Agility trials and games are one of the most recent additions to canine competitions, and probably the most fun. In agility trials, dogs compete against one another and against the clock to race through an obstacle course that involves weaving, jumping, balancing, and obeying the handler.

If you plan to participate, make sure that you as well as your dog are in good shape, since you both must run around the course (although you may skip the hurdles, and may take a course considerably shorter than the dog's). This is a gloriously demanding physical activity.

Flyball

Flyball is a kind of relay race with a twist. A dog races down a short course, leaping over a series of hurdles, and presses the lever on a box. This triggers a launcher that tosses a tennis ball, which she catches in her mouth. She races back over the hurdles to the starting line. As she crosses the line, the next dog in the team flies down the course. At the same time, another team of canine competitors is doing the same thing in the next lane. The faster team wins. The height of the hurdles varies with the size of the dogs competing.

■ **Agility competitions** *can involve any well-trained dog and its owner, and are fun for animal and human to take part in.*

■ **Flyball** *dogs compete in teams; the sport is not restricted to any one breed.*

INTERNET

www.agilityeye.co.uk

This site provides information on agility methods, trials, and games throughout Britain.

Dogs with missions

■ **Therapy dogs** *give a valuable service to the elderly or infirm; allowing themselves to be petted they give a healing touch to many.*

MEDICAL RESEARCH *shows that dog owners need to visit their doctors less frequently than non-dog owners, that we need fewer prescriptions for drugs and suffer from fewer minor health complaints. In late 1999, Dr Karen Allen from the State University of New York in Buffalo reported to the American Heart Foundation that stockbrokers suffering from high blood pressure who were given dogs experienced less of a surge in blood pressure when they were stressed than those treated with the same medication but not given dogs. (I would like to know how they stressed the stockbrokers. Did they whisper "market crash" in their ears?)*

We know our canine companions are good for us, if only because we are forced to exercise more; that alone is good for our health. But they can be beneficial, even therapeutic, to others too. In the last 25 years, new opportunities have arisen for pet dogs, well-rounded canine citizens, to help people in a practical way.

Therapy dogs are well-trained family pets with easygoing personalities, examined by a veterinary surgeon and found to be healthy, who visit people in hospitals, retirement homes, and residential institutions. Wherever they visit, they bring their no-nonsense honesty and unconditional love. They do not judge people by their age or physical condition. They allow themselves to be touched and stroked because they enjoy it. Think about it: touch is perhaps our most important sense yet people placed in institutions get precious little of it.

Search and rescue dogs

Earthquake, avalanche, and mountain rescue dogs do serious professional work, but most of them are, in fact, pet dogs trained to work when circumstances dictate.

After the great Han Shin earthquake in Japan a few years ago, when several people were rescued because their pet dogs located them in the debris, local dog training clubs started incorporating "hide and seek" games into standard obedience training.

> ### Trivia...
> *Appendix A in this book has the names and contact information for organizations involved in all the sports and activities I've mentioned in this chapter, including therapy dogs.*

■ **Search and rescue** *dogs help throughout the world in disaster zones and emergencies; their unique skills are invaluable.*

Search and rescue is simply "hide and seek" played at a more serious level. A dog uses his air and ground scenting abilities to seek out the lost individual. Large dogs are used in all professional search and rescue operations, although the Japanese experience shows that even smaller dogs such as Shelties are capable of being trained in these techniques. If you have a dog you believe is suitable for search and rescue training, contact your local club. You will also have to be capable of some physical exertion as you accompany your dog.

Service dogs

These are the true professionals of dogdom, acting as eyes, ears, and aids for disabled people. While many assistance dogs are bred for these roles, some are shelter rescues or just regular dogs with a naturally curious and responsive disposition. You can get involved by offering to foster a service dog puppy. Contact a local service dog organization for more information.

■ **Service dogs** *are the eyes and ears for the blind and deaf.*

A simple summary

✓ Dog shows are popular competitions where dogs are judged against their written breed standard.

✓ There is a variety of working events for all kinds of dogs, including mixed breeds.

✓ Getting involved in a dog activity will bring you closer to your dog and to other dog lovers in your community.

✓ Dogs can also quite literally assist humans, by rescuing those in disasters, working as service dogs, and visiting those in hospitals and nursing homes.

✓ Dogs are happier when they can be involved in activities that engage their minds and their bodies.

Chapter 24

Time Marches On

SOCIAL SCIENTISTS TELL US that with increasing life expectancy we must plan our retirement years carefully, because they will last as long as our working years. It's the same with dogs. A dog's life expectancy has increased 20 percent in my lifetime alone. Geriatrics has become the growth area in veterinary medicine. For a typical dog, at least one third of her life – perhaps the last four years – is spent in "retirement," a time when she wants to do what she always did but now finds it rather more difficult.

Organized activities wind down and are replaced by a more sedentary lifestyle. Now it is more important than ever to provide your dog with mental and physical stimulation to delay the deterioration of advancing years.

In this chapter...

✓ Age-proofing your buddy

✓ Diet changes through life

✓ Common problems of aging

✓ Introducing a new canine companion

PLAY WITH YOUR OLDER DOG CREATIVELY TO KEEP HER MIND OCCUPIED

Age-proofing your buddy

IT'S AS TRUE FOR DOGS *as it is for us: use it or lose it. Just as routine physical activity keeps your dog's body in the best condition, routine mental exercise helps postpone the natural decline in brain power that comes with age. When your dog was younger she coped well with a little exercise one day, then a 30-kilometre hike the next. Not now. As her age advances, her exercise periods should become more regular. Do not pay attention to what she might tell you. She might think she can cope with sudden extensive activity, but her body feels otherwise. It is up to you to ensure that she continues to enjoy the exhilaration of daily routines.*

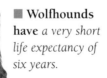

Never force activity on your older dog. Dogs are true stoics. They seldom complain. If your dog is unwilling to exercise, always assume something is wrong and that she may be experiencing pain.

■ **Miniature Poodles** *have one of the longest life spans of all the dog breeds, averaging 15 years.*

If your dog's ability to exercise is significantly reduced, make sure she still enjoys the stimulation of mental activity. Give her creative activities to do at home; rolling a toy that releases food is one that most seniors enjoy. Maintain her physical dexterity by giving her work to do with her forepaws. If her activity level is temporarily reduced through illness, massage her muscles. You know how you feel after a period of bed rest. Dogs experience the same exhaustion and need a similar build-up of strength.

■ **Wolfhounds have** *a very short life expectancy of six years.*

■ **Massage your** *dog to help stimulate her muscles after a period of illness.*

THE LIFE EXPECTANCY OF DOGS

Have reasonable expectations about your dog's life expectancy. According to an extensive survey of Pet Plan insurance records, published in December 1999, here are the median life expectancies, in years, for a number of breeds:

Breed	Years	Breed	Years
Miniature Poodle	14.8	Golden Retriever	12.0
Miniature Dachshund	14.4	Scottish Terrier	12.0
Toy Poodle	14.4	Standard Poodle	12.0
Tibetan Terrier	14.3	English Cocker Spaniel	11.8
Bedlington Terrier	14.3	Irish Setter	11.8
Whippet	14.3	Old English Sheepdog	11.8
Border Terrier	13.8	Welsh Springer Spaniel	11.5
Jack Russell Terrier	13.6	Corgi	11.3
Chow Chow	13.5	Gordon Setter	11.3
Shih Tzu	13.4	Airedale Terrier	11.2
Beagle	13.3	English Setter	11.2
Pekingese	13.3	Samoyed	11.0
Shetland Sheepdog	13.3	Cavalier King Charles Spaniel	10.7
Cairn Terrier	13.2	Boxer	10.4
Greyhound	13.2	German Shepherd Dog	10.3
Random-bred	13.2	English Toy Spaniel	10.1
Border Collie	13.0	Norfolk Terrier	10.0
Chihuahua	13.0	Staffordshire Bull Terrier	10.0
Collie	13.0	Weimaraner	10.0
Dalmatian	13.0	Dobermann	9.8
English Springer Spaniel	13.0	Rottweiler	9.8
Wire Fox Terrier	13.0	Scottish Deerhound	9.5
Bull Terrier	12.9	Flat-Coated Retriever	9.5
Irish Red and White Setter	12.9	Rhodesian Ridgeback	9.1
Basset Hound	12.8	Bullmastiff	8.6
West Highland White Terrier	12.8	Great Dane	8.4
Yorkshire Terrier	12.8	Bernese Mountain Dog	7.0
Labrador Retriever	12.6	Bulldog	6.7
Lurcher	12.6	Irish Wolfhound	6.2
Cocker Spaniel	12.5		
Hungarian Viszla	12.5		
Bearded Collie	12.3		
German Shorthaired Pointer	12.3		
Dachshund	12.2		
Collie	12.2		
Afghan Hound	12.0		

■ **On average,** *Lurchers live for 12.6 years.*

Diet changes through life

As dogs age, their dietary needs change, especially when specific health problems arise. Generally speaking, an older dog needs about 20 percent fewer calories than she did in her physical prime. At the same time, she needs more vitamins, minerals, and antioxidants.

If you do not reduce her calorie intake, the supply of energy going in is greater than the amount of energy used up in activity. The surplus is stored as fat. That is the simple reason why many dogs get fatter as they get older. Of course, there are also individuals that require as much food or more in their golden years. That's why you must continually assess your dog's condition, and feed accordingly.

A gradual change

Any diet change should be done gradually. Sudden changes upset the living environment of digestive microorganisms in your dog's intestines. This is why diarrhoea occurs so often when a dog's diet is changed. When changing your dog's diet to one more appropriate for her advancing years, gradually increase the percentage of new food mixed with the old over a ten-day period.

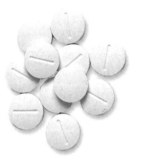

■ **Calcium**
Essential for puppies and pregnant and lactating bitches.

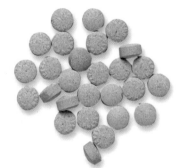

■ **Vitamin tablets**
Give only as directed by your vet.

■ **Bonemeal**
An extra source of calcium: buy it sterilized.

Weigh your dog routinely, at least once a month. Steady weight is one of the best signs of good health. Weight increase is usually associated with excess calories in the diet, while weight loss almost always means illness.

Antioxidants

> **DEFINITION**
>
> Free radicals *are atoms in the body that destroy cell membranes.*

The value of antioxidants in our diet was first emphasized by practitioners of complementary medicine, and is now accepted by even the most straight-laced conventional medical people. Antioxidants are substances, such as vitamins C and E or zinc, that destroy *free radicals*. Dogs (and people) have their own natural free-radical scavenging systems, but consuming extra antioxidants may boost these natural systems. All major dog food manufacturers now supplement their senior dog foods with extra antioxidants.

Protein

Finally, a word about protein. For many years veterinary surgeons were taught that older dogs should be fed less protein. Too much protein, we were told, gave the kidneys too much work to do. This became an unquestioned "fact." It was wrong. Older dogs do not need a reduction in protein. They benefit from extra micronutrients and more digestible protein.

If a dog has kidney problems, the most important part of treatment is to reduce the amount of the mineral phosphorus in her diet. At the same time, she needs highly digestible protein. Only in very advanced stages of kidney disease should she be fed a low-protein as well as a low-phosphorus diet.

■ **Older dogs** *need more vitamins, minerals, and antioxidants but less food than when they were younger.*

Common problems of aging

THERE IS MUCH *that is predictable about your dog's health, and within breeds even more is predictable. Most of the age-related conditions that dogs experience are similar to those that we have, from bad breath to cancer. All of these problems seem to be more frequent now than they once were, but that is only because dogs are living longer than ever before. This raises difficult ethical problems, which I will talk about in the next chapter. Here are some of the common problems you might find, and suggestions about how to either prevent these conditions or deal with them.*

THE SENIOR CHECK-UP

With any age-related condition, the earlier it is diagnosed the easier and cheaper it is to treat. At some time between seven and ten years of age, depending on the breed of your dog, arrange for a full preventive health check-up. The details of this check-up will vary from breed to breed, but some aspects are similar for all. Your vet will carry out a full physical examination and take a blood sample when your dog has not had a meal. I have carried out these check-ups on thousands of golden oldies.

In my urban practice most dogs that look healthy outwardly are just as healthy inside. But for some, the examination reveals early heart conditions or internal lumps where there should not be any. A blood sample reveals strain on the kidneys, early liver disease, or other still benign conditions. As with us, prevention is the best form of medical treatment.

Bad breath and gum disease

Mouth problems will eventually occur in almost every dog, although some breeds, Poodles for example, are more at risk than others. The problem is simple: dogs today do not get to use their teeth and gums for their intended purposes. Ripping, tearing, and

■ **Elderly dogs** *often suffer from bad breath; good dental hygiene can remedy this.*

chewing is left to their friends in the wild, while pet dogs just swallow. The result is a build-up of slime on the teeth, leading to bacterial multiplication, gum inflammation, and bad breath.

Prevention is quite simple. Your dog needs routine dental hygiene. You can provide this by giving her rock-hard biscuits to chew on, providing rawhide, especially enzyme-treated rawhide under supervision, and by brushing your dog's teeth and gums. Oral antiseptic is also excellent for reducing smelly bacteria.

INTERNET

www.srdogs.com

The Senior Dogs Project has health and behaviour news, lovely stories, lots of links, and great advice for owners of older dogs.

Smelly skin

As dogs age they often produce increasing amounts of oily secretions from the sebaceous glands in the skin. This is called seborrhoea, and the condition develops as either an oily or a dry, flaking condition. Either way, your dog smells "doggy". Some breeds, such as the Cocker Spaniel, are more susceptible to seborrhoea than others. There are a variety of causes of seborrhoea. Your veterinary surgeon will discuss diet, external parasites, and skin hygiene with you, but at the core of treatment are shampoos.

■ **Older dogs** *need frequent grooming as they often suffer from more skin conditions than they did in their youth.*

Older dogs need to be bathed more frequently than younger ones. The problem is that older dogs sometimes get crotchety about baths. As your dog ages, make sure you maintain a high level of grooming, including frequent shampooing. This leaves your dog with healthier skin and you with a more socially acceptable house partner.

SIGNS OF OLD AGE

Hearing deteriorates, resulting in deafness in some dogs

Coat becomes thinner

Muscles shrink and body becomes weaker

Lenses in eyes become a cloudy blue-grey

Hair turns grey on muzzle and around ears

Joint fluid dries up, causing inflammation and discomfort

Painful joints

The incidence of painful arthritis increases with age. Although any dog can develop joint pain, this too is a problem that is more likely to occur in some breeds than in others. Breeds with a high incidence of hip dysplasia – poorly designed hip joints – include retrievers, shepherds, and some other large breeds.

■ **Some larger** *breeds such as retrievers suffer from a high incidence of hip dysplasia in old age.*

Over time, the smooth surface of the joint wears down. Eventually this causes chronic pain, but because the development of the problem is slow and insidious, some dog owners assume that their dog is simply winding down, when in fact he is in pain.

People think that a dog limps if he has joint pain, but in a condition such as hip dysplasia, if the deterioration occurs in both hip joints, there is no limp, just pain when a dog moves. You have to watch for other signs.

Dealing with joint pain

All of my Golden Retrievers have had joint pain in their later years, but fortunately, my more recent dogs have had (and Lex still has) their pain controlled with effective medication. But medicine alone is not the solution. Weight reduction, to a healthy weight that the dog's skeleton was meant to carry, is vital. A 10-percent surplus in weight can mean the difference between treatment success and failure. It was only when Lex dropped from 35 to 32 kilos that her activity increased and her medication became effective.

■ **It is important** *for older dogs to get plenty of gentle exercise to keep their weight down and to work their muscles.*

Routine exercise is important, too. It is the best way to keep muscles in fine tone, and for dogs with joint pain we want their muscles to carry a lot of weight so they can take the strain off inflamed joints. Finally, non-steroid anti-inflammatories (NSAIDs) have advanced beyond recognition in the last five years. These are the most effective non-narcotic pain killers to become available since I began in veterinary practice over 30 years ago. At my practice we routinely use injectable NSAIDs during every surgical procedure and in liquid or tablet form for most dogs with acute or chronic pain.

The longer your dog has experienced chronic pain, the longer it will take NSAIDs to break through the pain threshold. If your veterinary surgeon recommends using them, persevere.

As well as NSAIDs, consider dietary supplements to reduce the pain of joint inflammation. There is good evidence that certain fatty acids found in oil of evening primrose, borage oil, flax oil, and fish oil have anti-inflammatory effects. There is similar evidence that natural substances such as chondroitin and glucosamine may benefit a dog's joints.

Heart disease

Heart disease is the second most common cause of death in dogs, accounting for almost eight percent of fatalities. Some breeds, Cavalier King Charles Spaniels and Dobermann, for example, are more susceptible. Heart conditions are often picked up early during routine preventive physical examinations. Generally speaking, the earlier medical treatment begins, the longer you can expect your dog to live. If your dog has any form of heart disease, discuss medication, weight, exercise, and diet with your veterinary surgeon.

Regardless of the type of heart condition your dog has, there is convincing evidence that a concentrated supplement of marine fish oil may be beneficial to the functioning of heart muscle. Some veterinary schools now incorporate marine fish oil into their treatment of heart and joint problems in dogs. This is something you can discuss with your veterinary surgeon.

■ **Fish oil has** *anti-inflammatory effects that ease joint pain.*

MORE ON NATURAL SUPPLEMENTS

If your veterinary surgeon is not familiar with the therapeutic uses of marine fish oil and other natural supplements, the British Association of Homeopathic Veterinary Surgeons (BAHVS) can help you find a member in your area who can direct you and your vet to more information.

BAHVS
c/o Mrs Third-Carter, 29 Finlayson St, Buchan House, Fraserburgh, AB4 4UP or
Mr Hoare, 12 Martins Road, Hanham, Bristol, BS15 3EW. www.bahvs.com/vetmfhom.html

Senior moments

Dogs have them too. When Dr Benjamin Hart, Professor of Animal Behaviour at the University of California Davis' veterinary school, investigated age-related behaviour changes in dogs, he observed that most of the signs of senile dementia that we might have, dogs have too. A typical age-related change in dogs is standing at the wrong place when he wants to go in or out. Other dogs bark at nothing. Collectively, these changes are known as *canine cognitive dysfunction*.

Trivia...

The poet who wrote, "The old dog barks backward without getting up. I can remember when he was a pup", was an accurate observer of aging in dogs.

DEFINITION

The term canine cognitive dysfunction, *or CCD, has been coined to describe the deteriorating behaviour changes of old age. The term itself is a mouthful, but it is useful because it recognizes this as a medical disorder. When vets and pet owners acknowledge that there is a problem, it is then possible to look for a solution.*

A drug called selegeline, developed for use in us and used for delaying the development of advanced signs and symptoms of Alzheimer's Disease, is licensed for use in dogs with CCD. There is also a drug called Vivotonin that has been licensed specifically for dogs. If your dog is having senior moments, check his behaviour. Some aspects of aging are irreversible, but others can be delayed and even reversed with effective use of medications.

■ **Incontinence** *sometimes affects young Dobermanns after they have been spayed.*

Incontinence

Loss of bladder control occurs most frequently in younger dogs that have been spayed, especially Dobermanns and Old English Sheepdogs, and in older females who, with time, lose sphincter muscle control and dribble urine when sitting, lying down, or sleeping. Many people assume this is an inevitable component of growing older, but in most instances the nuisance of urinary incontinence can be controlled or eliminated with simple medication that increases sphincter muscle tone. If your dog occasionally dribbles urine, see your veterinary surgeon.

■ **Old English Sheepdogs** *sometimes develop incontinence if they have been spayed at a young age.*

Faecal incontinence, a condition where a dog involuntarily passes a bowel movement, usually when lying down, is more difficult to control. I take off my hat to the dog owners I know who cope with this unpleasant, usually age-related problem. If medication does not work, all I can do is modify a dog's diet so that her stools are hard and compact – little Easter eggs, as a conscientious owner once described them.

Lumps and bumps

Cancer is the most common cause of death in dogs. Almost 16 percent of dogs succumb to one form of cancer or another, but do not assume that all lumps and bumps are cancers.

They are not. Many skin lumps are simply cysts, which are blocked sebaceous glands. Others are unsightly but benign warts, technically called papillomas. One of the most common tumours a dog gets is called a lipoma, a lump of fat, usually between the skin and underlying muscle. Lipomas are not dangerous, but can grow from bean size to baseball size or larger. They are unsightly but only need attention when they are located in areas where they cause physical problems.

If your dog has any form of cancer, but especially if she has a lymphoma – a cancer of the lymphatic system – avoid a high-carbohydrate diet. There is ample evidence that carbohydrates give cancer cells extra energy. Instead, feed a diet of high-quality fat and protein, supplemented with extra micronutrients. Your veterinary surgeon will guide you on what diet is best for your dog.

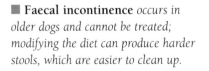

■ **Faecal incontinence** *occurs in older dogs and cannot be treated; modifying the diet can produce harder stools, which are easier to clean up.*

ACCORDING TO PET INSURANCE COMPANY RECORDS:

BREEDS MOST AT RISK OF DYING FROM CANCER ARE:
Irish Wolfhound
Rottweiler
Afghan Hound
Standard Poodle
Weimaraner
Staffordshire Bull Terrier
Boxer
Cairn Terrier
Old English Sheepdog
Golden Retriever
Flat-Coated Retriever

BREEDS WITH AN AVERAGE RISK OF DYING FROM CANCER ARE:
Dobermann
English Springer Spaniel
Labrador Retriever
Great Dane

THE BREEDS LEAST LIKELY TO DIE FROM CANCER ARE:
Border Collie
Cocker Spaniel
Random-breds
German Shepherd Dog
West Highland White Terrier
Shetland Sheepdog
Yorkshire Terrier
Jack Russell Terrier
Collie
Bulldog
Welsh Springer Spaniel
Airedale
Irish Setter
Dachshund
Cavalier King Charles Spaniel
Beagle

■ **Bulldogs are** *one of the breeds that are least likely to die from cancer.*

Diminished senses

All of my Golden Retrievers have lived beyond the average life expectancy for their breed. I put Honey to sleep at close to 17, Liberty at just under 15, and Lexington is now nearing 14 years. All of them lived so long that their senses diminished to the point where they needed help.

Eyesight

> **DEFINITION**
>
> A cataract is a crystalline development in the lens. Light reflects off the crystals, causing darkened starburst-like vision, but eventually light cannot get through the cataract to the retina at the back of the eye. This causes blindness.

All had deteriorating eyesight. Look at the eyes of any older dog and the lenses look cloudy. It looks like cataracts have developed. Dogs, especially certain breeds such as Toy and Miniature Poodles and Labrador Retrievers, may inherit a risk of developing cataracts. If cataracts do develop, the crystalline lenses are removed.

■ **Golden Retrievers** *are one of the few breeds that are susceptible to inherited cataracts.*

Cloudy changes in older dogs' eyes look like cataracts, but in most cases they are not. The cloudy change is really the result of connective tissue fibres in the lens, something technically called lenticular sclerosis.

Every single dog, if she lives long enough, develops sclerosis. She sees through a mist, can still see movement, especially at a distance of say 7 metres, but may have difficulty finding a tennis ball in front of her nose. This is a natural aging change.

■ **Older dogs** *with reduced vision may feel insecure and rest more.*

Hearing

All my Golden Retrievers went deaf, a common problem in older retrievers. At first we think they have selective hearing. "She didn't hear me when I told her to sit, but she sure can hear the fridge door opening from the next room." This is not selective hearing. It is a true hearing deficit. Initially, some sounds are lost while others are still heard.

Hearing aids would probably work, but of course they are not practical. If your dog is losing her hearing, it is up to you to compensate. Be more alert to dangers. Teach her hand signals, preferably early in life, so that she (and you) can cope better if her hearing fails. Keep her under your physical control, especially if she is going deaf and has senior moments.

■ **Teaching your** dog to understand your hand signals early on in her life will help her enormously if she becomes deaf later.

Introducing a new canine companion

IS IT FAIR to introduce a new dog into your home? This is one of the most common questions I am asked by owners of senior citizens. As with so much in life, the answer is yes and no. It depends on your dog's personality and your circumstances.

Case by case

I joke when I say we set up a 24-hour suicide watch on Lex when Inca came into our home, but it is true that Lex, well into her 14th year, was not amused by the antics of a youngster. Then again, Lex has never been amused by the antics of other dogs. She is a deadly serious "people dog" with a sense of humour bypass. She did not like the attentions of other dogs when she was younger and still does

■ **Think carefully** before introducing a new companion into your home if you have an older dog.

Trivia...

Does one dog year really equal seven human years? This may have been true in the first part of the 20th century, but no longer. As you can see from the chart of life expectancies for different breeds of dogs, the typical life expectancy has increased from ten to over 12 years. At the same time, our life expectancy also has increased. Each breed now has its own sliding scale of human-to-dog years. But as a rough guideline, one dog year now equals about five and a half human years.

not. Knowing her personality, it is unfair for us to get another dog while she is in her dotage. We knew Inca would be with us only for a few months before she and Ben, my son, moved out.

If, however, Lex's lifelong companion Libby were still around, even at her great age she would have considered Inca a gift from the gods. Libby was a "dog's dog". That is why, in fact, we got Lex. Libby enjoyed nothing more than communing with her own kind.

The decision of whether or not to get another canine companion when your present dog is maturing is an idiosyncratic one. In most instances, even the most aloof of dogs eventually comes around to the newcomer. Lex did when she realized we fed her more when Inca was around. Ultimately, this is a family decision. Your veterinary surgeon will be able to give you independent advice.

■ **Your resident dog** *will soon get used to a new companion if she receives rewards for their presence and her good behaviour.*

A simple summary

✔ A regular routine of physical and mental exercise is valuable for older dogs.

✔ Many dogs need less food as they age, and could benefit from increased antioxidants and high-quality protein.

✔ It's normal for senses – eyesight and hearing – to diminish as a dog ages.

✔ A variety of maladies become common as a dog ages. Preventive health checks can catch problems early.

✔ Introducing a new dog to an aged canine can be good or bad, depending on the older dog's temperament. Remember that every dog is an individual with a unique personality.

Chapter 25

The Cycle of Life

THE AGING AND EVENTUAL DEATH of your dog is inevitable, but do not assume that the slowing down of your older dog is always age-related. Sometimes it can be difficult to differentiate between aging and illness. While one is inevitable, the other is not.

As a vet, I know that most dogs do not die of illness or injury. In most circumstances we have to make life and death decisions on their behalf. I can say from professional and personal experience that the decision to end a dog's life can be made with equal measures of logic and compassion. Whatever begins, eventually ends. The great joy of canine companionship is that while your relationship with each dog is unique, the satisfaction of living with a dog is available from others, ever-eager to join a human family.

In this chapter...
✓ There's no cure for old age

✓ Letting go

✓ Grieving is normal

✓ Life moves on

There's no cure for old age

LEFT TO NATURE, *a dog's life expectancy is limited by his ability to find food, defend himself, and avoid illness and injury. By hooking up with us pushovers, good food is always available, preventive vaccines eliminate killer diseases, good obedience training reduces injuries, and when crises occur veterinary surgeons are there to help. The consequence is that many dogs live long enough to become true senior citizens.*

Aging versus illness

Aging is not an illness. With increasing age, your dog's body simply does not work as well as it once did. This means illnesses occur more frequently. We have little control over that. But there are signs of aging that are similar to signs of illness, and it is important to know the difference between the two. Older dogs that lack mental stimulation become dull and lethargic, but lassitude or depression is also one of the natural ways in which a sick dog's body responds to the stress of illness.

Trivia...

With age may naturally come increasing disorientation, changes in social relationships, and modifications in sleeping patterns. A majority of elderly dogs eventually involve themselves less with their family. They are likely to sleep more during the day and less at night. Many get befuddled, staring into space or walking into corners. A curious phenomenon of aging is that while neutered females generally become more aggressive, neutered males often get less aggressive as they grow older.

Never assume that changes in your dog's behaviour are simply the changes of aging. It is certainly true that with time, like us, older dogs get both wiser and sillier, but if your dog's behaviour changes, see your veterinary surgeon.

As a general rule, dogs in the last third of their natural life expectancy benefit from twice-yearly medical examinations. (See the list on page 367 of the Chapter 24 for life expectancies for a variety of breeds.)

Life depends on the immune system

With age, dogs naturally slow down, outwardly but also inwardly. Just as the clarity of vision or the acuity of hearing diminishes with time, so too does the efficiency of the immune system. It still works well most of the time, but not as it once did. Failures happen more frequently as dogs get older. The immune system may fail to detect and destroy a germ. This leads to a greater incidence of infections, for example bacterial skin infections, in older dogs. Or the immune system fails to detect a cell that duplicated incorrectly. This is why tumours, both benign ones such as lipomas and malignant ones such as bone cancers, are far more common in older dogs than in youngsters.

As a dog ages, his immune system sometimes under-reacts to threats, but it may also over-react. It may erroneously think that part of its own body is "foreign", and attack and destroy it.

This is the most common cause of thyroid gland failure in older dogs. In a more devastating scenario, his immune system may attack and destroy his own red blood cells, causing a life-threatening anaemia. These are called auto-immune conditions. The natural cycle of your dog's life is intimately associated with how his immune system works.

Older dogs have natural dignity

It is great fun having Inca, a rambunctious pup, in the house, but I must admit I prefer the companionship of older dogs. This is a topic we have discussed at my veterinary clinic, and I find I am not alone in my attitude. It may be an idiosyncratic fluke (after all, I hired the staff) but all my staff agree that they prefer tending to older dogs. When we talk about why this is so, the word "respect" keeps surfacing.

Older dogs are completely honest. There is a natural dignity to the way older dogs stoically cope with the irritations of aging. They seldom complain. Elderly Lexington may fall down, but simply picks herself up and gets on with life. Elderly dogs do what you and I are told to do but find difficult, if not impossible. That is, they do not look wistfully back on what they once could do, but rather concentrate now on what they are capable of doing. And that is why older dogs have such dignity and generate such respect.

Letting go

In a survey of the records of a large pet insurance company, the most extensive survey of aging in dogs, accidents accounted for fewer than five percent of deaths. Natural death occurred in just under eight percent of individuals, while illness was the cause of death in 35 percent of dogs. The most common cause of death, involving 52 percent of all dogs, was **euthanasia**. Euthanasia because of behaviour problems accounted for a very low two percent. In the majority of instances, euthanasia was carried out because owners and vets felt it was in a dog's best interest – in over 29 percent of individuals because of disease and in another 21 percent because of old age.

The toughest decision

I have gone through this experience with thousands of clients and with all of my own dogs, all of whom lived so long that my family and I had to make this difficult decision on their behalf. How do you do it?

DEFINITION

Euthanasia *means voluntarily ending the life of an individual who is suffering from a terminal illness or an incurable condition. The word comes from the Greek eu, which means good, and thanatos, death – a good death.*

Let me tell you a story. A women about my age brought Hamish, her middle-aged West Highland White Terrier, to my clinic because he was limping painfully and had lost his appetite. Hamish's shoulder was swollen and sensitive when touched. His breathing was laboured. I took shoulder and chest X-rays. Hamish's owner did not want to wait the few minutes for the results, preferring to go home where I could telephone her. I am sure that, like me, she suspected something terrible. The X-rays showed a devastating problem: bone cancer that had spread to the lungs. The condition took months to develop to this critical stage but Hamish, a typically tough terrier, had never complained. Now he was in pain and short of breath. With this kind of cancer, even the most heroic treatment would be futile. I telephoned his owner with the dreadful news. She had expected it, and we arranged that she would return with Hamish at the end of the day for euthanasia.

An hour after dusk, Hamish and his owner arrived. The woman was soaked with December rain, soaked to the skin, but she had kept Hamish perfectly dry. We gave her a towel to dry her face, and as Maxine, one of my nurses, and I prepared, I asked how she got so wet.

Every day in the nine years of his life, she told us, the two of them walked from their home to the local park where Hamish had a set routine, walking on the mile-long peripheral pathway. She felt that Hamish would, on the last day of his life, enjoy a final look at what he had always considered his turf, but his pain and difficulty breathing made this impossible. So she put a blanket in the basket of her bicycle, gently placed Hamish on it and took him for one last look. She held her umbrella over him so he would not get wet. She was letting go of Hamish with great dignity and the respect he deserved. Maxine and I found it difficult to work efficiently because of our tears.

Be honest with yourself

Be honest and rational when thinking about what is best for your dog. In the 1970s Bernard Hershhorn, a veterinary surgeon in New York City, suggested that dog owners ask themselves these questions. They are just as relevant today.

1. Is the condition prolonged, recurring, or getting worse?
2. Is the condition no longer responding to therapy?
3. Is your dog in pain or otherwise suffering physically or mentally?
4. Is it no longer possible to alleviate that pain or suffering?
5. If your dog recovers, is he or she likely to be chronically ill, invalid, or unable to care for him or herself?
6. If your dog recovers, will there be severe personality changes?

If the answer to all these questions is "yes" then euthanasia is the honest, simple, and humane option.

If, however, you answer "no" to several of these questions, then ask yourself these questions.

1. Can I provide the necessary care?
2. Will providing this care seriously interfere with or create serious problems for myself and my family?
3. Will the cost of treatment be unbearably expensive?

Any decision should not be yours alone. Your dog is a member of your family. Decisions should be family decisions.

Cultural considerations

Your consideration of euthanasia is influenced by the culture you live in, but also the culture you come from. In the Judeo-Christian tradition of Europe and North America we have little difficulty taking on the responsibility for making life and death decisions on behalf of our dogs. This comes from the cultural responsibility we feel for animals around us, a responsibility that has been translated in the last 30 years into stewardship. (In other cultures, for example the Buddhist-Shintoist tradition in Japan where all objects – animate like dogs and people or inanimate like rocks – have souls, the decision to euthanize a dog is fraught with cultural conflict.)

Within the European/American tradition I come from, I feel that these are valid reasons for ending your dog's life:

1. Overwhelming physical injury.
2. Irreversible disease that has progressed to a point where distress or discomfort cannot be controlled.
3. Old age wear and tear that permanently affects the quality of life.
4. Physical injury, disease, or wear and tear resulting in permanent loss of control of body functions.
5. Uncorrectable aggressiveness with risk to children, owners, or others.
6. An untreatable disease dangerous to humans.

CHARITIES CAN HELP

There was a time when decision making was left to you and your veterinary surgeon. Most of the cost involved was in his or her personal professional fee. Regrettably, with the increasing sophistication of available diagnostics and treatments, basic costs can be exceptionally high and cannot be avoided. For example, with diagnostic scans and chemotherapy, a dog with cancer can have a comfortable life extended for a considerable period of time. But the costs are substantial and somehow must be met. If your financial circumstances are such that you genuinely cannot meet these expenses, discuss this with your veterinary surgery. There are charities nationwide that may be able to help.

Grieving is normal

Most of us are deeply distressed when our dogs die, and rightly so. But then a complication occurs. Many of us, and other people too, think we're acting silly. "It was just a dog!" we say to ourselves, or our bluntest friends tell us, "Get over it". We feel embarrassed that our emotions are so raw.

INTERNET

www.scas.org.uk

The Society for Companion Animal Studies has a support group, useful books, and articles for people who want to talk to someone about their feelings when their dog dies.

My own story

About a year ago I put down Libby. It was a sad moment and a bit tearful when we buried her the next day. Six months later I was in Japan being interviewed by a national newspaper and was asked about my own experiences of euthanasia. I told the story of how we came to the conclusion that Lib should be euthanized, how we carried out the procedure with my wife's help (all vet's wives should learn to be emergency nurses!), with Lib on our bed, and how I took her to the country to bury her under her favorite apple tree – a tree she had always picked apples from and dropped at my feet when she wanted me to pay attention to her. I explained to the reporter the strange satisfaction Julia and I both got from the hard work of digging her grave. Then, as I was telling him how, after laying Lib in the ground, Julia went inside, brought out an apple and put it in the grave with her, I choked up. Six months later. In Japan!

What happened to me was embarrassing, because of the circumstances, but perfectly normal. The emotional pain we feel when our dogs die does not go away in a week. If you are an average dog owner, the stages of grief last, typically, about 11 months.

Denial

Sometimes dog owners show their distress by trying to find someone to blame – often themselves or perhaps the veterinarian who gave them the bad news. Anger is a natural part of our reaction to the loss of a pet or even to the suggestion that a pet will die. So too is the vain attempt to obliterate from our mind what has been said or what has happened. This is denial. It is not uncommon, when I give devastating news to a dog owner, that I am asked to trim the dog's nails or check a wart; to do something trivial. We want everything to continue as it was. But, just as most of us eventually come to terms with other losses, we come to terms with the loss of our pets. However, compared to the loss of a close friend, with our canine companions we have a unique opportunity.

Life moves on

I GREW UP WITH DOGS: Sparkie until I was an adolescent, Duchess and Misty until I left for the university. When I married, we acquired Honey, a Golden Retriever, who was there when the kids came along. Liberty and Lexington have seen my family grow up. Dogs fit so well into the natural cycle of life. Emotionally, the most difficult aspect of living with a dog is his death, but although we can never replace the uniqueness of a personality, it sure is easy to replace the dogginess.

Much of what we enjoy about canine companionship is there in all dogs: honesty, fidelity, companionship, constancy, and disgusting habits. Virtually any dog is a born expert in these fields. And if you have lived with a specific breed and admired its looks and temperament, it is even easier to find a dog that has the qualities you are looking for. Yes, every dog is unique, but when a void opens in your home and in your heart, there are literally thousands of individuals, little or large, capable, willing, and eager to fill it.

A simple summary

✔ Don't assume that changes in a dog's behaviour are simply the effects of aging. Old dogs do not have to become ill.

✔ Grieving is normal, and there are now associations, support groups, and hotlines offering help.

✔ Each dog is unique, but there's always another one waiting to share more doggy love.

✔ The most common cause of death in dogs is euthanasia. You may be called on to make this heart-wrenching decision for your dog.

More resources

Pet Charities

Royal Society for the Prevention of
Cruelty to Animals
Causeway
Horsham
West Sussex, RH12 1HG
England
(44) (0)1403 264 181

Irish Society for the Prevention of
Cruelty to Animals
300 Lower Rathmines Road
Dublin 6
Ireland
(353) 1 4977 874

Ulster Society for the Prevention of
Cruelty to Animals
Unit C
Boucher Business Centre
Apollo Road
Belfast, BT 12 6HP
Northern Ireland
 (44) 08000 280 010

Scottish Society for the Prevention of
Cruelty to Animals
Braehead Mains
603 Queensferry Road
Edinburgh, EH4 6EA
Scotland
(44) 0131 339 0222

RSPCA Australia
PO Box E369
Kingston, ACT, 2604
(06) 282 8300

Petlog National Microchip Registry
PO Box 2037
London W1A 1GP
(44) 020 7518 1000

Kennel Clubs

The Kennel Club
1-5 Clarges Street
London W1Y 8AB
(44) 0171 629 5828
www.the-kennel-club.org.uk

Federation Cynologique
Internationale (FCI)
Place Albert 1er, No. 13
6530 Thuin
Belgium
(32) 71 591 238

Australian National Kennel Council
Royal Showgrounds
Ascot Vale
Victoria 3032
Australia

Royal New South Wales Canine Council
PO Box 632
St Marys, NSW 2760
Australia
(02) 9834 3022

Victoria Canine Association
PO Box K9
Ascot Vale, Victoria 3032
Australia
(03) 9376 2255

New Zealand Kennel Club
Private Bag 50903
Porirua 6220
New Zealand

Kennel Union of Southern Africa
PO Box 2659
Cape Town 8000
South Africa

Veterinary Associations

Association of British Veterinary
Acupuncture
East Park Cottage
Handcross
Haywards Heath
West Sussex RH17 6BD
01444 400213

British Veterinary Association
7 Mansfield Street
London W1M0AT
(020) 7636 6541

British Association of Homeopathic
Veterinary Surgeons
c/o The Natural Medicine Veterinary Centre
11 Southgate Road
Potters Bar
Hertforshire EN6 5DR
01707 662 058

British Small Animal Veterinary Association
Kingsley House
Church Lane
Shurdington
Cheltenham
Gloucestershire GL51 5TQ
01242 862 994

Federation of European Companion Animal
Veterinary Associations
40 rue de Berri
75008 Paris
France
(33) 1 5383 9160

Irish Veterinary Asociation
53 Lansdowne Road
Ballsbridge
Dublin 4
Ireland
(353) 1 668 5263

Magazines –UK

Dogs Today
Pankhurst Farm
Bagshot Road
West End
Woking
Surrey GU24 9QR
01276 858 880

Dog World
Summerfield House
Wotton Road
Ashford
Kent TN23 6LW
01233 621 877

The Kennel Club Gazette
1-5 Clarges Street
London W1Y 8AB
0171 793 6651

Our Dogs
5 Oxford Road
Station Approach
Manchester M60 1SX
0161 236 2660

Magazines –US

AKC Gazette
American Kennel Club
260 Madison Avenue
New York, NY 10016
(212) 696-8314
www.akc.org

Dog Fancy
PO Box 6500
Mission Viejo, CA 92690
(714) 855-8822
www.dogfancy.com

Dog & Kennel
7-L Dundas Circle
Greensboro, NC 27407
(336) 292-4047
www.dogandkennel.com

Dog World
500 N. Dearborn
Suite 1100
Chicago, IL 60610
(312) 609-4340
www.dogworldmag.com

Books

Adopting a Great Dog by Nona Kilgore Bauer, TFH Publications

The British Veterinary Association Guide to Dog Care by David Taylor, Dorling Kindersley, 1989

The Complete Dog Book 19th Edition, Revised, by the American Kennel Club, Howell Book House, 1998.

The Consumer's Guide to Dog Food by Liz Palika, Howell Book House, 1996.

Dog Anatomy by Peter Goody, J A Allen & Co Ltd, 1997

The Dog Owner's Home Veterinary Handbook 3rd Edition, by James Giffin, MD, and Liisa Carlson, D.V.M., Howell Book House, 1999.

The Dog Owners' Questions and Answer Book by Don Harper, Ward Lock

The Dog Owner's Problem Solver by John Bower, Caroline Bower, Reader's Digest

The Dog Owner's Veterinary Handbook by John Bower, David Youngs, The Crowood Press,1994

Dog Training in Ten Minutes by Carol Lea Benjamin, Howell Book House, 1997.

Dogs: The Ultimate Care Guide by Lowell Ackerman, TFH Publications, 1998.

The New Encyclopedia of the Dog by Bruce Fogle, D.V.M., Dorling Kindersley, 2000.

The Holistic Guide for a Healthy Dog by Wendy Volhard and Kerry Brown, Howell Book House, 1999.

How to Be Your Dog's Best Friend by the Monks of New Skete, Little Brown, 1978.

How to Housebreak Your Dog in 7 Days by Shirlee Kalstone, Bantam, Doubleday, Dell, 1991.

Mother Knows Best: The Natural Way to Train Your Dog by Carol Lea Benjamin, Howell Book House, 1985.

101 Questions Your Dog Would Ask by Helen Dennis, Parkgate Books

Natural Dog Care by Bruce Fogle, D.V.M., Dorling Kindersley, 1999.

RSPCA Complete Dog Training Manual by Bruce Fogel, D.V.M., Dorling Kindersley, 1994.

Second Hand Dog: How to Turn Yours into a First-Rate Pet by Carol Lea Benjamin, Howell Book House, 1994.

Dogs on the web

THERE IS SUCH A HUGE AMOUNT *of dog-related web sites on the Internet that it's really quite bewildering! Everything from grooming and housetraining your canine friend, to in-depth breed information from kennel clubs around the globe. The sites listed here are just the tip of the iceberg – but I'm sure that you'll be able to find something of interest. Happy Hunting.*

www.acmepet.com/canine/
Acme Pet has a wide variety of articles on many canine subjects.

www.agilityeye.co.uk
This site provides information on agility methods and games throughout Britain.

www.air-transport.org
The Air Transport Association offers information on airline travel with your pet.

www.akc.org
The American Kennel Club site has a wide variety of information about purebred dogs, including national breeds clubs, rescue coordinators, and rules for AKC-sanctioned dog sports.

www.animalaunts.co.uk
This is the website of Britian's largest pet (and house) sitting agency. Animal aunts look after your pets, plants, and home when you are away.

www.apdt.co.uk
The website for the Association of Professional Behaviour Counsellors are primarily involved in overcoming behaviour problems.

www.arba.org
The home page of the American Rare Breed Association.

www.avma.org
The American Veterinary Medical Association site offers information for veterinarians and general pet care articles.

www.biddeford.com/~seadog/treats.html
Favorite Dog Treat Recipes gives you 101 ways to bake your own dog biscuits.

www. "breed rescue associations"
All breed clubs have breed rescue secretaries. Visit either the breed club website of your choice or this site for information on how to contact individual rescue secretaries.

www.bsava.com/petzone/petcare/vaccineq.html
The British Small Animal Veterinary Association site offers information for veterinarians and general pet care articles. This part of the site looks at vaccinations.

www.city.vancouver.bc.ca/police/structure/op-support/oas/dogs/dogsqd.html
For a really interesting overview of how dogs are used by the police, including a history of police K9 units and a look at training procedures, type in this long web address and visit the Vancouver, Canada, Police Department's Dog Squad.

www.clickandtreat.com

This site shows you how to use clickers and treats for effective dog training. You can make some clickers yourself. Others can be purchased through www.petspyjamas.com

www.cyberpet.com/cyberdog/articles/

For tips on pet-proofing your home, especially during the holidays, check out the articles on Cyberpet.

www.dmoz.org/Recreation/Pets/Dogs/Origins/

Try this site for a really interesting collection of articles about the history and evolution of dogs.

www.dmoz.org/Recreation/Pets/Pet_Travel/

Listings of many other web sites with specific travel information, from moving advice to accommodations to listings of boarding kennels and more.

www.doctordog.com/dogbook/dogch01.html

Doctor Dog's Emergency Section offers illustrated advice on what to do in a variety of emergencies, from burns to electrocution to shock.

.www.doglogic.com/vaccinemain.html

This page, written by Jean Dodds, D.V.M., looks at some of the controversies surrounding the traditional annual vaccination schedule.

www.fci.be/english/

The home page of the FCI, the largest international purebred dog association. If you're up to it, you can also view this page in French, German or Spanish.

www.identichip.co.uk

This site gives information on both the microchip and the Pet Travel Scheme.

www.k9netuk.com

This site contains everything that UK dog owners might need to know, including a list of stud dogs, help on training, breeds, services including kennels, and a bookshop.

www.ludin.com.au/~hollow/dogrec~1.html

Hollow's Hound Recipes contains a variety of dishes, from casseroles to cookies, that have been dog-tested.

members.aol.com/AHTerrier/allergies.html

This section in the website for the American Hairless Terrier offers basic information about pet allergies, a list of breeds recommended for allergy sufferers, and a page of links to other pet allergy sites.

www.mushing.com/68massa.html

This page offers a short lesson in basic massage techniques. It was written for mushing dogs, but the principles can be applied to any breed.

www.nashelter.org/crate.html

There's information here on crate training your dog.

www.ncdl.co.uk

National Canine Defence League provides valuable information on shelter dogs needing good homes and also on the responsibilities of dog ownership. You can learn about the peculiarities of "recycled" dogs.

www.petplan.co.uk

You can find details of Pet Plans insurance policies for home or abroad on this page.

www.petspygamas.co.uk

Pets Pyjamas sells an extensive range of tools and equipment.

www.pogopet.com

The Pogopet site has a variety of health-related features, including Ask the Vet and Symptom Centers that help explain why your pet may not be feeling well. There are also sections on legal issues, pet etiquette, and trivia. Pogopet information can be customized for your particular pets.

www.scas.org.uk

The society for Companion Animal Studies has a support group and useful books, articles and helpful hints for people who want to talk to someone about their feelings when their dog dies.

www.simplypets.com/Pet_Directory/Resources/Pet_Travel/

Listings of many other web sites with specific travel information, from moving advice to accommodations to listings of boarding kennels and more.

www.srdogs.com

The Senior Dogs Project has health and behaviour news, lovely stories, lots of links, and great advice for owners of older dogs.

users.bigpond.com/winron/training.html

For an overview of canine socialization needs, visit Collar & Lead Obedience Training at this site.

www.wolfpark.org

To learn more about wolves, visit Wolf Park. This wildlife education and research facility studies wolf behaviour.

www.wonderpuppy.net/canwehelp/index.htm

This site, called Can We Help You Keep Your Pet?, offers links to a wide variety of pages that deal with common canine problems, such as aggression, housetraining, barking, and destructiveness.

www.workingdogweb.com

This is a list of links with a lot of information on testing, training, and getting started in many canine activities.

Complete list of breeds

The American Kennel Club has registered 148 dog breeds and classifies them into seven different groups:

Sporting (1)
Hounds (2)
Working (3)
Terrier (4)
Toy (5)
Non-sporting (6)
Herding (7)
Breeds awaiting full registration are in the Miscellaneous Group (8)

Affenpinscher (5)
Afghan Hound (2)
Airedale Terrier (4)
Akita (3)
Alaskan Malamute (3)
American Eskimo Dog (6)
American Staffordshire Terrier (4)
American Water Spaniel (1)
Anatolian Shepherd (3)
Australian Cattle Dog (7)
Australian Shepherd (7)
Australian Terrier (4)
Basenji (2)
Basset Hound (2)
Beagle (2)
Bearded Collie (7)
Bedlington Terrier (4)
Belgian Malinois (7)
Belgian Sheepdog (7)
Belgian Tervuren (7)
Bernese Mountain Dog (3)
Bichon Frise (6)
Black and Tan Coonhound (2)

Bloodhound (2)
Border Collie (7)
Border Terrier (4)
Borzoi (2)
Boston Terrier (6)
Bouvier des Flandres (7)
Boxer (3)
Briard (7)
Brittany (1)
Brussels Griffon (5)
Bull Terrier (4)
Bulldog (6)
Bullmastiff (3)
Cairn Terrier (4)
Canaan Dog (7)
Cavalier King Charles Spaniel (5)
Chesapeake Bay Retriever (1)
Chihuahua (5)
Chinese Crested (5)
Chinese Shar-Pei (6)
Chow Chow (6)
Clumber Spaniel (1)
Cocker Spaniel (1)
Collie (7)
Curly-Coated Retriever (1)
Dachshund (2)
Dalmatian (6)
Dandie Dinmont Terrier (4)
Doberman Pinscher (3)
English Cocker Spaniel (1)
English Setter (1)
English Springer Spaniel (1)
English Toy Spaniel (5)
Field Spaniel (1)
Finnish Spitz (6)
Flat-Coated Retriever (1)
Fox Terrier (Smooth) (4)
Fox Terrier (Wire) (4)
Foxhound (American) (2)
Foxhound (English) (2)
French Bulldog (6)
German Shepherd Dog (7)

German Shorthaired Pointer (1)
German Wirehaired Pointer (1)
Giant Schnauzer (3)
Golden Retriever (1)
Gordon Setter (1)
Great Dane (3)
Great Pyrenees (3)
Greyhound (2)
Harrier (2)
Havanese (5)
Ibizan Hound (2)
Irish Setter (1)
Irish Terrier (4)
Irish Water Spaniel (1)
Irish Wolfhound (2)
Italian Greyhound (5)
Jack Russell Terrier (4)
Japanese Chin (5)
Keeshond (6)
Kerry Blue Terrier (4)
Komondor (3)
Kuvasz (3)
Labrador Retriever (1)
Lakeland Terrier (4)
Lhasa Apso (6)
Löwchen (6)
Maltese (5)
Manchester Terrier (Toy) (5)
Manchester Terrier (Standard) (4)
Mastiff (3)
Miniature Bull Terrier (4)
Miniature Pinscher (5)
Miniature Schnauzer (4)
Newfoundland (3)
Norfolk Terrier (4)
Norwegian Elkhound (2)
Norwich Terrier (4)
Old English Sheepdog (7)
Otterhound (2)
Papillon (5)
Pekingese (5)

Petit Basset Griffon
  Vendéen (2)
Pharaoh Hound (2)
Plott Hound (8)
Polish Lowland Sheepdog (8)
Pointer (1)
Pomeranian (5)
Poodle (Miniature) (5)
Poodle (Toy) (5)
Poodle (Standard) (6)
Portuguese Water Dog (3)
Pug (5)
Puli (2)
Rhodesian Ridgeback (2)
Rottweiler (3)
St. Bernard (3)
Saluki (2)
Samoyed (3)
Schipperke (6)
Scottish Deerhound (2)
Scottish Terrier (4)
Sealyham Terrier (4)
Shetland Sheepdog (7)
Shiba Inu (6)
Shih Tzu (5)
Siberian Husky (3)
Silky Terrier (5)
Skye Terrier (4)
Soft Coated Wheaten
  Terrier (4)
Spinone Italiano (8)
Staffordshire Bull Terrier (4)
Standard Schnauzer (3)
Sussex Spaniel (1)
Tibetan Spaniel (6)
Tibetan Terrier (6)
Vizsla (1)
Weimaraner (1)
Welsh Corgi (Cardigan) (7)
Welsh Corgi (Pembroke) (7)
Welsh Springer Spaniel (1)
Welsh Terrier (4)
West Highland White
  Terrier (4)
Whippet (2)
Wirehaired Pointing Griffon (1)
Yorkshire Terrier (5)

List of Kennel Club Breeds

**The Kennel Club in London
has classified 192 breeds
into seven groups:**

Gundogs	**(1)**
Hounds	**(2)**
Working dogs	**(3)**
Terriers	**(4)**
Toy dogs	**(5)**
Utility dogs	**(6)**
Pastoral	**(7)**

Affenpinscher (5)
Afghan Hound (2)
Airedale Terrier (4)
Alaskan Malamute (3)
Anatolian Shepherd Dog (7)
Australian Cattle Dog (7)
Australian Shepherd (7)
Australian Silky Terrier (5)
Australian Terrier (4)
Basenji (2)
Basset Bleu De Gascogne (2)
Basset Fauve De Bretagne (2)
Basset Griffon Vendéen
  (Grand) (2)
Basset Griffon Vendéen
  (Petit) (2)
Basset Hound (2)
Bavarian Mountain
  Hound (2)
Beagle (2)
Bearded Collie (7)
Beauceron (3)
Bedlington Terrier (4)
Belgian Shepherd Dog
  (Groenendael) (7)
Belgian Shepherd Dog
  (Laekenois) (7)
Belgian Shepherd Dog
  (Malinois) (7)
Belgian Shepherd Dog
  (Tervueren) (7)
Bergamasco (7)
Bernese Mountain Dog (3)
Bichon Frise (5)

Bloodhound (2)
Bolognese (5)
Border Collie (7)
Border Terrier (4)
Borzoi (2)
Boston Terrier (6)
Bouvier Des Flandres (3)
Boxer (3)
Bracco Italiano (1)
Briard (7)
Brittany (1)
Bull Terrier (4)
Bull Terrier (Miniature) (4)
Bulldog (6)
Bullmastiff (3)
Cairn Terrier (4)
Canaan Dog (6)
Cavalier King Charles
  Spaniel (5)
Cesky Terrier (4)
Chihuahua (Long Coat) (5)
Chihuahua (Smooth
  Coat) (5)
Chinese Crested Dog (5)
Chow Chow (6)
Collie (Rough) (7)
Collie (Smooth) (7)
Coton De Tulear (5)
Dachshund (Long Haired) (2)
Dachshund (Miniature Long
  Haired) (2)
Dachshund (Miniature
  Smooth Haired) (2)
Dachshund (Miniature Wire
  Haired) (2)
Dachshund (Smooth
  Haired) (2)
Dachshund (Wire Haired) (2)
Dalmatian (6)
Dandie Dinmont Terrier (4)
Deerhound (2)
Dobermann (3)
Dogue de Bordeaux (3)
Elkhound (2)
English Setter (1)
English Toy Terrier (Black
  and Tan) (5)

Eskimo Dog (3)
Estrela Mountain Dog (7)
Finnish Lapphund (7)
Finnish Spitz (2)
Fox Terrier (Smooth) (4)
Fox Terrier (Wire) (4)
Foxhound (2)
French Bulldog (6)
German Longhaired
  Pointer (1)
German Shepherd Dog
  (Alsatian) (7)
German Shorthaired
  Pointer (1)
German Spitz (Klein) (6)
German Spitz (Mittel) (6)
German Wirehaired
  Pointer (1)
Giant Schnauzer (3)
Glen of Imaal Terrier (4)
Gordon Setter (1)
Grand Bleu De Gascogne (2)
Great Dane (3)
Greyhound (2)
Griffon Bruxellios (5)
Hamiltonstövare (2)
Havanese (5)
Hovawart (3)
Hungarian Kuvasz (7)
Hungarian Puli (7)
Hungarian Vizsla (1)
Hungarian Wirehaired
  Vizsla (1)
Ibizan Hound (2)
Irish Red and White
  Setter (1)
Irish Setter (1)
Irish Terrier (4)
Irish Wolfhound (2)
Italian Greyhound (5)
Italian Spinone (1)
Japanese Akita (6)
Japanese Chin (5)
Japanese Shiba Inu (6)
Japanese Spitz (6)
Keeshond (6)
Kerry Blue Terrier (4)

King Charles Spaniel (5)
Komondor (7)
Kooikerhondje (1)
Lakeland Terrier (4)
Lancashire Heeler (7)
Large Munsterlander (1)
Leonberger (3)
Lhasa Apso (6)
Lowchen (Little Lion
  Dog) (5)
Maltese (5)
Manchester Terrier (4)
Maremma Sheepdog (7)
Mastiff (3)
Mexican Hairless (6)
Miniature Pinscher (5)
Miniature Schnauzer (6)
Neapolitan Mastiff (3)
Newfoundland (3)
Norfolk Terrier (4)
Norwegian Buhund (7)
Norwegian Lundehund (2)
Norwich Terrier (4)
Nova Scotia Duck Tolling
  Retriever (1)
Old English Sheepdog (7)
Otterhound (2)
Papillon (5)
Parson Jack Russell
  Terrier (4)
Pekingese (5)
Pharaoh Hound (2)
Pinscher (3)
Pointer (1)
Polish Lowland Sheepdog (7)
Pomeranian (5)
Poodle (Miniature) (6)
Poodle (Standard) (6)
Poodle (Toy) (6)
Portugese Water Dog (3)
Pug (5)
Pyrenean Mountain Dog (7)
Pyrenean Sheepdog (7)
Retriever (Chesapeake
  Bay) (1)
Retriever (Curly Coated) (1)
Retriever (Flat Coated) (1)

Retriever (Golden) (1)
Retriever (Labrador) (1)
Rhodesian Ridgeback (2)
Rottweiler (3)
Saluki (2)
Samoyed (7)
Schipperke (6)
Schnauzer (6)
Scottish Terrier (4)
Sealyham Terrier (4)
Segugio Italiano (2)
Shar Pei (6)
Shetland Sheepdog (7)
Shih Tzu (6)
Siberian Husky (3)
Skye Terrier (4)
Sloughi (2)
Soft Coated Wheaten
  Terrier (4)
Spaniel (American
  Cocker) (1)
Spaniel (Clumber) (1)
Spaniel (Cocker) (1)
Spaniel (English
  Springer) (1)
Spaniel (Field) (1)
Spaniel (Irish Water) (1)
Spaniel (Sussex) (1)
Spaniel (Welsh Springer) (1)
Spanish Water Dog (1)
St. Bernard (3)
Staffordshire Bull Terrier (4)
Swedish Lapphund (7)
Swedish Vallhund (7)
Tibetan Mastiff (3)
Tibetan Spaniel (6)
Tibetan Terrier (6)
Weimaraner (1)
Welsh Corgi (Cardigan) (7)
Welsh Corgi (Pembroke) (7)
Welsh Terrier (4)
West Highland White
  Terrier (4)
Whippet (2)
Yorkshire Terrier (5)

Comparing breeds

In the chart that follows, I've rated most attributes on a scale of 1 to 5, where 1 is the least and 5 is the most. Remember, these are the average characteristics of the average dogs of each breed. Individuals dogs are as different as individual people.

BREED	SIZE	GOOD FIRST DOG?	SPACE	TRAINABILITY	EXCITABILITY	CARE NEEDS	NOISE	GOOD WITH KIDS
Afghan Hound	4	no	5	1	2	5	2	2
Airedale Terrier	3–4	no	4	2	4	3	4	3
Akita	5	no	4	3–4	1	3	1	2
Alaskan Malamute	3–4	maybe	3	3	2	3	1	3
Australian Shepherd	3	yes	2	5	1	3	1	5
Basset Hound	4	maybe	2	1	1	2	2	5
Beagle	3	yes	4	1	4	1	5	4
Bichon Frise	2	yes	1	4	4	4	5	5
Bloodhound	4	maybe	1	2	1	1	1	5
Border Collie	3–4	no	5	5	4	3	3	2
Boston Terrier	2	yes	1	3	4	1	4	4
Boxer	4	maybe	5	3	4	1	2	4
Brittany	3	maybe	4	4	3	2	2	5
Bulldog	3–4	maybe	1	1	1	2	2	4
Cairn Terrier	2	yes	1	3	4	2	5	4
Cavalier King Charles Spaniel	2	yes	1	4	3	3	3	5
Chesapeake Bay Retriever	4–5	yes	4	5	1	1	1	5
Chihuahua	1	no	1	2	5	1–2	5	2
Chow Chow	4	no	2	1	1	4	1	1
Cocker Spaniel (American/English)	3	yes	2	3–4	3	3–4	3	5
Collie	4	yes	3	4	2	1–3	2	5
Dachshund	1–2	maybe	1	2	3	1–2	4	2
Dalmatian	4	no	4	3	3	1	3	2
Dobermann	4	maybe	4	5	2	1	2	3
English Springer Spaniel	3	maybe	5	5	3	3	3	5
Fox Terrier	2	no	3	1	5	1–2	5	1

BREED	SIZE	GOOD FIRST DOG?	SPACE	TRAINABILITY	EXCITABILITY	CARE NEEDS	NOISE	GOOD WITH KIDS
German Shepherd Dog	4–5	no	4	5	3	3	3	3
German Shorhaired Pointer	4	maybe	4	3–4	3	1	3	4
Golden Retriever	4	yes	3	5	1	3	1	5
Great Dane	5	no	4	3	1	1	1	4
Hungarian Vizsla	4	yes	3	4	2	1	2	5
Jack Russell Terrier	2	no	3	2	5	1–2	5	1
Labrador Retriever	4	yes	4	5	1	2	1	5
Lhasa Apso	2	yes	1	3	4	2	3	4
Maltese	1	yes	1	3	5	4	4	4
Newfoundland	5	no	4	3	1	5	1	5
Norwegian Elkhound	4	yes	4	3–4	2	3	2	4
Old English Sheepdog	5	no	4	2	2	5	1	3
Pekingese	1	maybe	1	2	3	3	3	4
Pomeranian	1	yes	2	3	4	3	3	5
Poodle (Miniature and Toy)	1–3	yes	2	4–5	4	3	5	5
Poodle (Standard)	4	yes	3	5	2	4	3	5
Pug	2	yes	2	1	3	1	4	4
Rottweiler	4–5	no	4	3–4	1	1	1	2
St. Bernard	5	no	4	2	1	5	1	4
Samoyed	4	maybe	3	2–3	2	4	3	3
Schnauzer (Miniature)	3	yes	2	3–4	5	3	5	4
Scottish Terrier	3	maybe	2	2	5	2	4	2
Shar–Pei	4	no	4	2	3	5	3	2
Setters (Irish and English)	4	yes	5	2	5	3	4	4
Shetland Sheepdog	2–3	yes	2	5	3	3	4	4
Shih Tzu	1–2	yes	1	3	5	2	3	5
Siberian Husky	4	no	4	3	3	2	3	2
Staffordshire Bull Terrier	3	maybe	2	3	4	1	4	4
Weimaraner	4	maybe	4	4	2	1	4	3
Welsh Corgi (Cardigan and Pembroke)	3	maybe	2	4	3	1	3	2
West Highland White Terrier	2–3	maybe	2	1–2	5	4	5	1
Yorkshire Terrier	1	maybe	1	1–2	5	4	5	1

My dog's life

1. My dog's registered name is ....

2. My dog's call name is ....

3. My dog .... is registered at ....
....
....
....
....

4. My dog .... was born on..

5. My dog ....'s breed is ....

6. My dog ....'s breed group classification is ....

7. My dog ....'s mother is named ....

8. My dog ....'s father is named ....

9. My dog .... has......brothers and sisters........................

10. My dog ....'s breeder's name is ....

11. My dog ....s breeder's address is ....
....
....
....
....

12. My dog ....'s microchip number is..................................

13. My dog ....'s microchip is registered at ....
....
....
....
....

14. My dog ....'s veterinarian's name is ....

15. My dog ....'s veterinarian's address is ....
....
....
....
....

16. My dog .... was wormed on ....
....
....
....

17. My dog .... was vaccinated for...........on ....

18. My dog .... is due the next vaccination for............on...........

19. My dog .... was vaccinated for..........on ....
20. My dog .... is due the next vaccination for............on ....
21. My dog .... was vaccinated for..........on ....
22. My dog .... is due the next vaccination for............on ....
23. My dog .... was vaccinated for..........on ....
24. My dog .... is due the next vaccination for............on ....
25. My dog ....'s weight at 6 months is ....
26. My dog ....'s height at 6 months is ....
27. My dog ....'s weight at 1 year is ....
28. My dog ....'s height at 1 year is ....
29. My dog ....'s weight at 5 years is ....
30. My dog ....'s height at 5 years is ....
31. My dog ....'s normal heart beat is ....
32. My dog ....'s normal temperature is................................
33. My dog ....'s groomer is ....
34. My dog ....'s first learnt the command "Sit" on.......................
35. My dog ....'s first learnt to walk off leash on...........................
36. My dog ....'s first learnt to walk on leash on ....
37. My dog ....'s first understood the command "Fetch" on...........
38. My dog ....'s first understood the command "Come" on ....
39. My dog ....'s has won ....

....
....
....
....
....

40. My dog .... is champion of ....

....
....
....
....

41. My dog ....'s first season was on ....
42. My dog .... was neutered on ....
43. My dog ....'s first litter was on ....
44. The father/mother of the litter is...
45. The names of the puppies are ....
46. The puppies went to their new homes on ....

A simple glossary

Allergen Any substance that triggers an allergic reaction.

Antioxidant A substance that destroys free radicals – atoms in the body that destroy cell membranes. Antioxidants, because they destroy free radicals, are good for dogs as well as good for preserving food.

Aversion therapy A type of behavioural therapy in which a dog learns not to do something because it is mildly unpleasant. If you use a chew deterrent, the bad taste teaches the dog not to chew.

Biopsy The removal of a small sample of living tissue to use for diagnosis.

Call name The name you call your dog every day.

Canine cognitive dysfunction The deteriorating behaviour changes of old age.

Cataract A crystalline development in the lens. Light reflects off the crystals, causing darkened starburst-like vision, but eventually light cannot get through the cataract to the retina at the back of the eye. This causes blindness.

Cesarean section Usually called simply c-section, this is surgical intervention to open the womb to deliver the puppies. It must be done in a veterinary hospital.

Chamois cloth A soft cloth used to polish and shine short coats.

Clicker training Long a favourite of those who train marine mammals, this type of training is now becoming very popular among dog trainers. A clicker is one of those little cricket toys you may have had as a child. If you click the clicker and then give your dog a treat, eventually the dog will come to regard the sound of the clicker alone as a positive thing.

Crate A portable enclosure with a top and a door, made from metal bars or molded plastic. It comes in a variety of sizes. Crates are for security, safety, housetraining, and just general control.

Crossbred A dog that is the result of mating two dogs from two different recognized breeds.

Dander Little bits of dog skin that naturally flake off as the skin renews itself.

Drop ears Ears that hang down, like the ears on Basset Hounds and Labrador Retrievers.

Euthanasia Voluntarily ending the life of an individual who is suffering from a terminal illness or an incurable condition.

Free radicals Atoms in the body that destroy cell membranes.

Go to ground To follow a burrowing animal into its underground den, and there to do fearless battle. Dachshunds and other terriers were bred to burrow after and kill rabbits, badgers, weasels, and foxes.

Guard hairs The outer, coarser hairs that project above the undercoat.

Half-check collar A collar where the part that tightens around the dog's neck can only close to a certain degree, unlike the traditional choke chain.

Hound glove A glove with a slicker brush on one side. Some also have rubber studs on the other side.

Houseline A long, light leash that you can use around the house to keep control of your dog. It's important to make sure your dog obeys you during training, and a houseline can help you do that.

Invisible fencing Wiring buried under the ground around the perimeter of your yard. Your dog wears a special collar that receives a signal from the buried wiring. The signal causes your dog's collar to buzz. The buzz is a warning that if the dog continues, she will receive an electrical shock. The dog must be trained to understand what the whole thing means, of course.

Kong A natural rubber puncture-resistant toy that is made to be chewed. It looks a little bit like a snowman made from three balls, but without the face. The inside is hollow, giving you a place to stuff peanut butter or cheese or some equally mushy food. Kongs come in several sizes to accommodate dogs from Great Danes to Pomeranians.

Laparoscopy A medical procedure where a rigid viewing instrument called a laparoscope is used to view the inside of the pelvis and abdomen through small abdominal incisions.

Lie of the coat The direction in which the hair grows. On dogs, it usually grows back toward the rump and down toward the toes.

Microchip An electronic transponder, the size of a rice grain, that is injected under the skin between the shoulder

blades. A unique number held in the transponder is read by a handheld reader that is run over a dog's neck. Through a computer database, that number helps to trace the dog's owners.

Mismating When your bitch breeds with a stud dog other than the one you had planned for her.

Multivalent vaccine A single injection that protects against a variety of diseases. Because it contains modified versions of several diseases, there are concerns about possible interactions, and about overloading the immune system.

Muzzle Anything used to hold your dog's mouth closed. It's also the long, flat top of the nose and mouth, from behind the nostrils to the forehead.

Neutering Removing the sex-hormone-producing apparatus from the male or female. In males the testicles are removed. In females the ovaries and uterus are removed.

Oestrus The period when the female dog is fertile and will accept a male dog for breeding.

Pack animals In the wild, dogs have learnt to live together in a pack. Every pack has a social structure, called a hierarchy, and every dog has a place within the hierarchy. Dogs defer to all the dogs above them in the hierarchy. For a domesticated dog, your family is his pack.

Point The body position a hunting dog assumes to indicate that he has located game. When a hunting dog is on point, his body is tense and stiff. His back is straight, one front leg is lifted off the ground, his tail is straight out, and his neck is extended so that he is indicating the game with his nose. The idea is for the dog to hold still so as not to disturb the game, while the hunter sneaks up to shoot.

Positive reinforcement A term taken from behavioural psychology. It is a reward given immediately following a behaviour which is intended to increase the likelihood that the behaviour will occur again.

Prick ears Ears that stand up, as on German Shepherds and Malamutes.

Purebred A dog produced by mating two dogs of the same breed.

Random-bred A dog produced by a random mating.

Registered name The official name your dog has on file with the kennel club where you registered her.

Rose ears Ears that fold partway, like the ears on Greyhounds and Bulldogs.

Shock The failure of blood to be transported throughout the body.

Scenthounds Dogs that hunt by tracking the scent of their prey. Bloodhounds, Basset Hounds, and Foxhounds are scenthounds.

Scruff shake Similar to what the mother dog does when she is annoyed by puppy mayhem. You hold some loose skin around the neck and give your dog a gentle shake. Use this form of discipline sparingly and wisely. You do not want your dog to become shy of your touch, nor do you want to provoke an aggressive response.

Separation anxiety An extreme reaction some dogs have when their owners leave the house. They may react by being very destructive or self destructive (licking or chewing themselves), or by excessive barking or whining. Dogs with separation anxiety need the help of a well-thought-out program of training, behaviour modification, and lifestyle enrichment.

Sheath The skin covering the dog's penis.

Sighthounds Breeds that hunt by chasing a moving prey animal, tracking it by sight. Lean, leggy breeds such as Greyhounds, Whippets, and Salukis are sighthounds.

Slicker brush A brush with bent wire bristles set into a flat pad.

Undercoat The soft, downy hairs that lie close to the skin.

Withers The very top of the dog's shoulders where the neck and the back meet.

Index

Acknowledgements

All photography by Dorling Kindersley except:
Animal Photography: © Sally Anne Thompson 2, 25, 27, 38, 48, 56t, 56b, 57t, 62, 86, 102, 104, 118, 132, 134, 150, 160, 162, 176, 190, 204, 218, 234, 250, 252, 262, 280, 294, 310, 324, 336, 338, 354, 356b, 358, 359t, 361t, 361b, 364, 380; © R.T. Willbie: 289t
Ardea: © S. Roberts 40b
Bryan Hawkins: 299
Mary Evans Picture Library: 67, 356t
RSPCA Photolibrary: © Des Cartwright 260t; © Robin Culley 58l, 58r; © Angela Hampton 272t, 272c, 272b, 274, 275, 363r; © Marina Imperi 276b; © Ken McKay 257l; © Tim Sambrook 255t, 255b; © Colin Seddon 362; © Alan Towse 60; © Nick Withey 256
S & O Mathews: 142t, 142r, 142b, 143tl, 143tr, 143c, 143bl, 143br
Sporting Pictures: 360t
Still Pictures: © Bryan and Cheery Alexander 41b, 45l; © Klein/Hubert 42t, 167t
Topham Picturepoint: 363l
Cartoons by Barry Robson, © Dorling Kindersley